Employee Engagement for Organizational Change

T0295738

The success of organizational change in a world of increasing volatility is highly dependent on the advocacy of stakeholders. It is the link between strategic decision-making and effective execution, between individual motivation and product innovation, and between delighted customers and growing revenues. Only by engaging stakeholders does change have a chance to be successful.

This book presents a coherent and practical view of how organizations might engender engagement with organizational change within their operational, tactical and strategic practices. It does this by providing a comprehensive review of the theoretical and empirical works on engagement and change from a variety of academic and practical perspectives. The academic research presented in this book is reinforced by research from consultancies as well as insights from practitioners that provide timely evidence. Ultimately the aim is to help raise awareness of the need to foster engagement with OC through a stakeholder perspective and how this can be done successfully within organizations across the globe.

Employee Engagement for Organizational Change is a valuable textbook for advanced undergraduate and postgraduate students of organizational change, employee engagement, human resource management and leadership. Its balance of theory and practice also makes it a reliable resource for HR and organizational development practitioners.

Julie Hodges, PhD, is an Associate Professor at Durham University Business School and Associate Dean. Julie first joined Durham University Business School in 2006. Prior to joining the School she worked for over 20 years in international business and is an experienced consultant and facilitator of organizational change, as well as an author and academic. She has written several books on organizational change and published in a number of international journals. Julie is also a Senior Fellow of the Foundation for Management Education (FME).

Employee Engagement for Organizational Change

The Theory and Practice of Stakeholder Engagement

Julie Hodges

Routledge
Taylor & Francis Group

LONDON AND NEW YORK

First published 2019
by Routledge
2 Park Square, Milton Park, Abingdon, Oxon OX14 4RN

and by Routledge
711 Third Avenue, New York, NY 10017

Routledge is an imprint of the Taylor & Francis Group, an informa business

British Library Cataloguing in Publication Data
A catalogue record for this book is available from the British Library

Library of Congress Cataloging in Publication Data
Names: Hodges, Julie, author.Title: Employee engagement for organizational change : the theory and practice of stakeholder engagement / Julie Hodges.Description: Abingdon, Oxon ; New York, NY : Routledge, 2018. | Includes bibliographical references and index.Identifiers: LCCN 2018019027| ISBN 9781138331259 (hardback) | ISBN 9781138331273 (pbk.) | ISBN 9780429447419 (ebook)Subjects: LCSH: Organizational change. | Organizational behavior.Classification: LCC HD58.8 .H6295 2018 | DDC 658.4/06–dc23LC record available at https://lccn.loc.gov/2018019027

ISBN: 978-1-138-33125-9 (hbk)
ISBN: 978-1-138-33127-3 (pbk)
ISBN: 978-0-429-44741-9 (ebk)

Typeset in Bembo
by Taylor & Francis Books

To Michael for his unerring support, patience and advice.

Contents

List of illustrations   viii
Acknowledgements   ix

Introduction   1

PART 1
Overview of context and key theories   7

1   The accelerating business environment   9

2   Key concepts   24

3   Theoretical perspectives of organizational change   42

4   Theoretical perspectives of engagement   59

PART 2
Dilemmas and drivers of OC engagement   73

5   The dilemma of OC engagement   75

6   Antecedents and outcomes of OC engagement   87

PART 3
OC in practice   115

7   Creating an environment for OC engagement   117

8   Fostering OC engagement   150

9   Conclusions and reflections on OC engagement   179

References   188
Index   210

Illustrations

Figures

1.1 Velocity trends   10
6.1 Antecedents and outcomes of OC engagement   89
7.1 Power and influence of stakeholders   129
8.1 Principles of OC engagement   152
8.2 Approach to creating sustainable culture change   174
8.3 The Fresh Start Programme   176
9.1 Engaging people to change   182
9.2 The safety-net of engagement   185

Boxes

1.1 The end of business as usual   11
5.1 Creating an environment for engagement with change in a stockbroking
     company in Mauritius   82
6.1 Engagement – the right and wrong way within a public sector organization 97
6.2 Harnessing forces of change and innovation   108
7.1 Principles of stakeholder management   124
7.2 Stakeholder management for success   126
7.3 HR change management in Hitachi   143
8.1 Engaging staff with transformation in a South African public water utility 166
8.2 Adopting a top-down and bottom-up approach to culture change   173
9.1 The Story of Perkin   181

Acknowledgements

I am very grateful to everyone who has supported me in writing this book and provided their thoughts and advice, from which I hope a great number of people engaged in organizational change will benefit. My special thanks go to Kamales Lardi, Roshan Romaly, Andy Davies, Duncan Sperry, Greg Longley, Stephen Pierce, Fiona Sweeney, Lindsey Agness and Mark Crabtree. Each of these individuals has taken the time to write their own stories which help illustrate the challenges of engaging stakeholders in change. Thanks also to Michael for reviewing each word I have written, and providing valuable support and advice. Finally, I am exceedingly grateful to all at Routledge who have given me the opportunity to write this book and provided support and guidance throughout the process.

Introduction

We are living through one of the greatest inflection points in history as the speed of change and the increase in complexity accelerates. The implications of advances in technology, economic shifts, demographic and social trends, populist revolts against globalization and continuing climate changes are redistributing power, wealth, competition and opportunities around the globe. The transformations we are facing are unequalled since Johannes Gensfleisch zur Laden zum Gutenberg, a German blacksmith and printer, launched the printing revolution in Europe, paving the way for the Reformation. What is remarkable about this metamorphosis is that it has been sustained for so long.

The world is not just rapidly changing, it is also being dramatically reshaped and starting to operate differently. This transition is happening faster than many organizations are able to reshape themselves. As a result industries are facing varying levels of turmoil, including being disintermediated, out-Googled, or otherwise made irrelevant. Not surprisingly, when asked to describe the environment in which their organizations are operating, business leaders use adjectives such as 'uncertain', 'complex' and 'challenging' and consider navigating change as their most salient priority. It is not just a question of adjusting to one change but rather adapting to multiple waves of change in order to survive and thrive in turbulent times.

Adaptation is vital if an organization is to keep up with and get the most out of the accelerating changes and cushion against their worst impacts. In order to be adaptable there is pressure on organizations to be agile: to swiftly turn decisions into actions, to manage change effectively, to focus on customers and to optimize the value of knowledge and innovation. Along with building agility organizations also have to enhance their resilience in order to be able to bounce back from adversity.

In a context where speed and agility are crucial, a failure to adapt can result in a failure to recognize and capitalize on opportunities. As Hillary Clinton (2017: 195) writes in her book, entitled *What Happened*:

> we don't always spend enough time thinking about what it takes to actually make the change we seek. Change is hard. That's one reason we're sometimes taken in by leaders who make it sound easy but don't have any idea how to get anything done. Too often we fail to think big enough or act fast enough and let opportunities for change slip away.

This failure to adapt is evident in companies, such as Blockbuster's – the film and video game rental company – denial of digital trends; HMV – the entertainment retailer – ignoring streaming services such as Spotify; Clinton Cards – the card retailer – disregarding the threat of e-cards; and Borders – the book and music retailer – overlooking the rise of the e-book. Ultimately, a lack of adaptation due to complacency or inertia can result in business casualties in terms of bankruptcy, wasted investments and shareholder dissatisfaction. Indeed as Thomas Friedman (2016) warns in his book, *Thank You For Being Late*, the greatest danger in times of turbulence is not the turbulence but it is acting with yesterday's logic due to inertia. In The *Self-Destructive Habits of Good Companies*, Jagdish Sheth (2007: 75) writes at length about the causes and nature of complacency which he describes as the illusion that "bad things can't happen here". Complacency, he says, "breeds in the assumption that the future will be like the present and the past, that nothing will change. [It] is like blindness". Complacency likes the status quo and it is quite natural because, deep down, most organizations are uncomfortable with change. As Witzel (2015: 59) points out, "growth and change of direction and risk taking all imply uncertainty, and we don't like uncertainty". Doing things that they have always done makes people in organizations feel comfortable and secure but, as Witzel goes on to say, individuals don't recognize that "not changing actually makes us less secure". Failing to adapt can be detrimental to an organization but even when the need for change is recognized its implementation may not be successful.

Organizations are littered with the debris of change initiatives that have failed to deliver their expected benefits and promised results. Successful change is still viewed as elusive, for despite the many approaches to managing changes in organizations and the plethora of advice and advisers, it is commonly agreed that the vast majority of transformation initiatives fail (Burnes & Randall, 2016). A wide range of reasons is given for the failure of change ranging from impractical theories to ill-informed practice. More often than not, change driven from the top down fails to engage properly with the front-line operational staff who are essential for the delivery of high-quality products and high levels of customer service. Successful change does not just happen due to the efforts of one leader who drives the change on their own and takes all the credit, but instead is due to the involvement of those impacted by the change and amongst whom responsibility needs to be distributed.

Change can only be achieved if stakeholders – those affected by organizational change – are given a chance to engage with it. When organizations are faced with the prospect and speed of change, they often fail to include relevant people. It is, however, important to ensure stakeholders are involved in transformations in order to achieve organizational effectiveness. Stakeholder engagement is vital for enabling organizations to change.

The success of organizational change in a world of increasing volatility is highly dependent on the advocacy of stakeholders. It is the link between strategic decision-making and effective execution, between individual motivation and product innovation, and between delighted customers and growing revenues. For although leadership envisions and drives change, success is largely contingent on the engagement of stakeholders. Only by engaging stakeholders does change have a chance to be successful. Engagement of stakeholders with organizational change is 'a must-do, not nice-to-have' activity as there are benefits for the organization when people engage across functional and business unit boundaries to bring a range of perspectives and drive change and innovation. Studies show that highly engaged employees tend to support organizational change initiatives and are more resilient in the face of change (for example, Holbeche & Matthews, 2012). Organizational change should, therefore, whenever it is feasible, be constructed or negotiated *with* rather than *to* stakeholders, thereby reflecting the plurality of stakeholder interests.

Despite being presented as a good thing that organizations should do there is rather little in the literature about how they should achieve stakeholder engagement with change. Existing theory and research have taken us some way towards addressing how change can be effective. However, given the importance of change to organizations, combined with the need to ensure it succeeds and achieves benefits, a key issue is how to promote the inclusivity of stakeholders. The academic and management literature is relatively silent on action to be taken apart from the provision of tools to assess levels of engagement in the form of attitude surveys. For academics, the recommended tool is something like the Ultrecht Work Engagement Scale, while for managers it is the Gallup Q^{12} or the equivalent offered by various consultancies. Action to enhance engagement, thus, appears to consist of conducting a survey or more general activities, none of which are in any way uniquely linked to engagement with change. To address how engagement with change can be generated we need to look further than attitude surveys and generic actions.

To start to build approaches for engaging people in transformations there is a need to lay some foundations by refining the concept of engagement within the context of organizational change, developing a much deeper understanding of why engagement with change is important and what drives it, before moving on to what is required to stimulate it. Understanding more about what engagement with organizational change is, the impact of its presence or absence, the factors that influence it, its potential outcomes and how it can be fostered to improve stakeholders' experience of change is essential if organizations are to succeed in an era of complexity and chaos.

This book aims to discuss such issues and in doing so to identify how stakeholders, particularly employees, can be engaged in change in order to realize effective transformations in organizations and sustain their benefits.

Overview of the book

In this book we examine the role of engagement with organizational change – referred to as OC engagement which comprises two concepts: (i) Organizational Change (OC) which is a complex, multidimensional, emotional process and has an impact on individuals in the workplace; and (ii) Engagement which is a multifaceted concept that can be experienced, like OC, in different ways by different individuals. Based on these concepts the case is made in this book for the role and significance of OC engagement as a core capability and a necessary condition for organizational effectiveness. We do this by examining OC engagement from two dimensions. First, rather than thinking about it purely as a leadership process in some sort of stage model it is considered from organizational, team and individual perspectives. This approach supports research that explores engagement from different levels and also echoes the literary appreciation of the human element of OC, asserting that change is an individual and an organizational level phenomenon (Hodges, 2016). Individual as well as organizational engagement with OC is, therefore, a critical focus of study within this book. Second, as it is important to continue to bridge the scholar–practitioner divide in the OC field, we examine and translate the theories and empirical evidence into practical implications for action. This approach is supported with the inclusion of insights and stories from the experiences of practitioners actively involved in promoting engagement as part of OC and forms an important part of the process of demonstrating that OC engagement is worth taking seriously. The approaches outlined in the practitioners' stories should not, however, be interpreted as best practices that are readily transferable to other organizations but rather, as providing valuable ideas that may be adapted by other organizations to inform their actions and approach to effective OC engagement.

To address both the dimensions outlined earlier, the evidence for this book is drawn from three distinct perspectives: (i) academic studies; (ii) research by consultancies; and (iii) practitioner insights and stories. Each of these perspectives has its own strengths and weaknesses, but the combined weight of this evidence provides grounding for the theory and practice of OC engagement that indicates that organizations cannot afford to ignore it. In this way, the book will help you to appreciate in more depth the nature of OC engagement, why it is important, its antecedents and outcomes, and how a clearer understanding of OC engagement advances theory, research, practice and the effectiveness of organizational change.

How the book is structured

The premise in this book is that a key way for organizations to transform successfully is through OC engagement. This involves firstly understanding what engagement with change is before identifying how to generate and maintain it in order to improve organizational effectiveness. To achieve this, the book is structured into three parts. Part 1 – Overview of context and key theories – is devoted to setting the stage for what OC engagement is. In Chapter 1 we begin contextualizing the key themes of the book by exploring some of the global velocity trends that are driving the acceleration of change in organizations. These trends are multifaceted, relentless and seditious, and have the potential to disrupt traditional business models. The impact which these trends is having, and might have, on organizations and the work within them is considered.

Chapter 2 focuses on the key concepts of 'engagement' and 'OC' which are central to the subject of the book. This chapter explores the meaning of each of these concepts with reference to various definitions and with a distinction made between academic and management perspectives. In particular, the chapter draws on the body of evidence demonstrating that OC is a complex, multidimensional emotional process and that engagement is a multifaceted concept that can be experienced in different ways. In Chapter 3 – Theoretical perspectives of organization change – the contemporary debates that populate the literature on the nature of change are critically examined. Our aim in this chapter is to review theories relevant to OC engagement which include the nature of change, how change emerges, patterns of change and its magnitude, focus and level. Consideration is given to some of the fundamental theories of OC, with attention drawn to their respective strengths and weaknesses. The theoretical perspectives of engagement are the focus of Chapter 4. These are critically evaluated and consideration is given to which of the theories are most applicable to OC. The uniqueness and similarity of engagement to other constructs such as job involvement, satisfaction and commitment are also examined.

Part 2 – Dilemmas and drivers of OC engagement – of the book explores the critical perspectives of OC engagement and what influences it. Since debate has raged, particularly in academia, about whether or not engagement is a sound construct for organizational effectiveness as well as its applicability across cultures and sectors, this part begins by exploring the more critical views of engagement and examining the dilemma of whether or not OC engagement is a viable construct across the globe. In the first part of Chapter 5 we review whether or not OC engagement is just another consultancy fad or if it has validity. Attention is given to the darker side of OC engagement and the risks it brings to individuals of becoming willing slaves of change in organizations and of ultimately burning out. This raises questions over the line between ethically acceptable and unacceptable behaviour in relation to both employees and management during OC. The ethical issues are, therefore, examined which potentially may be raised when stakeholders are expected to participate in change that may ultimately affect their jobs and well-being. In the second part of Chapter 5 the discussion focuses on cross-cultural perspectives and whether OC engagement is a construct which is applicable across borders. In order to understand what drives OC engagement, its antecedents and outcomes are explored in Chapter 6. Common themes are identified and a model proposed of the principal antecedents (context, process and individual factors) and outcomes of OC engagement.

In Part 3 – OC in practice – the attention is on the applied side of OC engagement in the sense of how it can be fostered and maintained in organizations. Chapters in this part focus on application, with a grounding in theory and research. It begins with Chapter 7 discussing the pivotal role played by leaders and managers in creating an environment in which stakeholders can engage with OC. The chapter explores the differences and similarities between the different roles as well as the impact of effective and ineffective leadership and management. Although a distinction is made between leadership and management, the chapter concludes that both are required to effectively create engagement with change. Since our proposition is that OC engagement is a shared and mutual responsibility consideration we also explore the role of the individual in the OC engagement process, which is important since change is usually seen from the point of view of leaders and managers rather than its recipients.

In an attempt to address how OC engagement can be developed, the aim of Chapter 8 is to identify some key principles and practices underpinning the way that OC engagement can be generated and sustained. We propose that the antecedents of OC engagement can be influenced through the following principles: inclusivity; connectivity; transparency; co-creation; equity and empathy. These principles provide ways for stakeholders to connect with change effectively.

The book is then brought to a close with a summary of the key issues discussed in previous chapters. Importantly, it proposes possible lines of inquiry and theory building for OC engagement which may further consolidate its position at the centre of 21st century organizations and enhance its role in sustaining organizational effectiveness and success.

Overall the structure supports the aim of the book which is to present a coherent and practical view of how organizations might engender engagement with organizational change within their operational, tactical and strategic practices. It does this by providing a comprehensive review of the theoretical and empirical works on engagement and change from a variety of academic and practical perspectives. The academic research presented in the book is reinforced by research from consultancies and insights from practitioners that provides timely evidence. Ultimately the aim is to help raise awareness of the need to foster engagement with OC through a stakeholder perspective.

It is my hope that this book will provide essential knowledge and understanding of how OC engagement can be reshaped so that it creates change that is anchored in an organization and, importantly, that the book sparks conversation, research and challenges to the ideas within it, to move the field forward, as well as identifying further implications for practice.

Part I

Overview of context and key theories

Chapter 1

The accelerating business environment

Learning outcomes

After reading this chapter you will be able to:

- discuss global trends affecting organizations;
- explore the impact of velocity trends on the workplace;
- identify changes in the employee–employer relationship;
- examine orthodoxies for organizing the workforce in response to global drivers for change.

Introduction

To set the scene we begin by considering the context in which organizations are operating by exploring some of the global velocity trends that are driving the acceleration of change in organizations. These trends are multifaceted, relentless, seditious and have the potential to disrupt traditional business models. The only way to survive and thrive is, according to some researchers, by maintaining dynamic stability, which is the ability to stabilize and standardize while also keeping pace with fast-moving disruptive innovations (Christensen et al., 2015). This is like riding a bike where you cannot stand still, but once you are moving it is actually easier. It is not a natural state but it is the state that organizations have to learn to exist in. To achieve dynamic stability there is a need to understand these forces of velocity that are reshaping organizations. We use velocity here in a broad sense, to signify the pace at which technological, social, economic, demographic and climate trends are accelerating. Such trends can also be defined as "crucibles", in which concentrated forces interact and where the direction of the reactions under way is unclear (Greenberg et al, 2017). These crucibles are spaces to watch as each of them alone is driving major change but in combination each has the potential to create radical consequences for organizations. In other words, the intensity of change impacting organizations is being driven by global velocity trends. This chapter will explore some of these trends as illustrated in Figure 1.1. It begins by discussing the trends, then goes on to explore the impact of them on the world of work.

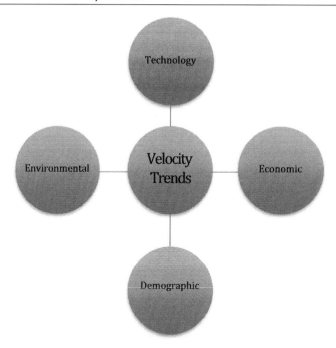

Figure 1.1 Velocity trends

Technology velocity

Technology is a major driver of social and business change. Globally and virally it is providing opportunities for organizations. Hirt and Willmott (2014: 1) note that technology is profoundly changing the strategic context in which organizations operate by "altering the structure of competition, the conduct of business, and ultimately, performance across industries". This is evident in the tremendous increase in electronic data, machine learning, cognitive computing, the ubiquity of mobile interfaces and the growing power of artificial intelligence (AI). Together these developments are reshaping consumers' expectations and creating the potential for virtually every sector with a distribution component to have its borders redrawn or redefined, at a more rapid pace than has previously been experienced.

The most radical technological advances which organizations are facing have not come from linear improvements within a single subject or expertise, but from the combination of seemingly disparate inventions and disciplines. As Arthur (2009) says, the overall collection of technologies bootstraps itself upward from the few to the many and from the simple to the complex. This is illustrated in how the increase in online connectivity, cryptography and advanced analytics have combined to create 'blockchain', a distributed, global database for transactions which is potentially a game changer, since transaction costs represent a substantial share of the world's commercial costs. The combinatorial effects of technology are creating more scope to innovate and to conceive new business models.

Although technological advances bring advantages, concerns are also being raised about the disruption they cause. Alarmists warn that this could be the first great technological revolution that ends up displacing more jobs than it creates. Some econo-mists estimate that automation will result in a third of all American men aged 25 to 54 being out of work by 2050. The fears about automation have been a cyclical phenom-enon for more than 70 years as Markoff (2015) says in his book *Machines of Loving Grace: The Quest for Common Ground between Humans and Robots*. This is worth remembering as the perils of the 'fourth industrial revolution' are pronounced. The phrase 'fourth industrial revolution' is not new but was first used in 1940 by US author Albert Carr (1940), who argued that only a new technological revolution could save western democracy. Advocates propose that the change is incremental rather than radical. In an article entitled 'Why automation may be more evolution than revolution', in the *Financial Times* newspaper, Thornhill (2018) provides the example, of Yandex Data Factory, the Amsterdam-based offshoot of the Russian tech company. The Factory has been working with Russia's Magnitogorsk Iron and Steel Works to optimize its pro-duction processes, leading to a 5 per cent reduction in ferroalloy use and an annual saving of $4m. Yandex has studied seven years of smelting data and used a real-time machine-learning system to calculate the optimal recipe of ingredients to produce the best steel with the least energy. Thornhill (2018) concludes that the accumulation of such incremental improvements can lead to transformational change.

While technological change can be uncomfortable or even destructive, it can also contain the seeds of opportunity (as illustrated in Box 1.1 by Kamales Lardi). Hirt and Willmott (2014) identify the following benefits of technology for organizations: (i) enhancing interaction between customers, suppliers, employees and other stakeholders; (ii) improving management decisions by processing big data and information from the internet of things; and (iii) creating new business models, such as crowdsourcing. To achieve such benefits organizations need to make sure that it is working for them rather than against them. If not managed effectively, the negative impacts of advances in tech-nology on employment levels and disposable incomes could affect economic growth across the globe. A report by the US Technology CEO Council (2016)[1] highlights that the technologies are a game changer and estimate that the effects of the information revolution have transformed just 30 per cent of the US private-sector economy, and that applying such technologies to the rest of the private sector could boost the size of the US economy by $2.7tn by 2031. The report concludes that with the arrival of powerful new technologies, the world is standing on the verge of a productivity boom. The critical question for organizations is, therefore, to what extent the latest generation of technol-ogies is going to change the workplace.

Box 1.1 The end of business as usual

Written by Kamales Lardi, Founder & Managing Partner, Lardi & Partner Consulting GmbH

Digital disruption has hit the global business landscape, effectively transforming the way traditional organizations operate. Digital technologies are creating opportunities across the business value chain, including driving new growth strategies, customer interaction models, digital products and services, as well as optimization of back office functions. A majority of the next generation of employees has been raised 'digital' – technology savvy, mobile and con-nected. They are looking to enter workplaces that are digitally enabled, and able to offer superior employee experiences through the use of digital technologies. Conversely, organiza-tions still employ a large community of traditional workers, remnants of the pre-disruption era.

Provision of a compelling workplace and employment experience will depend on how well organizations are able to understand the evolving workforce needs, as well as utilize digital technologies to drive collaboration, engagement and creativity. Digital disruption has triggered several critical changes in the workplace environment, including the following:

A few short years ago, companies were struggling to implement 'bring your own device' strategies into the corporate technology architecture as employees increasingly used their own smart mobile devices at work. Today, companies are faced with a new wave of challenges as disruptive technologies make their way into the workplace. In 2017, a report by McKinsey entitled 'Harnessing automation for a future that works[2]' concluded that 49 per cent of work across 800 occupations from entry to C-Level can be automated. As companies increasingly explore the use of new technologies such as robotics and artificial intelligence (AI) to improve productivity and efficiency, the traditional workforce faces displacement.

Virtual personal assistant technology, such as Siri and Cortana, are actively being used in the workplace as front-end interfaces to help people find information, collaborate and engage. The rapid development of AI, virtual or augmented reality, robotics and Internet of Things (IoT) are taking front-end interfaces to new heights. For example, the Edge, the smart office building located in Amsterdam, is connected with smartphone apps that recognize individual worker preferences, including workspace location, lighting, temperature and humidity.

Although AI has the potential to dramatically improve our world in many ways, there are notable concerns regarding its potential impact on employment and the workforce. Monotonous tasks could be easily automated, gradually rendering certain roles obsolete. However, AI actually has the potential to improve employee skillsets and create more interesting job profiles across a wide range of industries. In addition, companies are also deploying chatbots as personal assistants, for customer support, data mining, as well as responding to employee questions. Chatbots, which are programs that facilitate text conversation fuelled by AI, are expected to result in efficiency gains of up to 30 per cent.[3]

The IoT, described simply as connected devices, offers clear opportunities for the future workplace. For example, a company with a large, mobile sales team could deploy an integrated, organization-wide communication program through any device within their corporate network. In 2017, a Swedish start-up hub, Epicenter, offered to implant its workers and start-up members with microchips the size of grains of rice that function as swipe cards: to open doors, operate printers or buy smoothies with a wave of the hand. The idea was well received and Epicenter has now implanted more than 150 people.

More than 53 per cent of the world's population is now online, while 68 per cent are connected via mobile devices.[4] People have the option to work from anywhere, without being confined to a single, corporate location. There is a growing number of collaborative workspaces available that encourage interaction, connectivity and creativity. Technology is also making it easier for companies to manage the mobile or virtual workforce. For example, mobile performance management (MPM) solutions enable employers to effectively manage essential areas creating a highly successful mobile workforce such as access and security, performance and expense control. In addition, emerging technologies are creating possibilities for new strategies to identify, engage and manage mobile or digital workforces. For example, Blocklancer offers a freelancer marketplace built on blockchain technology, a distributed ledger system that was initially developed to manage cryptocurrencies. The company has created a Distributed Autonomous Job Marketplace (DAJ) that is entirely self-regulating for finding clients/projects and ensuring jobs are completed efficiently and fairly. On the flipside, increased mobility has raised concerns about cyber security. Mobile employees use a range of access points for connectivity, such as public Wi-Fi, increasing the possibility for malware or cyber-attacks. Organizations that employ a mobile or digital workforce need to deploy robust end-point strategies for threat detection and prevention.

Digital technologies have enabled flexible and transformative working models. By giving teams and individual employees access to the right technologies, organizations are able to develop custom team structures and working models. Based on a study published by Vodafone[5], three in four companies worldwide offer employees flexible hours and work from home.

Digital business models are changing the traditional definition of an employee, as more fluid employment opportunities arise, for example as offered by Uber. Additionally, digital business platforms such as LinkedIn are flattening organizational structures, as employees are now freely able to access even top management directly. The traditional hierarchical organization structures are making way for flatter, holocracies that drive speed, agility and adaptability.

I am personally passionate about the opportunities that digital technologies create in managing diversity in the workplace. New working models create opportunities for a wider range of people, particularly those with non-traditional situations such as working parents or even those with physical disabilities. Additionally, the increasing use of digital platforms helps connect a broader range of ideas and crowd-sourced solutions that promote creativity.

Based on a study by Altimeter Group, 'The 2017 state of digital transformation'[6], the top challenge for companies facing digital transformation is the low digital literacy or expertise among employees and leadership. Digital technologies offer a range of self-directed education and training opportunities that are cost efficient. For example, LinkedIn Learning and MOOC (Massive Open Online Courses) platforms offer a range of competent training and development across a range of topics.

Traditionally, organizations were responsible for managing employee learning and development programmes. The cost burden on the company and the time required to attend trainings were discouraging for on-going skills development. However, with easily accessible online courses, this process has become lighter and more manageable. Companies are also incorporating virtual and augmented reality into training programmes to offer immersive experiential sessions, particularly required for highly specialized skills. These trainings provide near-real experience within a fail-safe environment, generating a workforce that already has a certain level of field experience before day one of work. For example, several UPS training facilities are now offering drivers fundamental driving, delivery and package handling training within a simulated environment.

Incorporation of digital technologies in the workplace is not only resulting in demands for new skillset, but also new roles relating to digital, innovation and specific technologies. For example, over the last two years, companies have begun creating new leadership roles such as Chief Digital Officer, Chief Experience Officer and Innovation Manager to help drive transformation in the organizations.

Digital transformation in the workplace will dominate organizational change initiatives, as companies focus on productivity and efficiency improvements through the use of digital technologies. Digital disruption is impacting practically every phase of the employee lifecycle, from recruitment and on-boarding, through to leaving and alumni management. However, based on the 'The digital workplace report' published by dimensiondata.com in 2017[7], some 60 per cent of organizations did not have a comprehensive strategy around how they deploy, or plan to benefit from, workplace technology.

> A digital workplace could impact the way people work, promoting transformation of business operations that improve collaboration, agility and customer engagement. In order to truly be successful in the digital age, organizations will need to develop strategies that close the gap between people, technologies and the surrounding environment in which they work.

Economic velocity

Economically, globalization is changing the map of consumerism. A report by Ogilvy and Mather (2016) notes that future global economic growth will be reshaped by velocity countries with an epicenter in South Asia, principally India, Pakistan and Indonesia but extending up to China in one direction, and to Egypt, Nigeria, Mexico and Brazil in the other, which comprise more than half of the world's population. The increase in growth of a new middle-class consumer is emerging in these velocity countries, which is expected to create a critical tipping point as the middle-class moves from a minority to the majority of the local population in many of these markets. In conjunction with this Muslim Futurists are reshaping the direction of business growth, consumer demand and social change, by combining consumerism and faith, pairing eco-concern and social activism with a love of luxury and premium brands. It is estimated that global consumption could grow by \$23 trillion between 2015 and 2030, and most of this will come from the expanding consuming classes in emerging economies (Manyika, 2017). As incomes rise, consumers will spend more on all categories but their spending patterns are also predicted to shift, creating more jobs in areas such as consumer durables, leisure activities, financial and telecommunication services, housing, health care and education (Ogilvy & Mather, 2016). Consequently, this next generation of consumers will not only play an important economic role, they will also become key agents of social change, influencers on their governments, arbiters of local lifestyles and empowered consumers in brand attraction and interaction. All of this will have a profound impact on the way companies develop marketing activities, communications and stakeholder relations with these global middle-class consumers.

For businesses to operate in this changing marketplace they will need to focus on differentiation. This means being aware of the nuances, the institutional differences, the regulatory differences and the differences in social perspectives which are creating a demand for a local capability inside a global footprint (Vorhauser-Smith, 2012). In an article in the *Harvard Business Review* on the 'The new rules of globalization', Bremmer (2014) points out that the approach to going global has changed since the governments of developing nations have become cautious, selecting the countries or regions with which they want to do business, picking the sectors in which they will allow capital investment, and selecting the local companies they wish to promote. At the same time traditional business models are being challenged. For instance, there is the evolution of the 'gig economy', a system of employment in which freelance workers sell their skills and services, through online marketplaces, to employers on a project or task basis. Sundarajan (2015) describes how not so long ago, the only people who looked for gigs were musicians, whereas,

> today, more and more of us choose, instead, to make our living working gigs rather than full time. To the optimists, it promises a future of empowered entrepreneurs

and boundless innovation. To the naysayers, it portends a dystopian future of disenfranchised workers hunting for their next wedge of piecework.

As globalization is progressing and changing, so too are anti-globalization sentiments growing, and governments are responding, for example, the UK is moving ahead with leaving the European Union (Brexit); while the USA has stepped back from the Trans-Pacific Partnership (TPP) and made changes to the North American Free Trade Agreement (NAFTA). Across the globe populist revolts are also occurring like those seen in Catalonia in Spain, as well as ethnic cleansing in parts of Asia and the Middle East, which have made discussions about erecting borders and walls more common. Such moves have the potential to restrict the flow of labour between countries and change the economic rules of globalization.

Demographic velocity

Demographic trends are making the workforce culturally more diverse and also older and younger. On the one hand, Generation Y (individuals born between 1980–1994) make up more than half the workforce; while on the other hand, the workforce in industrial economies is ageing and the proportion of the population who have retired from employment is growing relative to the population still in work. By 2030, it is estimated that there will be at least 300 million more people aged 65 years and above than there were in 2014 (Manyika, 2017). This unprecedented increase in ageing and life expectancy is fundamentally changing the organizational assumptions about retirement, about the employment of the over-65s and about the provision of pensions.

Not only is the population ageing and living longer but the proportion of the global population living in urban areas is also increasing. The Development Concepts and Doctrine Centre (DCDC) (2010) in a report entitled 'Global strategic trends', predicts that by 2040 around 65 per cent, or six billion, of the world's population will live in urban areas, attracted by access to jobs, resources and security, with the greatest increases in urbanization occurring in Africa and Asia. Such trends are supported by the United Nations (2014) report on the 'World urbanisation prospects' which outlines that urbanization is integrally connected to the three pillars of sustainable development: (i) economic development; (ii) social development; and (iii) environmental protection. The report highlights the need to forge a new model of urban development that integrates all facets of sustainable development, to promote equity, welfare and shared prosperity in an urbanizing world and concludes that:

> accurate, consistent and timely data on global trends in urbanization and city growth are critical for assessing current and future needs with respect to urban growth and for setting policy priorities to promote inclusive and equitable urban and rural development.
>
> (2014: 4)

So urbanization, along with longevity, has the potential to impact upon and reshape organizations across the globe.

Environmental velocity

A herd of environmental 'black elephants' is gathering which is in danger of trampling on energy resources. A 'black elephant' is a cross between a 'black swan' – a rare, low probability, unanticipated event with enormous ramifications – and the 'elephant in the room' – a problem that is widely visible to everyone, yet no one wants to address it, even though they know that it will one day have vast black swan like consequences. Environmental 'black elephants' include global warming, deforestation, ocean acidification, mass biodiversity, extinction and so on. At a Climate Action Conference in 2016, the President of the World Bank Group, Dr. Jim Yong Kim, was very clear on the dangers of these black elephants:

> . . . with each passing day, the climate challenge grows. Record hot days and months have now become the new norm. The Artic is melting at a record pace, with temperatures this winter 6 degrees Celsius above long term averages. Over 90 percent of reefs in and around Australia's Great Barrier Reef system have succumbed to coral bleaching. We also know that climate volatility in places like the Sahel in Africa contribute to instability and fragility. Continued migration of people, whether from conflict or from lack of opportunity, will stretch demand for natural resources even further.[8]

The solutions for organizations to address such challenges lie not only in climate change projects but also in effective risk management and ensuring that all the thinking and work in organizations is designed with the threat of the herd of black elephants in mind. Jim Yong Kim concludes by referring to the quote by Martin Luther King:

> We are confronted with the fierce urgency of now. In this unfolding conundrum of life and history, there 'is' such a thing as being too late. This is no time for apathy or complacency. This is a time for vigorous and positive action.[9]

To summarize, the velocity trends are linking the world more closely, even as others are causing rifts. Globalization and technology have jointly enabled a massive increase in trade and financial flows and global online traffic. This level of interconnectivity has raised engagement with stakeholders and forced society to think about how information is accessed and consumed. These trends will continue to transform the world. But in which direction? Are we entering an age of de-globalization or can we usher in a new era of inclusive global growth? Global trade wars could disrupt supply chains and drive up prices, hurting both companies and consumers. Economic and political uncertainties could deter investment and dampen innovation, and perhaps even bring about another worldwide economic recession.

Organizations will need foresight and agility to adapt to the trends, as well as original ideas and creativity to continually target and re-tune their products and services to very diverse and still evolving customer bases across the globe. Companies will also need to understand new markets, regions and cities that are perhaps less familiar to them. The progression of demographics will pose challenges over time for some markets as the population ages and labour forces shrink. Populist uprisings, pollution and resource degradation, and cyber security crimes can deter both internal growth and external investment.

Velocity trends are serving as catalysts for organizational change, such as adapting to technology advances, addressing the needs of an ageing population and the demands of younger generations and expanding consuming classes, raising energy efficiency and meeting climate challenges. These trends are powerful and demand thoughtful responses, as they are threats as well as opportunities.

Impact of velocity trends

As a result of these velocity trends, and others not mentioned, the workplace is being digitized, and robotized at a speed, scope and scale never seen before. It is hard to think of any organization not being touched by such trends which are posing a fundamental challenge to organizing people at work.

To adapt and survive, organizations need to review their business models. In a classic 1960 *Harvard Business Review* article, Levitt asked readers to consider, "What business are you really in?" Due to the velocity trends, Levitt's question needs an addendum: "and what's your ecosystem?" In response to the velocity trends any-to-any models are emerging and organizations which are able to adapt to such models are at the centre of platform-based ecosystems, and are distinctly asset-light. For example, Facebook, the online social media and social networking service, creates no content; Alibaba, the Chinese e-commerce, retail and technology conglomerate, owns no warehouses; and Airbnb, the hospitality service, owns no rooms. In response to the rapidly evolving landscape an increasing number of industries are converging under newer, broader and more dynamic alignments – that is digital ecosystems (Atluri et al., 2017).

An ecosystem is a highly customer-centric model, where users can enjoy an end-to-end experience for a wide range of products and services through a single access gateway, without leaving the ecosystem. Ecosystems comprise diverse players who provide digitally accessed, multi-industry solutions. The relationship among these participants is commercial and contractual, and the contracts, whether written, digital or both, formally regulate the payments, the services provided and the rules governing the provision of, and access to, ecosystem data. Apple's introduction of the iTunes store platform, for example, gave birth to a major mobile-app industry. Similarly, the YouTube platform has spawned online multichannel networks (known as MCNs) that aggregate microchannels to attract advertisers looking for new ways to target spending. These developments have in turn created new jobs in areas such as content creation and digital production.

Critical to ecosystems is collaboration since to succeed requires taking advantage of the whole ecosystem of partners including clients, suppliers, start-ups and even universities. Competitive advantage will go to those with the greatest capacity to develop such networks and relationships based on trust, sustainable values and purpose.

Impact on work

How work will continue to evolve in response to the velocity trends is a complex and an unanswered question, but old orthodoxies are already starting to fall. Organizations need to become more agile and resilient so that they can flexibly embrace the global drivers for change, while employees need to have the capabilities and adaptability that will help create a more flexible work environment. Some of the key contours of this change can be considered through a set of orthodoxies which suggest new principles for organizing the workplace. These orthodoxies fall into the following categories: (i) the nature of work; (ii) the supply of labour; (iii) the demand of work; and (iv) employment deals.

(i) The nature of work

The impact of the velocity trends will change the nature of work. Traditionally, organizations hire most people for well-defined jobs and although these employees might eventually move to other positions elsewhere, the nature of the jobs themselves tend not to change substantially. This assumption is starting to evolve as work in marketing, finance, research and development (R&D) and other functions breaks away from set boundaries and hierarchies, morphing into more on-demand and project-based activity. Research by Manyika and colleagues (2016) shows that as work is more likely to be designed and performed by teams, either formally or informally assembled, an organizational model of a network of teams is on the rise in which companies build and empower teams to work on specific business projects and challenges.

Digitization, AI and learning machines are likely to extend commoditization of all forms of work, including professional, highly skilled work. Automation is likely to further destabilize jobs since it allows them to be disaggregated into their component tasks and subtasks and the hiving off of those that can be automated. The nature of work will change, with some jobs being automated, such as service work, while computing power will complement other human skills such as creativity and decision-making. Workers of the future will spend more time on activities that machines are less capable of, such as managing people, applying expertise and communicating with others.

As the nature of work becomes more fluid, jobs are less likely to be defined by a clear description and instead will be more about encapsulating the processes and outcomes of how work is structured, organized, experienced and enacted. These are likely to be made up of constantly changing activities or by a role in a work process, or responsibility for a specific outcome. Thus employee flexibility will become mandatory, as employers will increasingly expect employees to shift roles, responsibilities and tasks quickly. This will put organizational and employee needs on a potential collision course since in traditional bureaucracies, people knew where they stood and where responsibility lay, whereas in flexible networks, it can be hard to discern where responsibility lies or how problems should be resolved. The resulting lack of clarity may lead to low morale, confusion, duplication and job strain. This destabilization of jobs also has the potential to speed up work processes, creating ever greater demands which puts increasing pressure on ensuring that the experience of work is meaningful. As Overell and colleagues (2010: 17) point out there is little merit in adopting high performance models of work organization without a "concomitant willingness to pay attention to the quality of the experience of work [since] they are two sides of the same coin." Additionally, the rapid pace of technological advancement requires employees to understand more than just the current program or system they are working with since it may soon be obsolete, so continuous learning is essential to ensure continued employment.

Even 'emotionally intelligent' work is susceptible to replacement, since for instance, AI chat 'bots' are replacing customer-service assistants and are already being trialled by

Facebook while robotics are being used for some surgical procedures which can be remotely controlled by specialists who may be based on the other side of the globe from the patient. Professor Stephen Hawking warned that as AI advances further, it could take off on its own and redesign itself at an ever-increasing rate since humans, who are limited by slow biological evolution, could not compete, and would be superseded. Digital Darwinism will, therefore, be unkind to organizations which stand still (cited in Cellan-Jones, 2014).

While technologies advance, and hypotheses about their impact multiply, executives are struggling to sort through the implications. On the one hand, techno-pessimists are concerned that the use of technology in the workplace may be revitalizing scientific management practices, which some critics term 'digital Taylorism' (Brown et al., 2010), as they fear it is enabling a high level of managerial control over employee work practices. There is also concern that work no longer has any real boundaries of time or space due to mobile technology, such as Wi-Fi, which means that work can be, and is, performed from anywhere, leading to a blurring of boundaries between work and other aspects of life for many people and which is fuelled by the always available work culture that technology supports. On the other hand techno-optimists see considerable productivity gains for the economy that will, in turn, help create new work opportunities. The growth of new jobs could more than offset the jobs lost to automation. None of this will happen by itself, it will require businesses to seize opportunities to boost job creation. The workforce transitions ahead will be enormous. Manyika and colleagues (2016) estimate that as many as 375 million workers globally (14 per cent of the global workforce) will likely need to transition to new occupational categories and learn new skills, in the event of rapid automation adoption. In response to this companies need to find ways to get the workforce they need, by engaging with policy makers and their communities to shape secondary and tertiary education and by investing in development and training to keep their organizational capabilities relevant. Technology will, therefore, enable new forms of work activity.

The emergence of a new category of knowledge-enabled jobs will become possible as machines embed intelligence and knowledge that less skilled workers can access with a little training. In India, for example, Google is rolling out the Internet Saathi (Friends of the Internet) programme in which rural women are trained to use the internet, and then become local agents who provide services in their villages through internet-enabled devices. The services include working as local distributors for telecom products (phones, SIM cards and data packs), field data collectors for research agencies, financial services agents and para-technicians who help local people access government schemes and benefits through an internet-based device.

Changes in the nature of work will also impact on the expectations of employees, many of whom may look to their managers to slow things down, take a hammer to the velocity trends or just give them a simple answer to make their anxiety and uncertainty about the changes go away. To close the anxiety gap organizations need imagination and innovation and not scare tactics or simplistic solutions that will not work. This means reimagining and redesigning the nature of work in order to keep pace with the velocity forces and thus generate stability while continuing to adapt.

(ii) The labour supply

The global trends are not only changing the nature of work within organizations but also enabling it to break out beyond them. Research indicates that about 25 per cent of the people who hold traditional jobs would prefer to be independent workers, with greater autonomy and control over their hours (Manyika et al., 2016). Digitization and the creation of the gig economy are helping to facilitate the switch to skills-based self-employment or even to hybrid employment combining traditional and independent work. For example, TopCoder, a crowdsourcer of software development, has built a community of more than 750,000 engineers who work on tasks that are often for companies other than those that employ them. Online labour platforms, such as Upwork, Freelancer.com and apps like TaskRabbit, connect freelance workers with employers and customers across the globe. This is also illustrated by the example of fruit pickers who previously looked on their own for work during fruit harvesting season, but who are now organizing themselves, via online communities, and presenting their joint forces directly to employers. Australia's Fruitpickingjobs.com.au, for example, not only enables pickers to join together but also helps them with services such as visas and accommodation. Similarly, the US Freelancers Union is not a union in the traditional sense of negotiating wages on behalf of its members but rather a community of independent freelancers and self-employed professionals which offers its members networking events and online support. Thus global trends are impacted not only on flexible employment arrangements but also the matching of jobs and workers within and across companies.

Collaborative working is also becoming a growing feature of communities, such as the fruit pickers, between organizations and among groups who share a common purpose. In particular, organizations in the digital and gig economies tend to be more horizontal, collaborative, flexible with more blurred boundaries than their traditional counterparts and work towards new conceptions of value. These more fluid structures are leading to new forms of management and leadership. For example, in open-software communities such as Linux, leaders arise because others rate their skills and trust them. Gandini (2016) defines this as the 'Reputation economy', where people's reputation is generated through collaborative relations. The challenge is how to integrate individuals and networks so that they can work sustainably beyond person-to-person collaboration. This is becoming an increasing challenge as the traditional boundaries and roles separating industries, companies, technologies and customers are disappearing. As a result, this requires organizations to be innovative in their approach to the supply and demand of work.

(iii) The demand of work

The velocity trends are creating demand for workers with new and different capabilities. Advances in technology mean that the skilled part of each job will require different capabilities and the routine, repetitive part, which can be much more easily automated, will pay minimum wages or be given over to a bot (Friedman, 2016). The proficiencies increasingly in demand will be in Cloud and distributed computing, big data, marketing analytics, data analysis and user–interface design. Research by Manyika and colleagues (2015) indicates, however, that there are shortages in these areas and insufficient levels of digital literacy which represent threats for organizations seeking to invest in new forms of digital capital. Organizations will not only require digital skills but they will also need good problem–solvers and people with interpersonal skills, such as communication, collaboration, teamwork, creativity, relationship management and emotional skills. As LRN's (previously referred to as Legal Research Network) Dov Seidman explains it, companies and leaders that recognize and put the human connection at the centre of their strategy will be the enduring winners. Indeed, machines can be programmed to do the next thing right. But only humans can do the next right thing. As Friedman (2017) writes in an article in *The New York Times* "The technological revolution of the 21st century is as consequential as the scientific revolution and it is forcing us to answer a most profound question: 'What does it mean to be human in the age of intelligent machines?'" The growth of automation may lead to people being liberated from dull, repetitive tasks and able to focus on the higher value-added job elements. From an employee perspective, the latter option of course would be preferable. People increasingly, over time, will have to be complements to the work that machines do, as technologies which involve robotics or AI work side by side with human beings. To find these employees, organizations are increasingly tapping into a more diverse hiring pool and looking across borders, as well as focusing on the future structure of work (Moritz, 2017).

Individuals, too, need to be prepared for the rapidly evolving demands of work. There will still be demand for human labour, but workers everywhere will need to rethink traditional notions of where they work, how they work, and what talents and capabilities they bring to that work. Some employees may experience something similar to a Darwinian 'survival of the fittest' with some employees being able to absorb the increasing pace, while others, less able to sustain the pace, may face the possibility of obsolescence, and the 'spectre of uselessness' (Holbeche, 2017). Ultimately, we will all need creative visions for how our working lives are organized and valued, in a world where the role and meaning of work is starting to shift.

(iv) Employment deals

A further consequence of the velocity trends is the emerging differences in the aspirations of the workforce. The experience of growing up online is profoundly shaping the workplace expectations of younger generations who at a minimum expect the social environment of their work life to reflect the social context of the internet, rather than a mid-20th century bureaucracy. According to research by the Institute of Leadership and Management (2011), what younger people want is collaborative workspaces and access to the latest and fastest technologies where they can share, comment and collaborate as equals. This is supported by Erickson (2010) who says that younger workers in particular are strongly influenced by their exposure to multimedia stimuli which is causing a fractured and externalized sense of self that can only be experienced through their latest achievement. This, Erickson (2010) argues, leads to a desperate search for recognition at the individual level, and through Facebook and other social media sites, the construction of an ersatz life. As the most connected generations, Generation Y and other younger workers expect management to respect and trust them, to communicate with them in a dynamic, two-way manner, and provide a purposeful work experience. They also expect constant learning, development opportunities and dynamic career progression and to be likely to refuse a project that does not align with their personal values and morality. Organizations need to understand the kinds of motivational practices that work well for the different generations of workers.

In the future, three or four generations, each with different values, needs and expectations, such as working conditions, or work-life balance, will work alongside one another, raising new challenges for finding appropriate relationship contracts. The employer–employee relationship, which is reflected in the traditional psychological contract, has progressively grown in complexity, especially since globalization and technology are shifting organized work onto a different level, in terms of rate of change, connectivity and the mobility of people and activities. Holbeche (2017) warns that the change driven by such global trends represents a widespread violation of the old psychological contract, manifest for instance in the loss of professional autonomy, job security and the possibility of career progression. Consequently, organizations must cooperate in the crafting of a new societal deal that helps the diversity of individuals cope with the changing nature of work.

New strategies are needed that take into account the needs and expectations of a diverse and ageing workforce. This means rethinking conventional strategic HR processes, such as benefits and flexible working. By considering the mindset and behavioural preferences of younger and older workers when designing and implementing HRM (Human Resource Management) strategies, research shows that organizations can more efficiently manage and effectively engage talented employees (Bissola & Imperatori, 2014). If employers and HR fail to get to grips with the changing demographics of the workforce, it could have a detrimental effect on the employee–employer relationship.

Summary

The global trends outlined in this chapter present huge opportunities as well as threats to organizations and the people who work within them. Embracing such trends will require leaders to recognize the dramatic transformation needed in the way they organize work and in their relationships with their employees. To redefine the relationship with their employees, leaders need to understand the nature and potential impact of the on-going demographic, technological, economic and environmental trends, as well as the political, social and legal ones. On the one hand, organizations will demand ever more motivated and engaged employees willing to make extra efforts, while on the other hand, they will be able to offer less security and certain career prospects.

Left unaddressed the impact of the trends will create angst in organizations and will affect not only productivity and performance but also the well-being of employees. To avoid this, leaders will need to question their own assumptions and imagine new possibilities, engaging with others to do so (Greenberg et al., 2017). People need to be engaged to make the change work, as May and colleagues (2004: 13) point out, "Engagement is important for managers to cultivate given that disengagement, or alienation, is central to the problem of workers' lack of commitment and motivation." Yet despite the relevance and importance of engagement and the efforts to engender it, organizations report that employees have become increasingly disengaged (Imperatori, 2017). For without stakeholder engagement in the change process nothing will happen.

An inclusive approach to change which focuses on engagement is important to pursue, not as an end in itself, but as a means of improving change in organizations and working lives. Ultimately, it puts employees at the heart of change. Engagement can play a key role in aiding the successful implementation of change in organizations in response to global trends and is particularly important in enabling agility and resilience in organizations forced to adapt to the changing environments in which they operate. Engagement is, therefore, a key enabler of change.

Notes

1   www.techceocouncil.org/clientuploads/reports/TCC%20Productivity%20Boom%20FINAL.
    pdf
2   McKinsey Global Institute. (2017). Harnessing automation for a future that works. Washington:
    McKinsey Global Institute
3   Jia, M. (2016). How to have a 35% increase in customer service efficiency. Available at https://
    venturebeat.com/2016/12/04/how-to-have-a-35-percent-increase-in-custom
    er-service-efficiency/
4   Global Digital Report. 2018, We are social. Available at https://wearesocial.com/
5   Flexible: friend or foe? (2016). Vodafone study. Available at www.vodafone.com/content/
    index/media/vodafone-group-releases/2016/flexible-working-survey.html
6   Solis, B. and Littleton, A. (2017). The 2017 state of digital transformation. Altimeter Prophet.
7   The digital workplace report: transforming your business: understanding the trends that are
    driving the workplace evolution. Dimension Data. Available at www2.dimensiondata.com/
    en/microsites/digital-workplace-report
8   www.worldbank.org/en/news/speech/2016/05/05/remarks-world-bank-group-president-jim
    -yong-kim-climate-action-summit
9   www.worldbank.org/en/news/speech/2016/05/05/remarks-world-bank-group-president-jim
    -yong-kim-climate-action-summit

Chapter 2

Key concepts

Learning outcomes

After reading this chapter you will be able to:

- explain organizations as complex systems;
- discuss the meaning of change;
- compare and contrast different perspectives on engagement;
- define engagement within the context of organizational change.

Introduction

Due to the potential impact of velocity trends on organizations, which we considered in the previous chapter, it is important to identify how organizations can adapt in response to them. Our premise is that a key way for organizations to transform successfully is through OC engagement. This involves firstly understanding what engagement with change means before identifying how to generate and maintain it in order to improve organizational effectiveness. In this chapter we analyze how the concept of OC engagement is understood and defined from the different perspectives of researchers and practitioners. We do this by breaking down the different elements of the concept ('organization', 'change' and 'engagement') and examining the definition of each of these in turn. The first part of the chapter explores definitions of 'organization' and 'engagement', shedding light on similarities and differences in the definitions and drawing together common themes. A distinction is made between academic and populist definitions of 'engagement' which is not to say that one perspective is better than the other but that it is important to highlight that they might not reflect the same thing and may be based on different assumptions. Inevitably there is a degree of overlap, but the distinction goes beyond terminology to reflect differences in precision, theorization, level of analysis and empirical support.

The concept of OC is also explored, for although there is a growing academic and populist literature on OC, suggesting ways to manage change, there is limited research on engagement with OC. The majority of the literature on employee engagement is within the field of HRM and focuses on generic engagement. The second part of the chapter provides a review of some of the definitions of OC. Only then can we understand better what engagement is within the context of OC and what needs to be managed as part of an OC engagement strategy. Based on our analysis we conclude by proposing a definition of OC engagement applicable for theory and practice which forms the basis of our approach in this book.

Perspectives on organizations

Organizations pervade our physical, social, cultural, political and economic environment, offering jobs, providing goods and services, contributing to the existence of whole communities and shaping the existence and daily experience of individuals across the globe. Organizations are a "social arrangement for achieving controlled performance in pursuit of collective goals" (Buchanan & Huczynski, 2017: 8). This definition emphasizes that it is the preoccupation with performance and the need for control which distinguishes organizations from other social arrangements. As such entities organizations can be understood from several perspectives.

Organizations as metaphors

In his book, *Images of Organizations*, Morgan (2006) introduces the use of eight metaphors to describe organizations and suggests that organizations can be:

1   Machines where processes are implemented as efficiently as possible through highly specifying and standardizing systems and processes.
2   Biological organisms in which growth, adaptation and environmental relations are employed.
3   Human brains that can learn.
4   Cultures which are based on values, norms, beliefs, assumptions, manifestations, artefacts and rituals.
5   Political systems in which personal interests, conflict and power issues predominate.
6   Psychic prisons in which people are trapped by certain ways of thinking.
7   Systems of change and transformation where adaptation and change are prevalent.
8   Instruments of domination where the emphasis is on exploitation of employees.

   Each of these metaphors presents a way of thinking about organizations and of understanding their complex characteristics which makes it possible to identify innovative ways in which to design, change and manage organizations.
   Although researchers employ Morgan's metaphors for a variety of purposes, they also critique the assumptions that they see underlying them, particularly the notions of relativism and pluralism. Tinker (1986: 364) says that Morgan has institutionalized a type of "supportive, tolerant, uncritical, scientific free-for-all" in his set of metaphors. While Reed (1990: 38) contends that Morgan's set of images promotes "a form of cognitive relativism and theoretical pluralism that can be defended only on the basis of a social ontology which maintains that social reality is constituted through shared symbolic representations". In Reed's (1990) view, Morgan's relativism marginalizes the economic and material realities of organizations, even for images that embrace the political and domination metaphors of organizations. McCourt (1997) draws on Reed's (1990) arguments and criticizes Morgan's images as being ready-made products that are too easily consumed. Critics also raise

concerns about whether each of the eight metaphors has equal weight. In particular, Tsoukas (1993) contends that Morgan emphasizes the usefulness of all eight metaphors while implicitly favouring some of them over others. Other scholars aim their critiques at Morgan's treatment of metaphor itself, in particular its usefulness, links to creative thinking and common sense views of organizational reality and question whether metaphorical analysis has generated any truly new ways of thinking about organizations (Oswick et al., 2002). Criticism is therefore aimed at the relativism and pluralism linked to Morgan's typology as well as his implicit bias towards certain metaphors.

In response Morgan warns his critics that it is not an exhaustive account of every conceivable metaphor that can be used to understand and shape organizational life but is an attempt to:

> reveal, through illustration, the power of metaphor in shaping organizational management and how the ultimate challenge is not to be seduced by the power or attractiveness of a single metaphor – old or new – so much as to develop an ability to integrate the contributions of different points of view.
>
> (Morgan, 2006: xii)

It would appear that to understand organizations, there is a need to consider all eight metaphors simultaneously which is akin to seeing organizations as systems.

Organizations as systems

An organization can be viewed as a system which is an interconnected set of elements that is coherently organized in a way that achieves something. As systems, organizations can change, adapt, respond to external trends, seek goals and attend to their own survival. Such systems can be open or closed. As an open system an organization is compared to a human body, in that it imports resources, such as people, materials, equipment, information and money, then transforms these inputs through producing goods and services and then exports those products back into the external environment, as goods and satisfied customers. The open systems approach views the interaction with the external environment as vital for organizational survival and success which is in contrast to the closed systems approach which considers the external environment and the organization's interaction with it, to be for the most part inconsequential. Organizations as open systems are, thus, able to become more flexible and respond to changes in the external environment.

Despite the potential benefits of systems theory, it does have its critics. Kast and Rosenzweig (1973: 57) identify several weaknesses of systems theory. They contend that there should be caution in trying to make the analogy between living organisms and organizations. In other words, organizations may be systems but not necessarily natural systems. Second, on the dichotomy between closed and open systems, they contend that there are difficulties in applying this strict polarization to organizations as most organizations and their subsystems are partially open and partially closed. Thus, 'open' and 'closed' are a matter of degree. Based on such criticisms, it seems appropriate to consider organizations as more complex adaptive systems.

Complex adaptive systems

A complex system is defined as consisting of "aggregates of interacting subunits, or agents, which together produce complex and adaptive behaviour patterns" (Boal & Schultz 2007: 413). Complex adaptive systems (CAS) are systems that absorb information from their environment and create stores of knowledge that can aid action. The concept of CAS thus describes organizations as nonlinear systems whose behaviour is determined by the interaction of its adaptive parts.

Complex systems have a number of common characteristics. First is the presence of a large number of interacting elements within the system. The elements interact with one another, and such interactions are typically associated with the presence of feedback mechanisms in the system. The interactions in turn produce nonlinearities in the dynamics of the system. Any change in any elements of the system causes changes in other elements of it. Second, complex systems are dissipative structures, that is, a semi-stable configuration that does not correspond to external pressures and manipulations in a linear manner (Styhre, 2002). Third, complex systems have the ability for self-organization and adaptation. Self-organization happens as the various decentralized parts of the system interact and adaptation is the behaviours which allow the system to survive changes in its environment (Byeon, 2005). Finally, complex systems tend to exhibit emergent properties. This means that patterns emerge which are due to the collective behaviour of the components of the system. Examples of self-organization and emergence include development of new strategies, development of marketing tactics for specific prospects, self-directed teams and the growth of strategic alliances. As a complex system an organization is able to learn from its environment and change its internal structure and its functioning over time, consequently changing the behaviour of individual elements (Sherif, 2006). Thus, organizations can be considered as dynamic systems of adaptation and transformation that contain multiple parts which interact with one another and the environment.

Organizations have become more complex whilst becoming more transparent; they have become more interconnected whilst becoming more technology driven; and they have become more democratic whilst becoming more accountable (De Haan & Kasozi, 2014). Yet, organizations were not designed to be adaptable and change; they were designed to be disciplined and efficient. That is why, according to Hamel (2012: 131), getting an organization to change is like getting a dog to walk on its hind legs. If you dangle a treat in front of the dog's nose, "you may coax him into taking a few, halting steps on his hind feet, but the moment you turn your back, he'll be down on all four paws again [since] walking upright is not in his DNA". Similarly, most organizations do not have adaptability DNA in their genome as their core management processes were not built with adaptability in mind, so they must build such a capability. In practical terms, this means learning from systems which have demonstrated adaptability, such as the internet which has morphed in many ways from Google to Twitter, from YouTube to Facebook. Unlike organizational systems which are top-down models of control, the internet is all periphery and very little centre since its architecture is end-to-end not centre-to-end. The values of the internet are also in contrast to those in most organizations. Community, transparency, freedom, meritocracy, openness and collaboration comprise the fundamental ethos of the internet whereas within many organizations, the values of control, discipline, accountability, reliability and predictability tend to prevail.

To adapt to the velocity trends and survive, organizations need to integrate such counter posed values and consider the principles used by systems such as the internet which are: variety (need to try a lot of new things); decentralization (create mechanisms from the bottom-up for change); serendipity (create more opportunities for unexpected encounters and conversations); and allocation flexibility (make it easy for resources and ideas to find one another). The challenge is, of course, for organizations to operationalize these principles in everyday practice, which means changing.

Organizational change (OC)

Definitions of OC

Change is a powerful word but hard to define. Clinton (2017: 195) illustrates this with reference to the use of the word in American politics; she says that "in 1992 and 2008, change meant electing dynamic leaders who promised hope and renewal. In 2016, it meant handing a lit match to a pyromaniac". So what is meant by change can vary depending on the situation.

Although there is a growing body of research and literature on various aspects of change, including theories and practices (for example, Burke, 2002); perspectives on change (Burnes & Randall, 2016); ethics and change (By & Burnes, 2013); practical guidelines on leading and managing people through change (Hodges, 2016) and on creativity and change (Dawson & Andriopoulos, 2014), there is, as yet, no consensus about what is meant by OC. Writers from different academic disciplines and perspectives offer competing explanations and as a consequence there is a large, disparate and, at times, contradictory body of literature relating to classifications of change. For instance, the word 'change' is characterized as a container concept, and searching for the word's underlying values results in a whole range of meanings and guises, including transformation, development, metamorphosis, transmutation, evolution, regeneration, innovation, revolution and transition. The ambiguities in such terms are acknowledged, although they are not purely academic, as changes in organizations are believed to be never clearly defined (Dawson 2003). The various definitions of OC tend to carry the same connotation that change involves the introduction or experience of something that is different through new ways of organizing and working. In its broadest sense, change is considered to be "any alteration to the status quo" (Bartol & Martin, 1994: 199). The difference can be small (incremental) or radical (transformational). Moran and Brightman (2001: 111) expand this further and define change as, "the process of continually renewing an organization's direction, structure and capabilities to serve the ever-changing needs of external and internal [stakeholders]". In other words OC is alterations to the whole or parts of an organization. Such definitions are not only generic but also rather vague.

To provide a more specific working definition of OC it is important to include the content, process and context. The content is *what* actually changes in the organization, such as the strategy, structure, systems, goals, processes, behaviours and ways of working. What changes can also be at a strategic or operational level. Strategic changes have an impact on the way that the organization does business – its business systems – and on the way it has been configured – its organizational system. Strategic change involves company-wide transformation such as mergers, acquisitions or downsizing. For example,

Amazon made a strategic change by purchasing the organic grocery chain Whole Foods; the deal gives Amazon hundreds of physical stores and provides the company with an entryway into the competitive grocery and food industry. Operational change involves anything that affects the day-to-day operations. For instance, when Nike set up an extensive system for monitoring and remedying factory conditions in its supply chain, this was an operational change.

The process is *how* the change occurs, which includes the pace of the change, the sequence of activities, the way decisions are made and communicated, and how people are engaged in change initiatives and respond to transition. It is the process of moving over time from a present state to an emergent, uncertain, future state, that is sometimes planned and managed, with the intention of securing anticipated objectives and benefits and sometimes unplanned for and unforeseen ones. It is any adjustment or alteration in the organization that has the potential to influence the organization's stakeholders' physical or psychological experience. Such alterations include changes to the organizational structure, the implementation of new organizational practices, changes in employees' job descriptions, or even geographical relocations of the organization and its subsidiaries. They also include longer term cultural changes which are often harder to design and implement. Each of these changes has the potential to influence not only the organization's performance, but also its employees. The process of change is critical not only for recipients, given that their acceptance and engagement is a key determinant of success, but also for managers and leaders, since they are responsible for shaping and implementing strategy in order to effect required changes. The context is about the *environment* in which the organization is operating and the situation in which the change is being implemented. Hence the need for an awareness of the internal and external drivers for change and for the content and process of change to be adapted to the context in which an organization is operating.

Taking into account the various definitions provided in the literature, for the purposes of this book OC is defined as an on-going dynamic process characterized by content and context. It is a process that unfolds or emerges and as this happens engagement with change also unfolds or emerges. This broad definition accommodates the range of discussions that inform a pluralistic understanding of OC.

The meaning of engagement

The concept of engagement has been the subject of a great deal of interest with a vast amount of managerial literature and academic research being developed, particularly within the field of HRM. Despite its widespread popularity and the financial gains and losses attributed to engaged and unengaged workers, engagement has been criticized as a difficult concept to define because it is viewed by critics (such as Guest, 2014) as a repackaging of traditional concepts such as motivation, satisfaction and commitment. As Christian and colleagues (2011: 89–90) point out: "engagement research has been plagued by inconsistent construct definitions and operationalizations". This lack of clarity has not prevented engagement from being considered a key element to organizational effectiveness with research (Hayward, 2010) indicating that 70 per cent of business leaders believe that engagement is critical for their businesses.

As a concept that has developed over time, engagement has been defined in numerous, often inconsistent, ways, so much so that the term has become ambiguous to many and it is rare to find two people defining it in the same way. It has variously been conceived as: a psychological or affective state, such as commitment; involvement or attachment; a performance construct, such as role performance; effort; observable behaviour; organizational citizenship behaviour; or an attitude. Some researchers have related the concept to other specific constructs such as altruism or initiative (Macey & Schneider, 2008). While others suggest engagement is not conceptualized identically from organization to organization, even though there may be some similarities (Purcell, 2014). Indeed there is little consensus in the literature as to which of these approaches is the definitive, or at least best fit, model for defining engagement. It is, therefore, a challenging and complex concept to describe and study because it seems to manifest itself in many ways, defying initial attempts to box it into a single and simple definition.

There is a need for a definition of engagement within the context of OC in order to differentiate it from other constructs and to be able to identify how it should be generated and sustained. In an attempt to identify the meaning of OC engagement we begin with an analysis of how the concept of engagement has been understood, defined and used from the perspective of consultants, managers and academics.

Consultancy perspectives on engagement

Consultancy firms have conceptualized engagement by combining and relabelling existing notions, such as commitment, satisfaction, involvement, motivation and extra-role performance. For instance, according to consultancy firm PwC[1], employee engagement is an individual's commitment to, and passion for, their work and role within an organization and is the extent to which employees are motivated to contribute to overall business success. To support this definition PwC provides an enticing list of the benefits of engagement including accomplishing the organization's mission, performing better, innovating more, boosting customer satisfaction and reinforcing the organization's talent brand. All of which leads to increased profitability for the organization. Likewise, the Kenexa Research Institute (2012: 1) defines engagement as the extent to which employees are motivated to contribute to organizational success. Similar to PwC, the Institut emphasize that engagement involves how willing an employee is to apply discretionary effort to accomplish tasks that are important to the achievement of organizational goals. A focus on the behavioural elements is also stressed by consultancy firm Aon[2] who define engagement in terms of three general behaviours (Say, Stay and Strive) which they propose engaged employees consistently demonstrate. These behaviours, Aon states, are demonstrated by: consistently speaking positively about the organization to co-workers, potential employees and customers (Say); having an intense desire to be a member of the organization despite opportunities to work elsewhere (Stay); and exerting extra time, effort and initiative to contribute to business success (Strive). The focus of many consultancies is therefore on the engagement of individuals.

A similar approach is used by Gallup – a consultancy firm that many organizations draw upon when defining engagement. Based on employee surveys built up over the years and also on their understanding of employee behaviours that have maximum impact on a company's performance, Gallup defines engagement as "the individual's involvement and satisfaction with, as well as, enthusiasm for work" (Harter et al., 2002: 269). Similar to Aon, Gallup breaks their definition down further into three types of employee:

i. 'Engaged' employees who work with passion and feel a profound connection to their organization, drive innovation and move the organization forward.
ii. 'Not engaged' employees who have essentially checked out and are sleepwalking through their workday, putting in the time, but not the energy, nor the passion into their work.
iii. 'Actively disengaged' employees who are not just unhappy at work but act out their unhappiness and undermine what their engaged co-workers accomplish.

This view of engagement tends to overlap with traditional constructs such as job involvement and job satisfaction rather than providing clarity on the concept of engagement on its own.

A number of consultancy organizations have defined engagement along similar lines to Gallup, often emphasizing the importance of discretionary effort as the key outcome, or a distinguishing feature of an engaged employee. Like Gallup, Willis Towers Perrin has adopted an approach that relies on surveys and defines employee engagement in terms of the preferred characteristics (cognitive, affective or behavioural) that engaged employees' exhibit, as distinct from non-engaged employees. The three features of such engagement are, according to Willis Towers Perrin (Towers Watson, 2013), think, feel and act which are defined as:

i. Think: a rational/cognitive understanding of the organization's strategic goals, values and their fit within it.
ii. Feel: an emotional/affective attachment to the organization's strategic goals, values and their fit within it.
iii. Act: the motivation/willingness to do more than the minimum effort in their role, that is to be willing to invest discretionary effort, to 'go the extra mile' for the organization.

This definition of engagement is similar to that of Gallup in that it focuses on aspects of employee characteristics that have been found to enhance performance within organizations.

Taken together, these examples suggest that in business, engagement is defined as a blend of existing concepts such as job satisfaction, commitment to the organization and extra-role behaviour, which is the discretionary effort of an individual which goes beyond their job description.

Engagement tends to be conceptualized in a variety of ways by consultancy firms to illustrate its beneficial outcomes. Consultancy firms which are in the business of improving levels of engagement in organizations often claim that they have found conclusive and compelling evidence that work engagement increases profitability through higher productivity, sales, customer satisfaction and employee retention. For instance, according to Gallup[3], their employee engagement approach realizes performance gains at the individual, team and organizational levels. To achieve such desirable objectives consultancies tend to steer managers towards management practices which usually involve installing appropriate drivers to ensure significant improvements in engagement. This creates a sense that engagement is, therefore, something which can be 'done to' employees.

The message from consultants is clear: increasing work engagement pays off. However, with the exception of Gallup this claim is not substantiated. It is merely stated in reports as a positive relationship between employee engagement and a company's profitability. For the consultancy industry, engagement is portrayed with a narrow range of identities, all of which can be captured and measured through metrics of considerable semiotic persuasiveness. However, to dismiss such constructions as commercial hyperbole would be to critically underestimate the role consultants have played in constructing, promoting and driving the engagement narrative.

Management perspectives on engagement

Similar to consultants, managers refer to engagement as the willingness of employees to 'go the extra mile' on behalf of the organization, colleagues and customers. Many of the managerial definitions of engagement which do exist are, however, vague and lack substance. For instance, among HR managers, Luisis-Lynd and Myers (2010) found a diverse range of concepts in use which they defined as: 'engagement-in-the-wild'. This lack of clarity is also confirmed in a UK government sponsored review of employee engagement which found over 50 different definitions of employee engagement. In the end, the definition the review settled on was: "a workplace approach designed to ensure that employees are committed to their organization's goals and values, motivated to contribute to organizational success, and are able at the same time to enhance their own sense of well-being" (MacLeod & Clarke, 2009: 9). In its favour this definition differs from other approaches in highlighting employee well-being alongside more typical organizationally oriented outcomes as a goal of engagement – although the exact definition of employee engagement is still left unclear.

A number of professional organizations define engagement along similarly vague lines, often emphasizing the importance of discretionary effort as the key outcome or a distinguishing feature of an engaged employee. For example, the Institute of Employment Studies (IES) (Robinson et al., 2004) states that engagement is a positive attitude held by an employee towards the organization and its values and that an engaged employee is aware of the business context and works with colleagues to improve performance within their job for the benefit of the organization. IES notes that there are three important requirements that must be in place before engagement can exist: (i) a healthy psychological contract; (ii) a need for employees to identify with the organization, its values and a belief in its products and services; and (iii) a need for employees to understand the context in which the organization operates. Summarizing this, IES proposes that engagement is based on several factors: a belief in the organization; a desire to work to make things better; an understanding of the business context; respect and support of colleagues; and keeping up to date with developments in the field. So the managerial perspective tends to conceptualize engagement by combining various traditional constructs to emphasize the organizational benefits of it.

The management view has progressively expanded the range of constructs to be included under the umbrella term of engagement, in many instances not just stressing a sense of discretionary effort but also a strong emotional element as well. A synthesized definition of such elements is offered by the Conference Board (2006), which views engagement as a heightened emotional and intellectual connection that an employee has for their job, organization, manager and co-workers that, in turn, influences them to apply additional discretionary effort to their work. Similar views are held by the CIPD (2009), which refers to engagement as creating opportunities for employees to connect with their colleagues, managers and wider organization, where employees are motivated to want to connect with their work and really care about doing a good job. The CIPD (2009) stresses that engagement goes beyond job satisfaction and is not simply motivation but something an employee has to offer. So similar to that of consultancy firms, the management view of engagement tends to refer to engagement as an umbrella or overarching term that subsumes many different concepts (such as attitudes, behaviours, dispositions) relevant to the performance of an individual or the organization as a whole.

Limitations of consultancy and management definitions

There are a number of limitations in the consultancy and managerial perspectives of engagement. First, critics, particularly in the academic camp, point out that the management and consultancy views on engagement are not embedded in any validated theory (Sparrow & Balain, 2010), thus making them, in many cases, invalid. Second, the management and consultancy definitions are largely driven from their respective database surveys which are designed for problem description and not necessarily problem solution and are based on an empirical model rather than a theoretical one. The disadvantage of this approach is that information is gained from observation, experience and experiment, rather than by any structure analysis (a theory) that enables observations to be explained and linked back to an underlying reality that brings observations together. Third, consultancy and management definitions of engagement tend to link it to business performance outcomes that can only result from engaged employees. This is generally based on a performance recipe which in all too many businesses, even amongst line managers who support the idea of engagement, is based on an act of faith rather than any sound evidence.

The academic perspective

It has to be acknowledged that the definitions of engagement used by academic researchers are not any better than the practitioner ones in producing an operational definition that clearly differentiates the concept from other similar constructs. However, as Balain and Sparrow (2009) point out, a more theoretical approach does help to understand the phenomenon of engagement. In reviewing some of the main academic definitions we consider where they originated and what assumptions and theories they are based on, so that we can better understand what engagement is within the context of OC and how it can be fostered and sustained.

Academic approaches to engagement can be traced back to the notion of engagement proposed by Kahn (1990) which was based on his study of camp counsellors at an athletic summer camp. Drawing on the theory of self and of how different selves interact with the roles that they need to play in their workplace, Kahn defines engagement as "the simultaneous employment and expression of a person's preferred self in task behaviours that promote connections to work and to others, personal presence and active, full performance" (Kahn, 1990: 700). The more people draw on their selves to perform their roles within those boundaries, "the more stirring are their performances and the more content they are with the fit of the costumes they don" (Kahn, 1990: 692). Kahn points out that people can use varying physical, cognitive and emotional degrees of themselves in engagement. The physical aspect of employee engagement concerns the physical energies exerted by individuals to accomplish their roles; the cognitive aspect is employees' beliefs about the organization, its leaders and working conditions; and the emotional aspect is how employees feel about each of those three factors and whether they have positive or negative attitudes towards the organization and its leaders. Engaged employees thus put a lot of effort into their work because they identify with it.

Grounded in Goffman's (1961) work on symbiotic relationships, Kahn's definition suggests that the more people draw themselves into their various work roles, which is engagement, the better their performance and the more happiness they experience. Drawing on themselves means self-employment (effort, involvement, flow, mindfulness, intrinsic motivation and psychological presence) and self-expression (creativity, personal voice, emotional expression, authenticity, non-defensive communication, playfulness and ethical behaviour). For Kahn (1990), engaged individuals express and fully involve their sense of self in their role with no sacrifice of one for the other. An individual is, therefore, engaged when they are able to express their authentic self and are willing to invest their personal energies in their job.

Since Kahn first proposed his definition of engagement there has been a steadily growing stream of research that has sought to further explore the meaning and significance of engagement. Much of the research builds on Kahn's concept of engagement, for example Maslach and colleagues (2001: 417) refer to engagement as a psychological and emotional state, a "persistent, positive affective motivational state of fulfillment". Similarly, Hallberg and Schaufeli (2006) define it as being charged with energy and dedicated to one's work. Rothbard (2001) also supports and expands Kahn's definition to suggest that engagement is a two-dimensional motivational construct that includes: (i) attention – the cognitive availability and the amount of time one spends thinking about a role; and (ii) absorption – the intensity of one's focus on a role. Saks (2006) expands on Kahn's (1990) focus on role performance and defines employee engagement as a distinct and unique construct consisting of cognitive, emotional and behavioural components that are associated with an individual's role performance and is the extent to which an employee is psychologically present in a particular organizational role. Building on this premise that engagement is role related and that the two most dominant roles for organizational members are their work role and their role in the organization, Saks (2006) proposes a two-dimensional engagement model which consists of job and organizational engagement. Job engagement pertains to the extent to which an individual is psychologically present in their role, when performing specific job tasks and responsibilities; whereas organizational engagement pertains to an individual's psychological presence in the role that is related to the broader organizational mission and context. This highlights that there is a difference between individual and organizational engagement.

Drawing on Kahn's (1990) work, Alfes and colleagues (2010: 5) have defined engagement as "being positively present during the performance of work by willingly contributing intellectual effort, experiencing positive emotions and meaningful connections to others". Similar to other definitions, Alfes and colleagues (2010) propose that engagement has three facets: intellectual, social and affective. Intellectual engagement is the extent to which an individual is intellectually absorbed in work. Social engagement is the extent to which an individual is socially connected with the working environment and shares common values with colleagues. Affective engagement is the extent to which an individual experiences a state of positive affect relating to their role at work. Schaufeli and colleagues (2002) offer a more attitudinally focused variant on Kahn's definition, suggesting that work engagement is a positive, fulfilling work-related state of mind that is characterized by vigour, dedication and absorption. *Vigour* refers to energy and mental resilience of an individual at work and their willingness to invest high amounts of effort in work. *Dedication* refers to an individual being strongly involved in their work and experiencing a sense of significance, enthusiasm, inspiration, pride and challenge. This dimension has conceptual similarity with having a strong identification with one's work. *Absorption* refers to an individual fully concentrating on their work and the extent to which employees lose themselves in their work and experience a sense of engrossment when carrying out their work. When absorbed, people can feel as if time stands still. This construct is closely linked to the concept of 'flow' (Csikszentmihalyi, 2000) and 'timelessness' (Mainemelis, 2001) and has a stronger emphasis on thinking rather than feeling. Despite having slightly different perspectives there are core commonalities between the conceptualizations of engagement between Schaufeli and colleagues (2002) and that of Kahn (1990). Both definitions share similar physical energetic (vigour), emotional (dedication) and cognitive (absorption) components. Compared to other definitions, those of Kahn (1990) and Schaufeli and colleagues (2002) are multi-faceted and incorporate the notion of the entire or whole self being employed in the engaged state, characterized by energy and absorption which is reflected in attitudes such as commitment and involvement.

Although definitions of employee engagement in the research literature, such as Kahn's (1990), tend to describe it as a state, some others refer to engagement as a process. For example, for Macey and Schneider (2008), engagement is a process that subsumes several pre-existing organizational constructs and results in a specific type of performance. They distinguish between trait, state and behavioural engagement: trait engagement reflects that an individual disposition will be more or less engaged and provides a neces-sary reminder that not everyone will wish to be enthusiastically engaged, even when the circumstances might appear to merit it; state engagement reflects the feeling of being engaged and is characterized by energy and absorption and reflected in familiar attitudes such as commitment and involvement; and behavioural engagement is defined as extra-role behaviour and extends to forms of proactive activity such as job crafting. Empirical work has built on Macey and Schneider's framework (such as Christian et al., 2011), and consultants have applied the model in organizational interventions (Mone & London, 2010). However, it is not without its critics, for instance Saks (2008) points out that for Macey and Schneider, engagement serves merely as an umbrella term for whatever one wants it to be. More specifically Newman and Harrison (2008) argue that when engagement is broken up into the separate aspects of state, trait and behaviour, state engagement becomes a redundant construct and tells us nothing more than an indivi-dual's attitude towards their job which has been measured by other constructs in the past. Instead, Newman and Harrison (2008) propose that the defining features of employee engagement are the simultaneous presence of three behaviours in employees, namely their performance in the job, citizenship behaviour and involvement. This does, how-ever, shy away from defining the psychological state of engagement and merely describes its outcomes. Indeed these types of engagement may be viewed either as manifestations of engagement, in line with Kahn's (1990) perspective or as outcomes of engagement, in line with Schaufeli and colleagues' (2002) more attitudinal perspective. Within the con-text of OC, engagement as a process does have some appeal, especially at an organiza-tional level, however, it must also be considered at an individual and team level. In contrast to seeing engagement as a process, some view it as the opposite of other constructs, such as burnout.

Engagement as the opposite of burnout

Engagement is defined, by some researchers, as the opposite or antithesis of burnout which is the response to chronic emotional and interpersonal stressors on the job. On an individual level burnout represents a misfit between the person and his or her work environment – the job exceeds the individual's capacity in some form (Maslach, 2003). Burnout is, however, not just an individual's response to stressors, but it is also a reaction to the interchange between the individual and others in their workplace and the general work situation itself; it is, therefore, a social construct. Although some research has demonstrated a connection between burnout and a few demographic variables such as single vs. married, younger vs. older (Maslach et al., 2001), most findings lean towards situational context rather than demographic or dispositional factors. For example, excessively or chronically challenging jobs, imbalance of resources vs. demands, and consistent personal and role conflict consistently show up in the situations most likely to elicit burnout (Schaufeli & Enzmann, 1998).

The relationship between burnout and engagement is controversial. According to Maslach and Leiter (1997), engagement and burnout are the positive and negative endpoints of a single continuum. Initially, Schaufeli in research with Maslach (Maslach et al., 2001) seemed to support this view that burnout and engagement were opposite ends of a continuum but in later research he argued that they are conceptually and empirically distinct (Schaufeli et al., 2008). Others such as Cole and colleagues (2012) suggest that on the basis of the empirical evidence, engagement and burnout are best viewed as two sides of the same coin. This may, however, be a rather simplistic view as the dimensions of both are different.

Burnout is defined by the three dimensions of exhaustion, cynicism and sense of inefficacy (Maslach, 2003): exhaustion leads employees to distance themselves emotionally and cognitively from their work; cynicism is characterized by a negative and callous response to co-workers and to the job itself, and is highly correlated with exhaustion; and a sense of inefficacy relates to feelings of ineffectiveness and an inability to accomplish one's goals or job tasks. Exhaustion and cynicism can develop because of work overload and social conflict whereas inefficacy appears to be a result of a lack of resources to carry out the work. In contrast, the corresponding three dimensions of engagement – energy, involvement and efficacy – are the antipode of the dimensions of burnout. By implication that means that individuals who are high on engagement are inevitably low on burnout, and vice versa. In other words, engagement is the opposite of burnout.

Disengagement

In contrast to engagement, disengagement is when people withdraw and become passive in their roles. Kahn (1990: 694) defines disengagement as "the uncoupling of selves from work roles" and likens it to robotic or automatic behaviours, suggesting that people who are disengaged hide their identity, thoughts and feelings while at work. These people perform their roles in a thoughtless way, as opposed to being involved and connected with what they have to accomplish. Disengaged employees may push their work onto others or, if they are in a managerial role, they may excessively delegate to their employees, avoid challenging or questioning what others do and keep ideas to themselves. Disengagement or "unemployment of the self" (Kahn, 1990: 701) is thus akin to withdrawal.

Withdrawal is "a matter of degree, with voluntary turnover the most extreme and absenteeism less dramatic" (Fugate et al., 2012: 898). Some forms of withdrawal are similar to those noted by Kahn (1990), such as distancing of oneself and disconnecting from the organization or others. For example, during OC when employees are unclear on how the change will affect them, they may enter into a self-protective mode that involves psychological distancing, which is achieved through devaluing the organization and reducing organizational identification. Uncertainty about change may also trigger distancing in the form of a loss of affective commitment and satisfaction (Michela & Vena, 2012). Perceptions of inequity in relationships can also result in withdrawal (Taris et al., 2004). For instance, if employees feel that their line manager is not involving them in decisions about changes they may withdraw. This can be related to the Theory of Reasoned Action (TRA) (Ajzen & Fishbein, 1980), which is a motivational theory based on expectancy theory and posits that behaviour is a function of a person's intentions which are determined by individual differences and situational factors. Applied to individual withdrawal, TRA posits that individuals are motivated to avoid or mitigate harm or threats due to changes at work, or conversely motivated to pursue or realize benefits and challenges. In either case, avoidance often manifests as intentions and actual behaviours.

While some forms of withdrawal are similar to those noted by Kahn (1990), others are similar to those used for describing burnout, such as emotionally draining and exhausting work. However, there also appears to be a few key differences between disengagement and burnout. First, job burnout is a stress response that is a personal reaction to the work environment and its dynamics, whereas disengagement is referred to as a decoupling of the self from the job. Thus, disengagement may predict burnout. Second, burnout refers to a complete exhaustion level at which a person cannot perform their job and at which they become negative and cynical towards others and their job. In contrast, disengagement does not necessarily include physical exhaustion as individuals may complete their work but with an emotional detachment that removes their sense of identity with the work and the organization. Disengagement and burnout can therefore be considered different concepts.

Engagement as a transient experience

Affective Shift Theory

Research has generally conceptualized engagement as a relatively stable and persistent phenomenon because of the continued presence of specific job and organizational characteristics (for example, Macey & Schneider, 2008; May et al., 2004; Schaufeli, et al., 2002). In contrast to this is the argument that engagement is less consistent and something that fluctuates depending on the organizational context and individual experiences (George, 2010). This view is supported by Kahn (1990: 693) who refers to engagement as "moments of task performances", meaning that it is not a stable trait or characteristic of an individual; instead it is a moment-to-moment experience that naturally fluctuates depending on the work context, the individual themselves and other factors of the work and the job role. Engagement, thus, relates to an individual's experiences of working. The Affective Shift Theory seeks to explain the dynamic nature of engagement. The theory is based on the assumption that both positive and negative affect have important functions for engagement and proposes that a core mechanism underlying the emergence of high engagement is a shift from negative to positive affect. So as a dynamic process that varies over time, engagement will wax and wane as a person moves through their working day, shifting from one task to another and being exposed to various kinds of events.

Defining OC engagement

So what is engagement? The answer is equivocal. Or perhaps it is more correct to state that the answer depends on one's perspective. Within the academic world, engagement is viewed as a psychological state, as compared with the managerial sphere, where engagement is conceptualized more broadly as a workforce strategy. Taking a purely academic perspective, engagement can be defined as a unique positive, fulfilling, work related state of mind or attitude that is characterized by vigour, dedication and absorption. However, at the same time, although supported by empirical research, this perspective on engagement may be considered rather narrow because it does not include its consequential behaviour. The behavioural aspect is particularly important for management and consultancy, which is the very reason that in these contexts engagement is defined in broader terms and includes employee behaviours that are in line with organizational goals. The reasoning is that employees might feel 'engaged' in their work, but may nevertheless not contribute to organizational effectiveness because their engagement is not properly focused. Unfortunately, by defining engagement more broadly, as consultants tend to do, its uniqueness is lost because the distinction with other concepts such as extra-role performance and organizational commitment gets blurred. So, it seems that we are stuck in a dilemma: either engagement is defined narrowly as an experience such as a purely psychological state in which case its practical relevance is reduced, or it is defined in broader terms including its behavioural expression, in which case the concept gets fuzzy. In large part, as Macey and Schneider (2008) say, the confusion about the meaning of engagement can be attributed to the bottom-up manner in which the engagement notion has quickly evolved within the managerial community. This bottom-up method that flourishes in business is not only at odds with the top-down academic approach that requires a clear and unambiguous definition of the term, but it also hampers the understanding of engagement for practical purposes, particularly within the context of OC.

So how do we move productively forward in defining engagement within the context of OC when there appears to be several different definitions of employee engagement? We can do so by: creating a unifying definition that combines the relevant concepts across definitions; capturing the key components that make engagement with OC unique from other constructs; integrating key perspectives; separating the antecedent and consequence constructs from the definition itself; and considering engagement at different levels. Taking these into account for the purposes of this book we refer to OC engagement at different levels in an organization. At an individual and team level it is a *transient attitude*, where an individual or team is *focused* on and aligned with the goals of

OC, and channels their *emotional* and *cognitive* self to transform change into a *purposeful accomplishment*, whereas at an organizational level, OC engagement is a process by which an organization increases the involvement of its employees and other stakeholders with OC. OC engagement is, therefore, an *active role*; not something that is happening *to* people but instead something they are engaging *with*. In terms of what this means in more detail we will break the definition down and examine its component parts.

First, employee OC engagement is an *attitude*. Practitioners and academics still question whether the condition of engagement is an attitude having the three components of cognition, affect and behaviour; or is more akin to a motivation, that is a heightened state of goal directed behaviour as in vigour. Several existing approaches to engagement refer to it as a motivational state or use the language of motivation to describe engaged employees (for example, Halbesleben et al., 2009). OC engagement, however, is more than just motivation because an individual can be motivated in a direction that fails to support the goals of change, be directed with manipulative or purely instrumental intent, or be motivated without skill and thus counterproductive. Instead we propose, in line with research such as that by Schaufeli and colleagues (2002) and Robinson and colleagues (2004) that OC engagement is an *attitude* held by the employee towards OC and the connection and commitment employees exhibit towards an organization and leads to higher levels of productive and effective work behaviours. Ajzen and Fishbein (1980) make some important and useful points in this area highlighting that attitudes themselves are influenced by prior beliefs – it is beliefs that cause attitudes. What this means is that employees make a judgement about the ability of their organization and themselves to deliver change. These beliefs then shape the specific attitudes that they hold. As an attitude, OC engagement is a personal choice. It means that employees like to involve themselves and their ideas in change which in turn leads to positive emotions. OC engagement is, therefore, an attitudinal concept which embodies an individual's enthusiasm in the process of change.

Second, OC engagement is a *transient* attitude that can fluctuate with individuals, teams and across an entire organization. Our proposition that people cannot be engaged at all times is supported by research, such as Kahn (1992) and Macey and Schneider (2008). The degree to which OC engagement fluctuates and how long it can be sustained for will vary depending on the individual and the situation. This means that the intensity of the attitude is likely to vary over time, so stakeholders who are highly engaged with change today may feel less engaged tomorrow due to various personal and/or situational reasons. The scope of engagement will, therefore, vary from change to change, which by definition suggests how it manifests itself, or what results from engagement, varies to a degree as well.

Third, *focus* is a key part of the definition of OC engagement. A focus on OC needs to have a target on factors such as its rationale, goals, implementation and sustainability because including focus with no target leaves this component of engagement a little vague and fails to incorporate an important aspect of what is critical for engagement. Employees whose engagement appears to be focused elsewhere other than with OC may give a great deal of energy towards a goal that is not in the organization's change strategy and not where the organization wants them to expend their efforts or energy. Such individuals, in the worst case scenario, may have a great focus on fulfilling their own goals and, as a result, may even be considered as mis-using organizational resources or as creating a performance issue. Not every change will require the same amount of focus nor will it require employees to invest their focus to the same level at all times. The amount of focus needed will depend on the nature of the change.

Fourth, *emotional and cognitive self*: when stakeholders are engaged with OC, they employ and combine varying levels of their emotional and cognitive selves as they transform their work tasks and specific activities for OC into meaningful accomplishment. Not only do different types of change require different investments of an individual's cognitive and/or emotional self but people are also different in how they approach change and interpret it. Specifically, some people tend to be more logically focused, opting for a cognitive explanation for sense-making and decision-making while others are more likely to understand and make decisions through their emotions. In essence, OC engagement captures how workers experience change: as stimulating and energetic and something to which they really want to devote time and effort (the vigour component); as a significant and meaningful pursuit (dedication); and as engrossing and something on which they are fully concentrated (absorption) which supports Schaufeli and colleagues' (2002) and Kahn's (1990) perspectives of engagement.

Fifth, the synergistic mix of these aspects of an individual is directed towards a *transformation* of the tasks or activities of change into *purposeful accomplishment*, which is meaningful or has significance to the individual and/or team. Classical motivation theorists propose that individuals have innate needs for work that is meaningful. For example, Alderfer (1972) and Maslow (1968) developed theoretical models describing the inherent need of individuals to seek higher order values that translate into meaningfulness and purpose. In contrast, diminished accomplishment or lack of successful achievement at work is considered a component of job burnout (Maslach & Jackson, 1981). Thus, employees engage with OC to fulfil their need for purposeful accomplishment, and they do so by transforming the meaning of OC through the full expression of themselves. Finally, at an organizational level OC engagement is a *process* of enabling and encouraging stakeholders to become more effective in OC.

Researchers such as Kahn (1990) and Schaufeli and colleagues (2002) incorporate antecedents and consequences into their definitions. However, for our purposes a definition of engagement with OC only is wanted such that when an individual is asked, 'What is OC engagement?' they can answer without also saying what causes, triggers or promotes it. The definition used in this book does not therefore include the antecedents or the consequences of engagement which provides a distinguishing difference with most other definitions. So for the purposes of this book, engagement is defined as an attitudinal concept experienced by individuals in an organizational process in relation to change that is sufficiently distinct from other, similar constructs and regarded as worthy of consideration in its own right.

Levels of OC engagement

We also have to be cognizant of OC engagement manifesting itself at different levels in an organization. Critics point out that it is time for engagement to be considered at all levels within an organization – the individual, team and organizational (Balain & Sparrow, 2009). The most fruitful way of thinking about OC engagement is therefore to see it as an individual, team or organizational concept – rather than something to be managed merely at the individual level. Many organizations have not yet made this jump and still think about engagement at the individual level as gaining the 'hearts and minds' of their employees. Indeed this is one part of OC engagement but engagement with OC also manifests itself within teams helping to facilitate the development of a common purpose and cohesiveness. Likewise OC engagement is also manifest at an organizational level and as such needs to be managed across an organization and its various locations. Therefore, OC engagement needs to be considered at an organizational, team and individual level.

Summary

OC engagement is a dynamic multifaceted concept which is not just a one-off event for an organization but an on-going activity. At an organizational level OC engagement is a process by which an organization increases the involvement of its employees and other stakeholders with OC. While at an individual level OC engagement is an attitude, wherein an individual is focused on, and aligned with, the goals of change, and channels their emotional and cognitive self to transform change into a meaningful and purposeful accomplishment. This also translates to engagement at a team level. Engaged employees not only have the capacity to be energetic, they enthusiastically apply that energy to OC. When engaged, employees feel compelled to strive towards achieving change. They accept a personal commitment to attaining the goals and benefits of OC and become absorbed in change. The practical implication of this is that organizations need to articulate and share what OC engagement is. This will involve reviewing how they define and communicate the importance of engagement with change at an organizational, team and individual level.

Notes

1 www.pwc.com/us/en/people-management/fast-takes-talent-innnovation/employee-engagem
   ent.html
2 www.aon.com/unitedkingdom/trp/talent-solutions/employee engagement.jsp
3 www.gallup.com/workplace/home.aspx

Chapter 3

Theoretical perspectives of organizational change

Learning outcomes

After reading this chapter you will be able to:

- compare and contrast theoretical perspectives of organizational change;
- identify different patterns of change in organizations;
- discuss the different rates of occurrence of change and its focus;
- appreciate the critical perspective of change in organizations.

Introduction

Change is an ever-present feature of organizational life, both at an operational and a strategic level. The ability of an organization to change is, to an extent, a conflict between perceptions of stability, continuity, consistency and certainty, against the chaos, fluidity and uncertainty. To successfully change, an organization needs to be comfortable with this complexity and to understand fully what OC is and what is needed to successfully implement and sustain it. For as Burnes (2006: viii) says, we cannot understand OC sufficiently, "nor implement it effectively, unless we can map the range of approaches and evaluate what they seek to achieve, how and where they can be applied, and, crucially, the evidence which underpins them". In undertaking these tasks, theory plays a significant role, as Collins (1998: 1) suggests: "a key problem with much of the study of change in organisations is that the authors active in the field tend not to discuss, explicitly, the theoretical models and frameworks which guide their analysis". In an attempt to begin to address such issues the aim of this chapter is to engage in a discussion of some of the theoretical perspectives relating to change, and in particular, to consider the contemporary debates that populate the literature on the nature of OC. Our aim is not to provide an in-depth analysis of the theories of OC, as this has been done effectively elsewhere (for example, Burke, 2002), but instead to review theories relevant to OC engagement, which include the nature of change, how change emerges, patterns of change and its magnitude, focus and level. We do this by exploring the various theories of change that offer different exploratory lenses.

The OC phenomenon

As a heterogeneous phenomenon OC is inherently messy, complex and loaded with unpredictability. Consequently, many academic and consultancy studies conclude that it is difficult and "often ugly in organizations because of resistance [which means that] clever business plans [about change] rarely survive the first attempts to put them into practice" (Xenikou & Furnham, 2013: 183). This difficulty in achieving success is supported by Hamel and Zanini (2014: 1) who argue that the reality is that organizations were simply never designed to change proactively and deeply, instead, "they were built for discipline and efficiency, enforced through hierarchy and routinization". In an attempt to address this complexity the leadership and management of OC have become highly desirable capabilities. Graetz (2000: 550) goes as far as suggesting that "against a backdrop of increasing globalisation, deregulation, the rapid pace of technological innovation, a growing knowledge workforce, and shifting social and demographic trends, few would dispute that the primary task for management today is the leadership of organizational change." The successful leadership and management of change are accepted as a necessity in order to survive and succeed in a highly competitive and continuously evolving environment driven by velocity trends. This is not, however, easy since the need for transformational change is frequently unpredictable and tends to be reactive, discontinuous, ad hoc and often triggered by an organizational crisis. Success is often illusionary as according to some researchers there is a mismatch between the pace of change in the external environment and the fastest possible pace of change in most organizations, as Hamel and Zanini (2014: 1) say, "if it were otherwise, we wouldn't see so many incumbents struggling to intercept the future".

Transformations tend to degrade rather than visibly fail. The typical scenario is that leaders and their employees summon up a huge initial effort, results improve, sometimes dramatically, and victory is often declared too quickly. Then, slowly but surely, the organization slips back into its old ways and employees say things like 'we have undergone three transformations in the last eight years, and each time we were back where we started 18 months later'. This inability to sustain change indicates a fundamental lack of a valid framework for identifying, implementing and embedding change successfully, instead what is available is a wide range of contradictory and confusing approaches. In our attempt to bring some clarity as to how change can be effective through engaging stakeholders we will begin by examining some of the theoretical perspectives of change.

Theoretical perspectives on OC

There is something unique and un-chartable about OC since it creates the new that refines, combines, displaces and overlaps with what has gone before and can never be fully contained as it shifts, transforms and reshapes in unexpected ways over time. There are, however, a number of recurring patterns and dimensions to change that are evident in some of the theoretical perspectives. To review these we will use a classification process, which as well as being good academic practice, also informs the management of change. From the literature, the following four categories of OC have been identified which provide a structure to link the main theories of change characterized by: (i) how it happens; (ii) its pattern; (iii) the rate of occurrence; and (iv) its focus.

Change characterized by how it happens

Although change in organizations may be a constant, the nature of it is not always the same. When characterized by how change occurs, the literature is dominated by the planned and emergent theories of change.

Theories of planned change

The unpredictability of OC underlines the need for theories that are applicable which is the driving principle of Lewin (1951) who consistently advocated that a good theory should be of high practicable worth. In accordance with this view Lewin proposed the planned theory of change which posits that before a change can be adopted successfully, existing behaviours have to be revised by the three steps of (i) unfreezing the present behaviour, (ii) moving to the new behaviour and (iii) refreezing this new behaviour. The first step of *unfreezing* is where the need for change is identified; the next step of *moving* is where, through trial and error, the change slowly gets implemented; finally the objective of the *refreezing* step is to embed the change in the organization and ensure that new behaviours are consistent with the required changes. This model of change recognizes the need to discard old behaviours, structures, processes and culture before adopting new ones. This is not, however, a step approach that is meant to be applied in isolation since Lewin intended it to be used with the three other elements which comprise planned change – field theory, group dynamics and action research – and so form an integrated approach to analysing, understanding and bringing about change.

Lewin's theory has been enthusiastically adopted as a general framework for understanding and implementing planned change. The theory is, however, broad and has attracted criticisms. The three main criticisms are: first, it is open to question as to whether organizations are as amenable to control as a block of ice as critics argue that the notion of refreezing is not relevant for organizations operating in turbulent times since organizations needs to be fluid and adaptable rather than frozen into a certain way of functioning (Dawson, 2003). Second, the theory is criticized for ignoring the human element, as it treats individuals as blocks of ice or automatons rather than active participants in the change process, ignoring the views of individuals and instead focusing on the singular, partial story told by senior management (Buchanan, 2016). Third, the theory is considered to be rooted in North American assumptions of change and consequently difficult to adapt to other cultures. Marshak (1993) illustrates this by comparing Lewin's theory with the assumptions behind an Asian model. In the former, change is linear, progressive and managed by people intent on achieving goals, whereas in the latter, change is cyclical, processional, journey orientated, associated with equilibrium and managed in a way that is designed to create universal harmony. So even if Lewin's theory is appropriate to North American organizations, it may not be appropriate to OC in other countries and cultures. Criticisms of Lewin's theory thus raise concerns about how it views organizations and the role of individuals in OC as well as the cultural assumptions embedded in it which may limit its use across geographical and cultural boundaries.

Such criticisms have been countered by Burnes (2009) who through setting Lewin's work within its political and social context highlights that for most of his life Lewin's main preoccupation was the resolution of social conflict and, in particular, the problems of minority or disadvantaged groups. Managerialist accounts of Lewin's work tend to neglect this fact when evaluating his work in terms of contemporary management logic. Consequently, Burnes (2009) encourages a reappraisal of the work of Lewin, although Burnes remains the exception rather than the rule among academics in support of Lewin's theory.

Despite the criticisms, Lewin's approach has spawned a number of similar linear frameworks including: Beer's (1990) six steps for change; Luecke's (2003) seven steps for change; Kotter's (1996) eight-step model; and Kanter and colleagues' (1992) ten commandments for successful change. The number of steps in each of these models may vary, as well as the order in which they should be taken, but what unites them is that they advocate that change can be achieved as long as the correct steps are taken. Kanter and colleagues (1992) stress that with their ten commandments of change, it is an unwise manager who chooses to ignore one of the steps. Such proponents of planned change argue in favour of change occurring through carefully phased or sequenced steps. Similarly, Kotter (1996) maintains that although change is full of surprises, his eight-step model will produce a satisfying result as long as the steps are followed. In a review of the evidence relating to Kotter's model Appelbaum and colleagues (2012) found support for most of the individual steps. However, despite Kotter's argument about integrating the eight stages, no studies have evaluated the framework as a whole. On the other hand, there is no evidence to challenge the practical value of the approach which remains popular among managers and consultants because it is easy to understand and to use.

Planned linear models provide logical and sequential prescriptions for OC and attempt to codify and simplify the process in a planned sequence of stages. These models do provide useful checklists for managers and leaders in terms of what needs to be considered when planning change as they map out the process from the first recognition of the need for change through to the practicalities of implementation. However, critics point out that there are limitations to such prescriptive approaches. As Buchanan (2016: 13) rightly says, "unlike recipes in your kitchen cookbook these guidelines list ingredients without explaining how to cook the dish". Managers often have to work that out for themselves, which can be a source of frustration as they attempt to identify what works and what does not because these prescriptive guides simply identify what factors need to be addressed. The difficulty, according to Paton and McCalman (2008), is that most organizations view the concept of change as a highly programmed process which takes as its starting point the problem that needs to be rectified, then breaks it down into constituent parts, analyses possible alternatives, selects the preferred solution, and applies this relentlessly. However, this rarely changes the organization's underlying nature and problems usually recur.

By attempting to lay down various steps, objectives and methods in advance, it is suggested that the theory of planned change is too dependent on senior managers, who in many instances do not have a full understanding of the consequences of their actions. This is certainly evident in many of the models which tend to focus on the role of leaders in OC. In such situations, Hatch (2018) suggests that planned change can be an unethical, fear-producing vehicle for domination that extends existing top-down power structures. It is also argued that the emphasis of the planned theory on small-scale and incremental change is not applicable to situations that require rapid and transformational change (Senior, 2002). According to Vince and Broussine (1996) this is because there is an over-emphasis on the rational which does not take into account the complexity, ambiguity and paradox, acknowledged to be an integral part of an organizational transformation. This is supported by Dawson (2003) who argues that since change is a complex and dynamic process it cannot be solidified or treated as a series of linear events.

Critics also argue that the planned theory of change presumes that all stakeholders are willing and interested in implementing change, and that a common agreement can be reached (Bamford & Forrester, 2003). This presumption is criticized for ignoring organizational politics and conflict, and for assuming that politics and conflict can be easily identified and resolved (Buchanan & Badham, 2008). Furthermore the planned theory of change is open to criticism for being based on the assumption that organizations operate under constant conditions and that they can move in a planned manner from one stable state to another. Such assumptions are, however, questioned by those who argue that due to the accelerating pace of change in the environment OC is more an open-ended and continuous process than a set of pre-identified discrete and self-contained events (Burnes, 2006). The planned approach to change is, therefore, not without its limitations. It represents change as a programmatic, step-by-step process with a clear beginning, middle and end, largely choreographed and controlled from the top of the organization. Change within this context is about establishing a new order, setting new boundaries and putting in place new structures, systems and processes. The focus is on re-establishing order and stability. However, this approach tends to ignore the complexities and contradictory nature of organizations and side steps the concept of change as a naturally occurring, on-going phenomenon that emerges in an unplanned, complex way.

Complexity theories

Planned change theories imply equilibrium, order and predictability, whereas complexity theorists propose that change should not be perceived as a series of linear events within a given period of time, but as a continuous, open-ended process of adaptation to changing circumstances and conditions (Dawson, 2003). The origins of complexity theories can be traced to physics, mathematical biology, meteorology, computer science and systems thinking. The essence of complexity is the idea that natural systems are characterized by dynamism, non-linearity and unpredictability, rather than simply equilibrium, order and predictability. Within the context of complexity theories, organizations are viewed as natural systems that do not necessarily follow the strategic plans of managers, and within such systems OC is viewed as emergent, unplanned and iterative. This kind of change tends to be impossible for leaders to effectively identify, plan and implement because, unlike planned change, it is not based on pre-defined steps and a top-down leadership approach. Instead, emergent change is unpredictable and includes a great deal of uncertainty.

The emergent theory of change starts from the assumption that change is not a linear process or a one-off isolated event but a continuous, open-ended, cumulative and unpredictable process of aligning and re-aligning an organization to its changing environment. The rationale for this approach is that the nature of change is evolving and unpredictable. Weick (2000: 237) describes emergent change as consisting of "ongoing accommodations, adaptations, and alterations that produce fundamental change without a priori intentions to do so. [It] occurs when people re-accomplish routines and when they deal with contingencies, breakdowns, and opportunities. . . ." As such, emergent change is viewed as a continuous process and, consequently, attempts to impose a linear sequence of planned actions on what are untidy processes "which unfold in an iterative fashion with much backtracking and omission" (Buchanan & Storey, 1997: 127) are likely to fail.

To illustrate how emergent change evolves the metaphor of a jazz band is a useful one to consider. Orlikowski and Hofman (1997: 11–12) describe how members of a jazz band do not decide in advance exactly what notes each is going to play, but wait until the performance begins: "each player is free to explore and innovate, departing from the original composition. Yet, the performance works because all members are playing within the same rhythmic structure and have a shared understanding of the rules of this musical genre."

Similar to how a jazz band performs, emergent change occurs through the evolution of an iterative process that produces outcomes that cannot be predicted. A practical example of this occurred when a small group of trainee clinicians and improvement facilitators in the UK's National Health Service (NHS) developed and ran the first NHS Change Day. By raising awareness of the event through social media a grassroots movement of over 180,000 people emerged which pledged to take concrete action to improve healthcare outcomes. When Change Day was repeated the following year, the number of pledges exceeded 800,000. Advocates of such emergent change emphasize that it is the uncertainty of the external and internal environment that makes it more pertinent than the planned approach (Dawson, 2003). The essential unforeseeable character of emergent change means that the process cannot be predicted and that outcomes are often only understood in retrospect. Thus, change emerges from the way an organization as a whole acquires, interprets and processes information about the environment.

The theory of emergent change does, however, have a number of limitations. Research has found that an emergent approach to change takes longer to deliver results and can be messy, lack coherence and create confusion and uncertainty in an organization due to a lack of clear objectives (Shaw, 2002). Although advocates have suggested sequences of actions for emergent change that organizations should comply with (such as Pettigrew and Whipp, 1993), many of these suggestions tend to be rather abstract in nature and difficult to apply in practice. They consist of a disparate group of models and approaches that tend to be more united in their scepticism to the planned approach to change than to an agreed alternative. The emergent approach is, therefore, criticized as lacking in coherence and a diversity of techniques (Bamford & Forrester, 2003). The nature of emergent change can also create anxiety especially amongst people who find it difficult to tolerate the unknown and to cope with the paradoxes that emergent change brings about. Not everyone has the skills or the inclination to participate in such an unplanned, open-ended approach to change – or to play jazz.

The general applicability and validity of the emergent theory depends on whether or not one believes that all organizations operate in dynamic and unpredictable environments to which they constantly have to adapt. If so then "the emergent model is suitable for all organizations, all situations and at all times" (Burnes, 1996: 14).

Contingency theories

Instead of OC being either planned or emergent, the contingency theory advocates creating synergy between the two and adopting the most appropriate approach that matches the context/situation in which the organization is operating. The contingency approach to OC is founded on the premise that the structure and performance of an organization are dependent on the situational variables that it faces since no two organizations are alike, and will not necessarily face the same contextual variables as their operations and structures may be different.

Arguing that the complex nature of environmental conditions mitigates against the creation of a unitary model of change, the contingency theory proposes that managers and consultants need a model of change that is essentially a situational or contingency model that indicates how to vary change strategies to achieve optimum fit with the changing environment (Dunphy & Stace, 1993). So rather than a 'one best way for all', organizational success depends on securing a proper fit or alignment between the organization and its environment. Advocates of this theory argue that the environment determines the type of change required. Such environmental determinists see the organization as being in constant interaction with its environment which consists of 'actors' or 'networks' (Duncan, 1979). The actors and networks in the organization's environment can change a great deal, thus the degree of environmental determinism varies for each organization. Environmental determinists argue that because an organization is dependent on its environment, that environment constrains the choices an organization can make about how it structures itself. As the environmental situation changes, the organization–environment relationship also changes, so to be effective an organization has to structure and restructure constantly to retain alignment or 'fit'.

Critics of the contingency theory of OC argue that it assumes that leaders and managers do not have any significant influence nor choice over situational variables and structure. Instead critics argue that an organization does not necessarily have to adapt to the external environment but if managers want to maintain or promote a particular approach they can choose to influence situational variables to achieve this (By, 2005). So rather than having little choice and being forced to change their internal practices to fit in with external variables, organizations can exercise some choice over these issues.

To address such criticisms and to deal with the complexity of the contingency approach, Balogun and Hailey (2004) propose the 'change kaleidoscope' which identifies a number of contextual features, including the necessary speed of change, the scope of the change agenda, the need to maintain continuity with some dimensions, the diversity of attitudes and values among those affected, individual change capabilities, organizational capacity for change, readiness for change and the power of the change agent. These contextual features influence decisions concerning the starting point and path of change, the implementation style, specific change levers and mechanisms, and the nature of change roles (top down, bottom up, dispersed). The power of this model is that it recognizes that contextual variables as well as design choices will constantly shift according to the organization and the environment in which it operates. Thus, the framework provides a diagnostic tool in the spirit of the contingency theory. To some extent at least this guards against the risks associated with a best practice prescriptive approach.

The flexible nature of the contingency theory means that change can be adapted to the environment. It can be fast or slow, small or large, loosely or tightly controlled, driven by internal or external triggers, and appropriate to varying levels of uncertainty. It just depends on the situation. Overall, the contingency approach argues against a single generic change approach on the basis that it cannot be generalized to every context; instead the trajectory of contingency theory is towards change approaches that vary by situation and context, with the goal of aligning the change approach with the organization and its environment.

Processual theories

Processual theories of OC are based on the assumption that change occurs as a complex, dynamic, non-linear, temporal and emotional process. Such theories recognize that unplanned, unforeseen and unexpected events will happen and that, consequently, OC cannot be reduced to a list of simple sequential steps. In support of this view, Pettigrew and colleagues (2001: 700), drawing on the work of Van de Ven (1992), define processes as "sequences of individual and collective events, actions and activities unfolding over time in context". In other words change is continuous rather than as a movement from one state to another. Process theories of OC also spotlight how forms of equivocality, where multiple interpretations exist, may be progressively resolved through collective sense-making processes (Langley & Tsoukas, 2010), whilst also sustaining conflicting interpretations between different groups that may be further reinforced through processes of change (Buchanan & Badham, 2008). Although, as Dawson (2005) points out, it is recognized that in practice these elements often overlap and interlock; they ensure that the importance of choice and human experience within the political context of organizational life is recognized.

Although the processual approach offers a series of general practical guidelines, Burnes (2006) doubts the value of these guidelines in giving clear advice, since the problem with much of the advice is that it tends to be relatively cursory or abstract in nature and difficult to apply on a day-to-day basis. In response to this, advocates (such as Dawson & Andriopoulos, 2014) point out that in a theory that recognizes that there can never be any universal prescriptions or simple recipes for OC, the context, substance and politics of change interlock and overlap in an on-going dynamic process, that leaders and managers need to be politically astute and sensitive to the way that making sense and giving sense to change not only describes events but can also be used to shape the processes they are describing, and that managing OC is often about managing contradictory processes. It is perhaps not surprising therefore that any attempt to offer guidelines is limited.

In its defence, the processual perspective is not making a statement against planning for change, rather it is pointing out that change is unpredictable and, consequently, that there will be a need to accommodate and adapt to the unexpected, the unforeseen twists and turns, the omissions and revisions that are all part of managing the process of change over time.

Theories of cyclical change

Implicit and often explicit in the OC literature is the notion that each theory of OC is an improvement on earlier theories. The cyclical theory of change fits this view as it provides a more realistic perspective in terms of a better understanding of OC. This is supported by Cummings and Worley (2014) who argue for a spiral rather than a planned linear approach to change. This builds upon Prochaska and colleagues' (1993) cyclical theory of change which was initially developed to show the phases a patient goes through in their journey to change certain health behaviours. The phases comprise: pre-contemplation, contemplation, preparation, action and maintenance. *Pre-contemplation* is when an individual is unaware of the problems, or fails to acknowledge them, without engaging in any process activities. Individuals in this phase do not want to change their behaviour and may insist that their behaviour is normal. *Contemplation* occurs when the individual becomes conscious of the issue and begins to think about changing their behaviour, but they are not yet ready to commit to any changes. *Preparation* is when the individual is ready to change their behaviour and plans to do so. The *action* phase follows and is characterized by the individual coping with the behavioural change and engaging in change activities. *Maintenance* is the last phase where actions to reinforce the change are taken, along with establishing the new behavioural change as part of the individual's lifestyle. In this spiral model, individuals have the ability to exit at any time if they decide not to change. The model also takes into account a behavioural *relapse* or a return to the previous existing behaviour. In the case of a relapse an individual can revisit the contemplation stage and prepare for taking necessary action. The spiral pattern of the model suggests that many individuals learn from their relapses. Such theories of curvilinear or cyclic change assume that change in a certain direction creates the conditions for change in another (perhaps even the opposite) direction. Whereas, the theory of planned change assumes that change in a certain direction induces further change in the same linear direction.

There are a number of differences between the cyclical and planned, linear theories of OC. First, the planned theory of reducing change to n-steps suggests that change, which is usually complex and untidy, can be controlled and managed effectively in a more or less logical and predictable manner and that having to handle such a small number of issues appears to lessen the scale of the management challenge. Second, the steps are often used in rigid, finite and sequential ways, in effecting or responding to episodic change, whereas the cyclical models are concurrent and always at work. Second, linear steps are usually driven by a small, powerful core group, often at the top of an organization's hierarchy, whereas the cyclical approach can pull in as many people as possible from different levels of an organization. Third, the linear models are often designed to function within a traditional hierarchy, whereas the cyclical model can be adapted to the flexibility of different structures such as a network. A cyclical model for OC can also serve as a continuous and holistic approach and one that accelerates momentum and agility. This approach is, therefore, a more realistic way to view OC than the traditional linear approach.

Change characterized by scale

Change is seldom a linear or neat process and is best seen as a pattern. Key patterns of change which are evident in the literature and worthy of attention are referred to as discontinuous, gradualism, transformational and punctuated equilibrium.

Discontinuous change

Discontinuous change refers to change which is characterized by rapid transformations that can be triggered by major internal issues or by external crises. Discontinuous change is often a one-off event that takes place through large, widely separated initiatives, which signify a single, abrupt shift from the past and is followed up by long periods of con-solidation. Advocates of discontinuous change argue that this approach is cost-effective since it does not promote a never-ending process of costly change initiatives, and that it creates less turmoil than is caused by continuous change (Guimaraes & Armstrong, 1998). Critics point out, however, that this approach allows defensive behaviour, complacency, inward focus and inertia, which creates situations where major reform is frequently required (Luecke, 2003). Although the discontinuous approach to change is still employed in change initiatives there seems to be a consensus that the benefits from dis-continuous change do not last (Taylor & Hirst, 2001). Instead critics (Rieley & Clarkson, 2001) argue that change should be viewed as a normal and natural response to internal and environmental conditions and, therefore, it is of vital importance to organizations that a state of continuous change becomes a routine.

Gradualism

Gradualism posits that change is continuous and occurs through a process of successive, limited and negotiated gradual shifts. Such incremental change is about doing things better through a process of continuous fine-tuning, adaptation and modification. It is when individual parts of an organization deal increasingly and separately with one problem and one objective at a time. Different authors employ different terminology when describing the same approach, for example, Burnes (2006) differentiates between incremental and continuous change, while Senior (2002) distinguishes between smooth and bumpy incremental change. The John Lewis partnership – a chain of department stores – refers to it as 'logical incrementalism', in which change is implemented in small steps with lessons from each phase informing the next (cited in O'Regan & Ghobadian, 2012).

One of the key premises underlying gradualism is that if an organization is able to promptly respond to internal or external drivers of change it can maintain some kind of alignment with its operating environment and avoid the need to undergo transforma-tional change, unless some sudden external change warrants a dramatic change to its business model and product offering. This does not preclude the fact that gradualism can have a cumulative effect – where incremental changes can add up over time and trans-form an organization. Some researchers have, however, questioned the assumption that incremental change can lead to sufficient modification to achieve fundamental change on the basis that it is difficult to overcome inertia and equilibrium without a continuous 'jolt' to the system (Burke, 2002). One response to this argument is that leadership can stimulate incremental change by socializing the organization to value it. The pattern of incremental change tends to be continuous and on-going and for the most part impacts on the day-to-day operational processes of an organization which is in contrast to trans-formational change.

Transformational change

The velocity trends (outlined in Chapter 1) mean that the slow, plodding pattern of incremental change is not sufficient for all organizations. Instead there may be the need for transformational change which aims to redefine an organization's strategic direction, cultural assumptions and identity. Transformational change means doing different things that impact on the strategy, such as when Amazon moved from being an e-commerce bookseller to a content publisher, to a producer of programmes. This pattern of change is also referred to as strategic, radical or revolutionary. For some organizations this is the only way for change to happen, for as Gersick (1991) points out, OC cannot be accomplished piecemeal, gradually or comfortably. Instead transformational change can create a paradigm shift and completely new behaviours, not just in a single company but also across an entire sector or even in a country, such as in the case of the Chinese company Alibaba which revolutionized online shopping in China. An example of a whole sector that has been faced with patterns of transformational change is the publishing industry which in response to the development of iPads, Kindles and other e-readers has had to change how it produces, as well as distributes, books.

At an organizational level transformational change impacts on the deep structure – that is the culture, strategy, structure, power distribution and the systems (Tushman & Romanelli, 1985). This is evident in the advancement of technology innovations, such as Blockchain which is driving transformations in how companies carry out transactions such as with digital currency. The patterns of such transformations will vary in their magnitude as illustrated by Flamholtz and Randle (2011) who distinguish between three types of transformational change:

- *Type 1* transformation occurs when an organization changes its structure.
- *Type 2* transformation involves the revitalization of an already established company.
- *Type 3* transformation involves an organization fundamentally changing the business in which it is involved.

Each of these types of transformation will vary in intensity and impact.

Transformational change tends to be depicted as strategic, and evolutionary and incremental change as operational. However, Burke (2002: 67) suggests that "more than 95 percent of OCs are evolutionary". While other writers point out how the various approaches can be used in combination, Kotter (1996), for example, sees strategic change as comprising a series of large and small projects aimed at achieving the same overall objectives but which are started at different times, managed differently and which vary in nature. This is similar to Kanter and colleagues' (1992) description of what they term 'long marches' and 'bold strokes'. The latter are radical and transformational and often have to be followed by a whole series of smaller-scale changes over a more extended timescale (long marches) in order to embed the changes brought about by the bold strokes.

Patterns of transformational and incremental change are different, not just in terms of their objectives but also in terms of their processes, size, scope and breadth. Transformations are much more disruptive to what people do and the way they work and tend to reflect major shifts externally in the environment and internally inside the organization, whereas incremental change happens more frequently and is more focused on fine-tuning processes, systems, policies and so on. Transformations require enormous energy to realize the necessary degree of change. In fact many organizations rarely have the necessary capabilities and capacity needed to successfully implement and sustain a transformation, often because transformation is episodic and sufficiently infrequent that leaders and managers are more accomplished at running businesses in stable environments than in changing ones. For many organizations, this relatively placid experience leads to a steady state of continuity, which often makes them poorly prepared for transformations.

Punctuated equilibrium

Neither gradualism nor transformational patterns of change work well in isolation; instead the change history of the average organization tends to involve long periods of incremental tweaking punctuated by occasional bouts of frantic, crisis-driven change. As Nelson (2003: 18) points out, "change cannot be relied upon to occur at a steady state, rather there are periods of incremental change sandwiched between more violent periods of change which have contributed to the illusion of stability once assumed to be the case." This more dominant pattern of change is known as punctuated equilibrium which means that rather than change being either incremental or transformational, there is an interplay between the two. The inspiration for this pattern arose from two sources: the first from Gould (1978) who, as a historian with an interest in Darwin's theory of evolution, found evidence pointing to a world punctuated with periods of mass extinction and rapid origination among long stretches of relative tranquillity; the second inspiration comes from the research of Gersick (1991), who defines the punctuated equilibrium as relatively long periods of stability (equilibrium) punctuated by brief periods of intense and pervasive transformational change that fundamentally alters an organization and then leads to the initiation of new equilibrium periods. Balancing the tensions between transformational and incremental change, according to Brown and Eisenhardt (1997), tends to keep an organization on the edge of order and chaos and so helps to sustain its innovative capability.

Such patterns of incremental and transformational change will vary across sectors. Those who subscribe to the punctuated equilibrium pattern of change argue that not only do organizations and entire sectors go through periods of gradualism and transformational change, but that this pattern of change repeats itself with some degree of regularity (Nadler & Tushman, 1995). Patterns will, of course, vary across sectors, for example periods of transformation may follow a cycle of several years of gradualism in the higher education sector, but a cycle of a few months in the technology sector. However, in almost all industries, since the rate of change is increasing in response to the velocity trends, the periods between gradualism and transformations are decreasing.

Change characterized by the rate of occurrence

Perceptions of pace and of the need to respond by accelerating the rate of change accordingly are heightened by advice from management consultants and academics. Some argue that OC should be pursued at a slow pace while others argue that change needs to be done quickly. For example, Kotter (2012) describes eight 'accelerators' that are necessary to ensure rapid change. Similarly consultancies such as Deloitte (2013) advise clients using a framework called 'organization acceleration' based on the assumption that change programmes move too slowly. There are, however, those who caution against organizations following such courses of rapid change. Abrahamson (2004) in his book, *Change without Pain*, argues that this can be destabilizing and cause burnout. Instead he advocates 'painless change', interspersing major initiatives among carefully paced spells of small changes – which supports the theory of punctuated equilibrium. Abrahamson cites the example of Lou Gerstner who knew when to implement transformational change and when to stick to incremental change. In his first nine months at TRS, Gerstner launched a massive reorganization of the card and traveller check businesses, followed by the introduction of new products. TRS's nine-month transformation was, in Gerstner's words, like breaking the four-minute mile. But Gerstner knew when it was time to rest, since he was alert to how people were responding to the changes and to the early signs of fatigue, cynicism and burnout. He also recognized that the success of his overall change strategy depended on the stability of the business units involved, and was mindful about how and when to intersperse incremental changes rather than transformational ones. Consequently no new products were launched and no new executives were brought in from outside for 18 months after Gerstner's initial blitz at TRS but he did not sit back and do nothing. Instead he tinkered constantly with the structure, the compensation system and the product offerings, to prevent the company from drifting into inertia. The unthreatening nature of such incremental changes allowed the company to be ready for the next wave of product launches and restructurings when they came. Abrahamson (2004) reminds us that it is particularly easy for organizations in the hurlyburly of everyday business to forget the importance of slowing down, especially as being first does not necessarily mean being fastest. This is supported by Bruch and Menges (2010) who argue that fast-paced change leads to burnout which they call the 'acceleration trap'. Similarly, Amis and colleagues (2004) advocate that rapid change throughout an organization is not only insufficient to bring about transformational change but may even be detrimental to its outcome.

Achieving the right pace is, however, a challenge. Schrage (2012) cautions against both moving too fast and moving too slowly. Schrage quotes examples such as Ron Johnson, CEO of JC Penney, as moving too fast; and Meg Whitman of Hewlett-Packard, Jack Welch of GE, and Bob McDonald of Procter and Gamble as moving too slowly. Netflix is an example of a company which was driven to transform itself rapidly due to changing too slowly and this resulted in a great deal of negative publicity and loss of customers. The company has since gone from being a distributor of DVDs to a producer of programmes. In order to make this transformation the company changed its business model very quickly and did what many other companies in the entertainment industry have been unable to do which is to execute a transformation and survive. A study by Ji and Oh (2014) found that some organizations ('hares') respond rapidly and aggressively to changing conditions and instability while others ('tortoises') try to maintain consistency and make smaller adjustments. The study suggests that very high instability is damaging, as is very low instability, and concludes that a slow and steady approach is advisable, warning that changing too slowly can be a risk to an organization's survival whereas changing too quickly can overload and demotivate staff and can also threaten performance and survival. The case of Toyota is evidence of what happens when change is introduced too quickly. For decades, Toyota was a model of manufacturing excellence and quality production. However, when faced with a massive vehicle recall and the accompanying loss of customer trust, the company was forced to review its rapid expansion. In his written testimony to the US House Oversight Committee in 2011, chief executive Akio Toyoda said, "I fear the pace at which we have grown may have been too quick" (cited in Simon & Kirchgaessner, 2010). Thus the story of Toyota shows that a continual rapid pace of change can be detrimental to a company and can be difficult to sustain.

Slow-paced change facilitates learning and allows all organizational members time to understand what needs to be changed and how. When done effectively slow-paced incremental change can be a crucial part of short-term success, whereas fast-paced change over a long period may also lead to change fatigue. However, if a change process takes too long, the change may lose salience and people will not notice anything happening. A slow pace can also allow time for increased resistance. Ultimately, how fast or slow change is implemented will ultimately depend on the nature, context and type of change.

Change characterized by its focus

Either/or theories

Traditional theories of OC tend to view change as focusing on either processes or people. Beer and Nohria (2000), for instance, propose two theories: Theory E and Theory O. Theory E advocates a process focus based on a systems-driven strategy motivated by the need to achieve clear economic gains. It is a planned, programmatic approach, based on formal structures and systems driven from the top of an organization. The explicit goal of Theory E change is to dramatically and rapidly increase shareholder value, as measured by cash flow and share price. This type of change usually involves the use of economic incentives, drastic redundancies, downsizing and restructuring.

In contrast, Theory O is a people-driven approach in which organizational capabilities are built by investing in people and creating motivation and commitment. Organizations that follow this approach attempt to invigorate their cultures and capabilities through individual and organizational learning. The Theory O approach requires high levels of employee participation, flatter organizational structures, strong bonds between the organization and its employees and implicit contracts with employees are considered too important to break (which is the opposite of what happens with Theory E). Leaders who advocate Theory O are less interested in driving the success of OC themselves than in encouraging participation from employees and in fostering employee behaviours and attitudes that will sustain change.

Yet whilst each theory tempts advocacy, there are weaknesses with the paradox of seeing both as separate approaches. For example, Theory E suggests the prioritization of maximizing stakeholder value; however, it is unlikely that anyone implementing a Theory O approach would not advocate this priority in their model. Rather, their priorities are broader in order to incorporate multiple rather than single stakeholders. Paton and McCalman (2008) support the requirement to consider disparate stakeholders and argue that an effective Theory O approach would incorporate consideration of individual and group stakeholders. Although they argue that this requires an interaction with systems, structures and processes, which are Theory E priorities.

To address such dilemmas, Beer and Nohria propose that the best approach is a mix of Theory E and Theory O: "Companies that effectively combine hard and soft approaches to change can reap big payoffs in profitability and productivity . . . Those companies are more likely to achieve a sustainable competitive advantage" (Beer & Nohria, 2000: 134).

Similarly, rather than an either/or mixed approach, I propose in my book, *Managing and Leading People Through Organizational Change* (Hodges, 2016), a shift to the focus of a stakeholder approach to OC. The benefit of this is that it ensures that people are engaged in change and enabled to participate in the decision-making and are, therefore, able to influence the change interventions. In the traditional process approach to OC, the power to create change comes through positional authority; whereas in the stakeholder approach, power comes from relationships and the ability to influence through networks. The process approach focuses on change to achieve the mission and vision of the organization, usually this is change which is driven from the top down. In contrast, on the stakeholder side, the emphasis is on a shared purpose of the rationale and decisions for change. On the process side, change approaches are driven by logical, linear tasks, whereas the stakeholder approach emphasizes the connection with the emotional aspects of change. While the passion and energy for creativity and innovation is driven by leaders on the process side, in the stakeholder approach, the drive for creativity and innovation is sparked by people at different levels up, down and across the organization. The process approach utilizes traditional planning and improvement methodologies such as Lean and Six Sigma, whereas the people approach focuses on the increasingly open and connected world where there are many new opportunities to share ideas, compare data and co-create novel approaches to change, such as through the wisdom of crowds.

Many of the levers for change with the process approach are transactional, such as compliance, and people are accountable through transactional performance targets; instead with the stakeholder approach, change is about commitment and ownership, and people are accountable through shared commitments and how they work together. The process approach focuses on getting things done, completing them and moving on; while on the stakeholder side the emphasis is on capabilities and building capabilities for change which will be of benefit to the organization in the longer term. Traditionally, the process approach has been used in OC initiatives where the focus tends to be measurement and implementation while the people and the emotional dimensions of change are largely ignored. The move to a stakeholder approach means including those affected by change in its identification, design and implementation.

Summary

OC is complex and fluid and in reality it differs from the prescriptive guides that often over simplify what is a dynamic and chaotic process, especially as there are usually several different types of change going on concurrently in an organization. There is, however, no agreed theory of change; rather there are competing theories for different categorizations of change and a healthy debate about their respective value bases and biases. The theories of planned change tend to generalize and provide helpful but limited checklists as to how the change approach should vary in different organizational contexts. Change rarely happens in a linear manner and frequently there is a need to go back to a step not just once but perhaps several times in a cyclical way.

The 'Critical Perspective' offers a counterpoint to the reassuring concept of prescribed planned theories of OC. Complexity theorists, in depicting organizations as complex adaptive systems, have emphasized the non-linearity of change and the unpredictability of change. In a similar manner process theorists have questioned the planned step approach to change. Both complexity and process theories have captured the imaginations of more enlightened change practitioners, consequently encouraging managers to not regard OC as linear and predictable and avoid 'recipes' about the one best way to manage change.

The theories outlined in this chapter are all useful in capturing aspects of the complexity of OC. They do, however, need to be adapted to the context in which they are being applied. For although change in many organizations may be a constant, the nature of it is not always the same, as change comes in a variety of patterns. No approach can be rigidly planned, since that implies perfect foresight and no learning. Neither can it be purely emergent, as that implies no control and merely leaving events entirely to the forces within the environment. Thus, the nature of change is dependent on situational variables.

Implications

There are a number of practical implications which arise from the discussion in this chapter:

- Recognize the need for change early. Whether the need is for incremental or transformational change, the earlier the need is recognized, the greater the number of options managers will have when deciding how to manage it and there will be more time for planning and for the involvement of people.
- Consider how to enable change. There is a need to consider how to enable change to be effective. This involves choices on the pace, scope and nature of the change. No approach can be rigidly planned, as that implies perfect foresight and no learning. Neither can it be purely emergent, as that implies no control and simply leaving events entirely to the forces within the environment. In terms of the relevant approach taken, review how you will develop a people-driven approach to change.
- Review the sequence of the change. A change process involves a number of events, decisions and actions that are connected in a sequence. They are connected in the sense that each event is influenced by earlier events and also help to shape subsequent events. Several models do advocate a sequential progress of activities, (for example, do A first, then B, and finish the change process with E), and many even suggest that to miss one step or to fail to do it justice before moving on to the next is a grave error. Yet there is little agreement on what steps should be taken first and what should follow. Caution needs to be used when applying n-step models to organizational change. Rather than being used as best practice they should be adapted to the context of the organization and to the proposed change.
- Pace of change. Along with the sequence of change initiatives there is also a need to identify the appropriate pace of change. On the one hand, changes that are made too quickly may constrain problem-solving and adaptation. Slow-paced change can also facilitate learning and allow all organizational members time to understand what needs to be changed and how. However, on the other hand, if a change process takes too long, the change may lose salience and people will

not notice anything happening. A slow pace can also allow time for the mobilization of power and increased opposition, which· is often one of the main arguments behind implementing large-scale changes as rapidly as possible. Fast-paced change over a long period may also lead to change fatigue. So the pace at which the change is implemented depends on the nature, context and type of change.

Chapter 4

Theoretical perspectives of engagement

Learning outcomes

After reading this chapter you will be able to:

- describe the roots of engagement as a concept;
- compare and contrast theoretical frameworks of engagement;
- differentiate between OC engagement and traditional constructs;
- evaluate OC engagement as a unique and distinct concept.

Introduction

The first scholarly article on engagement at work was written by Kahn in 1990 and published in the *Academy of Management Journal*. Kahn's work initially had little impact on either practice or research as it took another decade before the topic was picked up by management consultants in the US and by academics in Europe. Since then engagement has been promoted by consultants as a good thing to do in order to improve performance and productivity and has spawned a mixed bag of academic studies based on a variety of theories. As a relatively new concept OC engagement lacks a unique theory. Instead, a number of theories exist that emphasize different aspects of generic employee engagement. To understand what causes OC engagement and, therefore, what it causes in turn, we need to embed the idea in a well-founded theory.

The aim of this chapter is to critically evaluate the theoretical perspectives of engagement which are applicable to the context of OC. We begin by exploring the roots of engagement. This is followed by examining some of the theories of engagement. The chapter then goes on to explore whether or not engagement is a unique construct that can be differentiated from other traditional constructs, such as job involvement, organizational commitment, job satisfaction, flow, as well as work addiction.

Roots of engagement

The roots of employee engagement lie in the field of the human relations and positive psychology schools. The former put the people back into the frame of organizational life, following the widespread adoption of scientific management practices during the early decades of the 20th century, in which the primary focus was on improving efficiency and dissecting work processes into discrete activities that only managers had an oversight of.

This approach was instrumental in driving forward mass production as it was widely believed that the partialization of work tasks and improvement of the physical working environment would lead to greater efficiency at work, although no thought was given to the person actually carrying out the work or to their well-being. In the 1920s, this view was challenged when a group of researchers carrying out a study in the Western Electric Company's Hawthorne Works, to determine what influence a change of working conditions had on work performance, were astonished to find that work performance improved significantly regardless of whether or not the physical conditions, such as lighting, were changed. The study concluded that work performance was not dictated solely by objective conditions but that effort and performance improved as a result of paying attention to factors affecting the well-being of employees. These findings acted as a trigger for the human relations movement. From then on, awareness was raised of the importance of the mental and social factors that affect workers. Subsequently, studies were increasingly carried out with the aim of increasing motivation and satisfaction in the workplace. Essentially, this was, and still is, about the influence of employees' engagement on an organization's productivity and about the ability to perform and be effective.

The other roots of engagement come from the school of positive psychology which was developed by a group of scholars working with Martin Seligman, the President of the American Psychological Association. Broadly speaking, positive psychology refers to the scientific study of optimal human functioning which aims to discover and promote the factors, such as engagement, that allow individuals, organizations and communities to thrive (Seligman & Csikszentmihalyi, 2000). The positive psychology movement created the fertile soil that helped the concept of employee engagement blossom. Since then the concept has attracted enormous interest, as Macey and colleagues (2009: xv) say, "rarely has a term […] resonated as strongly with business executives as employee engagement has". Despite its popularity it does lack a specific theory; instead there are a number of theoretical perspectives which can be related to engagement, specifically within the context of OC.

Theoretical frameworks

Job Demands-Resources (JD-R) theory

Although various theoretical approaches have been proposed to explain the underlying psychological mechanisms that are involved in engagement at work, so far the Job Demands-Resources (JD-R) theory has received most empirical support. The theory suggests that there are two groups of job components affecting engagement levels at work: job demands and job resources (Bakker & Demerouti, 2007). Job demands refer to those aspects of a job that require sustained physical and/or psychological costs, workload, time pressure and emotional and cognitive demands. When these demands are high, employees may feel overwhelmed and unable to meet them. For example, without enough staff on a hospital ward, it may not be possible for nurses to attend to patient needs for food, water and cleanliness in a timely manner, which is likely to make nurses feel incompetent, unable to control their work environment, and lead to feelings of being undervalued and under resourced. So job demands may turn into job stressors when meeting those demands requires major effort from an individual who feels under pressure.

Job resources refer to those physical, social or organizational aspects of the job that may: reduce job demands and the associated physiological and psychological costs; be functional in achieving work goals; or stimulate personal growth, learning and development. Job resources are assumed to play either an intrinsic motivational role because they foster employees' growth, learning and development, or an extrinsic motivational role because they are instrumental in achieving work goals. Resources can come from different levels: at the organizational level they include salary, career opportunities and job security; at the level of interpersonal and social relations they include supervisor and co-worker support and team climate; at the work level they include role clarity; and at the task level resources include autonomy and feedback. More specifically, JD-R theory argues that job resources, which fulfil the basic psychological needs of the Self Determination Theory for autonomy (experiencing choice and a sense of freedom), competence (succeeding at challenging tasks and achieving goals) and relatedness (a sense of belonging with others), are motivating and promote work engagement (Ryan & Deci, 2000). This is supported in a meta-analysis involving 99 studies by Van den Broeck and colleagues (2016) which shows that personal resources – including self-esteem and optimism – and job resources – including social support, autonomy and feedback – are related to each of the three needs of the Self Determination Theory and to engagement.

The JD-R theory suggests that when demands exceed resources, employees disengage and when resources exceed demands, employees engage because resources reduce the costs associated with on-going demands. Importantly, the JD-R model also includes a feedback loop which describes how employees who are engaged in their work are more able to create their own resources, which then, over time, foster further engagement. Based on these assumptions in order to improve OC engagement, job resources need to be increased to help individuals deal with job demands. The type and quality of resources that matter most will depend on the need for OC and on readiness for change both of which need to be reviewed before change is considered. The JD-R theory, therefore, suggests that resources are key to enabling engagement and the presence of job demands make resources much more salient.

Conservation Of Resources (COR) theory

Similar to the JD-R theory, the Conservation Of Resources (COR) theory proposes that job resources buffer the negative effects of various work settings or stressors on engagement. The theory defines resources as those entities that either are centrally valued in their own right, or act as means to obtain centrally valued ends and are considered to be objects, personal characteristics, situations or conditions that are valuable to the individual. Specifically, the theory contends that "people strive to retain, protect, and build resources and that what is threatening to them is the potential or actual loss of these valued resources" (Hobfoll, 1989: 516). The basic tenet of COR theory is, therefore, that people are motivated to obtain, retain, foster and protect resources.

COR theory assumes that people will invest their resources in order to deal with stressful conditions and protect themselves from negative outcomes. For instance, employees may use the social support which they receive from their colleagues, such as assistance with workload, in order to deal with an overload of change at work. Consequently, COR theory predicts that those with greater resources, such as more-supportive colleagues, are less vulnerable to stress, whereas those with fewer resources, such as less-supportive colleagues, are more vulnerable to stress. The theory also proposes that individuals strive not only to protect their current resources, but also to accumulate them. For instance, employees may learn new capabilities in order to increase their employability and reduce the risk of losing their job. Those who possess more resources are considered more capable of resource gain. In other words, as with the JD-R theory, initial resource gain gets future gain, thus constituting so-called *gain spirals* (Salanova et al., 2010). For example, increased employability not only reduces the risk of unemployment but also augments the possibility of getting a better job that offers additional opportunities for learning and development, and which enhances engagement at work. Hence, gaining resources increases an individual's resource pool. This accumulation and linking of resources creates resource caravans, that is, resources tend to not exist in isolation, but rather they aggregate such that, for instance, employees working in an environment where they have autonomy or receive coaching are likely to reinforce their beliefs in their capabilities and resilience, to feel valued and be optimistic about meeting their goals. Resource caravans will result in positive personal outcomes such as better coping, adaptation and engagement. So adequate resources to cope with OC may well increase engagement.

The needs satisfying theory

Kahn's (1990) engagement theory, also referred to as the 'needs satisfying' approach, is based on the premise that engagement is influenced by three antecedent psychological conditions: meaningfulness, safety and availability. In other words, workers are more engaged at work in situations that offer them more meaning and safety, and when they have the resources to invest in their work. Meaningfulness refers to the extent to which people derive purpose from their work and feel that they are receiving a return on their investments in their performance at work through the positive feelings and energy their job creates and the sense of personal value they derive from doing the job. Work that is experienced as challenging, clearly delineated, varied, creative, autonomous and provides feedback is considered most meaningful. Meaning is about connecting with others, having a sense of higher personal purpose and a heightened understanding of what is really important (Holbeche & Springett, 2004). When asked to describe times when they have experienced intense meaning at work, individuals describe feelings, identity and a sense of purpose as being important (Holbeche, 2017). It seems that what employees aspire to is akin to this statement by American author and historian Studs Terkel (1974: xiii):

> Work is about a search for daily meaning as well as daily bread; for recognition as well as cash; for astonishment rather than torpor; in short, for a sort of life, rather than a Monday to Friday sort of dying.

Employees do not always need outside recognition to feel their work is meaningful or to be assigned a job society considers meaningful. Ashforth and Kreiner (2013) write about finding meaning in dirty work. Dirty work, they say, refers to occupations which society views as socially unclean or physically ugly, such as funeral service, garbage, maintenance services or hospice care. The authors suggest that workers in dirty occupations create a cognitive shift in what work means, enabling them to derive meaning from it and to essentially transform their work into something that is meaningful. Employees who feel that the work itself makes a meaningful contribution to society, to something bigger than themselves, or inherently pays them back emotionally, physically and cognitively will feel meaningfulness. Meaning at work is about individuals making their mark on the world and finding answers to questions such as: 'What contribution am I making? Why am I doing? What difference do I make?' Given the length of time most people spend at work, having a role and work context which offers the chance to achieve something significant, to make a difference, is vital to the possibility of work being meaningful. People want their work to have a higher purpose and for workplace behaviour to be characterized by congruence, respect, integrity, authenticity and honesty. However idealistic, they want the chance to achieve something worthwhile and to be part of a community they can be proud of. When there is a lack of meaning at work, morale suffers and people start to look for other jobs or consider self-employment. Change also becomes more difficult to manage. Conversely when people experience greater meaning, they appear to be able to give their best and be willing to change (Holbeche & Matthews, 2012). So, meaningful work can help enable engagement.

Safety refers to the extent to which employees feel able to employ and express their true selves at work without fear of negative consequences to their self-image, status or career (Kahn, 1990). Work environments that are predictable, consistent and non-threatening provide a greater sense of safety. In contrast, an environment that promotes discrimination against individuals, stifles or fails to encourage positive and constructive criticisms, or has an excess of negative organizational politics, will inhibit safety. Employees who are treated inappropriately are unlikely to ask for help when they need it or may even retaliate against supervisors who are perceived as punishing them (Treviño & Brown, 2005), thus inhibiting organizational safety. So feeling and being engaged may be affected by the extent to which individuals feel safe.

Availability refers to an individual's belief that they have the physical, emotional and psychological resources required to invest themselves in their work. Kahn (1990) found that availability was negatively influenced by an individual's depletion of physical and emotional energy, job insecurity and their lives outside of work. This means that for employees to feel available they must feel physically and emotionally able to perform their job as required. Employees who feel their job is at risk may be inhibited from feeling available on the job. That is, if they are constantly worried about their job security, they will not feel able to focus on the job because they will be worried about making mistakes or doing something that puts the job at risk.

Individuals may vary their willingness to engage with OC according to the meaning or purpose they attribute to it, the safety they perceive exists or not, as well as their availability and the resources they perceive themselves to have. The combination of these three conditions – meaning, safety and availability – creates a state of presence from which organizational members are able to engage themselves physically, cognitively and emotionally in their work (Kahn, 1992). So in the context of the Needs-Satisfying theory, when OC is challenging and meaningful, the social environment at work is safe, and personal resources are available, then engagement is likely to occur.

In sum, although theories, such as JD-R and the Needs–Satisfying, indicate the psychological conditions that are necessary for OC engagement, they do not fully explain why individuals will respond to these conditions and the outcomes with varying degrees of engagement. A stronger theoretical rationale for explaining this can be found in the Social Exchange Theory.

Social Exchange Theory

Since engagement forms part of the social exchange that takes place within an organization, the Social Exchange Theory is a good theoretical foundation for understanding the concept of OC engagement. According to the Social Exchange Theory, reciprocal interaction forms the basis of group behaviour. Individuals who feel supported by colleagues are likely to reciprocate support by taking on more responsibility and performing extra-role behaviours (Blau, 1964). In essence, Social Exchange Theory proposes that relationships at work evolve over time into trusting, loyal and mutual commitments as long as all parties involved abide by certain rules of exchange between the employer and employee.

Rules of exchange usually involve reciprocity or repayment such that the actions of one party lead to a response or actions by another party. For example, when individuals receive financial resources or social support from their organization, they may feel obliged to respond in kind and repay the organization (Cropanzano & Mitchell, 2005). This is consistent with Robinson and colleagues' (2004) description of engagement as a two-way relationship between the employer and employee. Anything that threatens this social exchange relationship could result in disengagement (Agarwal & Bhargava, 2013). That is, issues with trust, lack of reciprocity, or psychological or social contract breaches may result in a weakening of the relationship, resulting in at least a reduction of engagement, if not actual disengagement.

Although there is no perfect measure of costs and benefits in social exchanges, the Social Exchange Theory proposes that feelings of loyalty, commitment and discretionary effort are all, in some form, a social reciprocation by employees to a good employer. Being an engaged employee is one of the ways employees repay their organization, and this engagement is paid back in two ways: first, job engagement, which is specific to the role task an employee is principally hired to perform; and second, organizational engagement, which is a more diffuse concept referring to other roles that an employee plays through being a part of the larger organization.

As with other theories of engagement, resources play a key part in Social Exchange Theory. Employees will choose to engage themselves to varying degrees and in response to the cognitive, emotional and physical resources they receive from the organization. When employees receive these resources from the organization, they feel obliged to repay the organization with greater levels of engagement. When the organization fails to provide these resources, individuals are more likely to withdraw and disengage themselves. Thus, the amount of resources that an individual is prepared to devote in the performance of their work is contingent on the resources they receive from the organization; that is the social exchange. Consequently, OC engagement may be considered a two-way relationship between the employer and employee.

Effort-Reward Imbalance theory

Related to Social Exchange Theory is the Effort-Reward Imbalance (ERI) theory, which is based on the exchange relationship and social reciprocity between employee and employer (Siegrist, 1996). The ERI theory has its origin in medical sociology and emphasizes both the effort and the reward structure of work. According to this theory, work-related benefits depend upon a reciprocal relationship between efforts and rewards at work. Efforts represent job demands and/or obligations that are imposed on the employee, such as time pressure, responsibilities, interruptions and working overtime. Rewards distributed by the employer consist of money, esteem, job security and career opportunities. An imbalance occurs when there is a lack of reciprocity between efforts and rewards. More specifically, the ERI theory claims that work characterized by both high efforts and low rewards represents a reciprocity deficit between high costs and low gains, which may elicit negative emotions which in turn might cause stress. This has been found to be valid in terms of responsiveness to OC. In research conducted by Niedhammer and colleagues (2006), links were found between the imbalance of low reward and levels of strain among workers exposed to major OC. Employees may therefore suffer from stress if they are not rewarded for their efforts when facing work demands as a result of organizational change.

In sum, social exchange theories provide a theoretical foundation to explain OC engagement with the focus on the relations at work being at the heart of it. This recognizes that OC engagement is not just top-down or a unitarist style of management but is pluralist and reciprocal and may be different from other similar constructs.

OC engagement versus other constructs

Whilst many theories and definitions of engagement exist, it is important to show if and how the concept is distinct from other similar constructs with which it is often confused. This is particularly important, as questions have been raised over whether engagement is indeed a unique concept or whether it is a rebranding of an existing construct. Therefore, this section will explore areas of similarities and differences between OC engagement and the following concepts which are most frequently linked to engagement – job satisfaction, organizational commitment, job involvement, organizational citizenship behaviour (OCB), job performance, flow, and workaholism – with a view to understanding how the concept is distinct.

Job satisfaction

Job satisfaction is defined in terms of employees' subjective judgements about their work situations. One of the most widely cited definitions of job satisfaction comes from Locke (1976: 1300) who describes it as "a pleasurable or positive emotional state resulting from the appraisal of one's job". This appraisal is based on multiple facets, such as satisfaction with pay, co-workers, supervisors and the work itself. Job satisfaction is a multi-dimensional response to the job that includes cognitive, affective and behavioural components (Hulin & Judge, 2003), giving it a conceptual link to engagement as defined by Kahn (1990). However, whilst there may be a connection between the concepts of engagement and satisfaction at work, there are also distinctions between them. Whereas engagement relates to individual behaviour and involvement in work, the expression of job satisfaction reflects an evaluation of how the desired and actual working conditions compare to one another.

Studies indicate that satisfaction is often not directly related to performance and business outcomes, whilst engagement can predict satisfaction and other business outcomes such as productivity and performance. For example, Macey and Schneider (2008) indicate that although someone may be satisfied with their job, this does not necessarily mean they are engaged. Indeed, Frese (2008) goes a step further to argue that engagement often occurs in situations other than where one is satisfied with their work, such as when imminent deadlines and time pressures require an individual to work particularly hard.

Overall, findings from research suggest two possibilities. First, satisfaction at work is actually a relatively minor outcome of, or even completely absent from, engagement. As such, whether an employee derives fulfilment and satisfaction from an action may be down to other factors, like whether they get a sense of fulfilment from completing a piece of work. This is consistent with the assertion of Macey and Schneider (2008) and Frese (2008). Second, satisfaction is related to engagement, but the behaviour that occurs as a result of stressors does not fall under the domain of engagement. It could be argued that an individual under pressure may display similar dedication and absorption, but it seems unlikely that they will experience the vigour and passion that tend to characterize engagement (Kahn, 1990).

So engagement and job satisfaction can be considered different constructs. The main difference is that engagement emphasizes the cognitive aspect of involvement with job task, whereas satisfaction focuses on affect (Wefald & Downey, 2009). This suggests that the concept of OC engagement is distinct from job satisfaction since engaged employees participate beyond the expected level and cooperate actively to achieve effective change.

Organizational commitment

Some managers may mistake organizational commitment for OC engagement. However, in comparison to OC engagement, commitment is a broad and all-encompassing notion defined as the strength of an individual's identification and involvement in an organization. According to Meyer and Herscovitch (2001: 301), "commitment is a force that binds an individual to a course of action of relevance to one or more targets".

Some researchers consider organizational commitment a one-dimensional construct, while others propose that commitment is multidimensional and includes affective, normative and continuance components (Meyer & Allen, 1991). Affective commitment refers to an attachment to a particular focus, usually the organization, where the emphasis is on feeling a sense of membership and desire to remain a member. This is the form of commitment most studies consider when referring to organizational commitment. Continuance commitment is about staying with the organization out of a recognition that the cost of leaving is not in an individual's best interests. So, the perceived cost of staying versus leaving, such as cost–benefit ratio, is what drives the desire to remain a member of the organization. This formative calculation is attributed to Becker's (1960) side-bets theory, which says a person makes a series of judgements that ultimately determine a final decision, which is either consistent with, or contradictory to, other decisions and actions the person takes. Side bets are not necessarily financial but can include other benefits such as seniority, social networks or status. Similarly, the 'golden handcuff' rule is that by staying with an organization for x number of years, an individual will get a lucrative (golden) remuneration package that continues to grow each year that they remain in the organization. However, if they leave the organization before x number of years are up, they will lose the package, so these golden handcuffs keep the person in place because they are too good to let go of, and the side bet is that if they leave, they are released from their golden handcuffs. The side bet or trade-off might, therefore, be made for an individual by the norms of the situation. Important in Becker's theory is the recognition of the cost of discontinuing the direction an individual is pursuing, because the theory is about consistency of actions. Without this recognition, Becker suggests there is no commitment.

Normative commitment is based on personal norms and refers to a sense of obligation to remain a member of an organization. Normative commitment may be more evident in religiously oriented or third sector organizations, for example, in which people join and stay because they feel obligated to those to whom the organization provides services, or perhaps they were helped by the organization at one time and they feel they need to reciprocate the support they were given. Normative commitment is more about personal norms, values and a sense of obligation rather than about society or external ties, such as with continuance commitment.

When the constructs of OC engagement and commitment are considered, it becomes clear that their content overlaps with regard to identification with work, but that OC engagement takes things a step further. OC engagement encompasses not only the emotional connection but also actual behaviour and participation for the sake of the organization's change goals. OC engagement is, therefore, related to, but distinct from, organizational commitment, in that it contains many of the elements of commitment but is by no means a perfect match.

Organizational citizenship behaviour (OCB)

Organizational citizenship behaviour (OCB) is defined as "voluntary individual behaviour that while not part of formal job requirements is still promoting the effective functioning of the organization" (Robbins, 2005: 28). This refers to extra-role behaviour that is above the formal responsibilities required by an individual in an organization and includes activities such as helping other team members, volunteering and a willingness to perform additional work without being formally rewarded. Konovsky and Organ (1996) identify five dimensions of OCB: (i) altruism; (ii) courtesy; (iii) sportsmanship; (iv) civic virtue; and (v) generalized compliance. Altruism refers to voluntary actions that help another person. Courtesy includes efforts to prevent a problem occurring and to avoid abusing the rights of others. Sportsmanship refers to behaviour demonstrating tolerance of less than ideal circumstances without complaining. Civic Virtue refers to constructive behaviours indicating a willingness to participate responsibly in the organization. Finally, generalized compliance involves discretionary actions beyond the expected minimum requirements of the organization. Employees who enact these dimensions of OCB demonstrate higher organizational commitment and higher job involvement than others.

Studies have shown similarities between the concepts of engagement and OCB. For example, like OCB, engagement is something that employees offer voluntarily in direct response to their organizational experience (Rich et al., 2010). However, while OCB involves voluntary and informal behaviours that can help co-workers and the organization, the focus of engagement is an individual's formal role performance rather than extra-role and voluntary behaviour (Saks, 2006). Engagement has also been found to be a potential antecedent of OCB (Kataria et al., 2013). So while there are some similarities between the two there are also differences which suggest OC engagement is distinct from OCB.

Job performance

Job performance is what people do on the job towards completing tasks assigned by the organization or tasks that contribute to achieving organizational goals – it is what an employee is actually hired to do. The job performance construct has been delineated into a number of dimensions or factors, with some common to most, if not all, jobs, and other dimensions specifically aimed at certain types of jobs. For example, the model of job performance proposed by Campbell and colleagues (1990) is derived from a study of US army personnel; while Murphy's (1994) model of job performance originates from a study of US navy personnel. Although both are based on military institutions, the models are quite different. For example, Campbell and colleagues' (1990) model has eight different dimensions, whereas Murphy's (1994) model has only four. The eight levels of Campbell and colleagues' model are intended to describe the senior executive jobs and focus primarily on positive or productive job performance. In contrast, Murphy's model covers a large and diverse set of jobs and is meant to be both broad and general. Dimensions of both models include the types of specific tasks employees perform or the technical aspects of the job (for example, joinery, typing, driving, surgery, communication), employees' management of themselves on the job (such as whether acting within safety guidelines or carelessly; emotion regulation) and how employees interact with others (for example, interpersonally, through others). Job performance, therefore, has various dimensions depending on the nature of the job which are different from OC engagement. Furthermore a number of studies also show that job performance is an outcome of engagement (such as Demerouti & Cropanzano, 2010). For example, Schaufeli and Bakker (2004) found that engaged Dutch employees receive higher ratings from their colleagues on job performance, indicating that engaged employees perform well. Job performance can thus be said to be distinct from OC engagement in that performance may be defined as an outcome of OC engagement.

Job involvement

Job involvement is "a cognitive or belief state of psychological identification" (Kanungo, 1982: 342). Originally defined as the "internalization of values about the goodness of work or the importance of work in the worth of the person" (Lodahl & Kejner, 1965: 24), job involvement refers to the centrality of work in a person's life, the importance of work and the connection to one's core self-image. It is the degree to which an individual is cognitively preoccupied with, and concerned with, their job or a cognitive or belief state of psychological identification which depends on the personal needs of the individual and the potential of the job to meet those needs. Job involvement is essentially about how an individual sees themselves with regard to their job, expressed as a cognitive judgement of whether the job can satisfy their needs. Moreover, job involvement, although relatively stable, increases with success on the job; hence, greater achievement leads to more job involvement (Rabinowitz & Hall, 1977).

Although findings from the research suggest that engagement may share some characteristics of job involvement, it also has distinct elements such as the emotional and physical elements that are not found in job involvement.

OC engagement can be considered to be different from job involvement in that engagement has to do with how individuals employ themselves in the performance of change. Indeed job involvement is conceptually different to OC engagement, as job involvement is a purely cognitive act, whereas OC engagement involves the active use of emotions and behaviours in addition to cognitions.

Flow

The notion of 'flow' is defined as the holistic sensation that people feel when they act with total involvement (Csikszentmihalyi, 2000). It is "the subjective state that people report when they are completely involved in something to the point of forgetting time, fatigue, and everything else but the activity itself" (Csikszentmihalyi & Rathunde, 1993: 59). As American photographer Annie Lebovitz describes it, "when I go into work, I am transcended" (cited in Galvin, 2011). When an individual experiences flow, all their attention is directed to the activity such that distractions or other random thoughts are ignored. Flow drives action for the sake of enjoyment and the reward of the action. Employees who are in a state of flow often find the process of performing their work more enjoyable and need no external rewards or goals to motivate them, as the activity itself presents constant challenges.

The idea of flow is not limited to the workplace and has wide application, for example to leisure activities such as playing a musical instrument. It would, however, be unrealistic to suggest it as a target for the experience of work in all circumstances. Although engagement shares some conceptual space with flow, it is not the same as flow. The cognitive processing, which is characteristic of OC engagement, resembles flow. Also consistent in the conceptualizations of both flow and engagement is that low demands or unchallenging tasks do not yield flow or engagement, instead they yield boredom. OC engagement is, however, different from flow in that employees may be in an engaged state and perceive the change as worth doing because it creates meaning and moves them closer to goal attainment, as opposed to doing the job or task for its own sake as with flow. Also, unlike flow, there is no precondition of possessing a skill to become engaged with OC. Flow requires "a balance between perceived challenges and perceived skills" (Csikszentmihalyi et al., 2005: 601). So, whilst flow is primarily the cognitive involvement of an individual in an activity on a momentary basis, OC engagement is a longer-term and more holistic involvement in change. Flow does, however, highlight the potential pay-off for employees who are fully engaged with OC.

Workaholism

Theoretical discourse has likened too much engagement to workaholism. Research suggests that when employees become excessively involved in their jobs, they can become compulsive workaholics (Mudrack, 2004). Although at first glance there might be some similarities between workaholics and employees engaged with OC, it is, however, important to distinguish OC engagement from workaholism as the latter implies a compulsive addiction to work that is associated with a lack of balance between work and leisure and complete surrender to work (Schaufeli et al., 2008). It is also argued that engaged employees lack the typical compulsive drive that is characteristic of any addiction, including an addiction to work (Schaufeli et al., 2006b). Evidence from two Dutch studies by Taris and colleagues (2010) indicates that workaholism, as measured in terms of working excessively and working compulsively, can be distinguished from work engagement. Engaged employees work hard because work is challenging and fun, and not because they are driven by a strong inner urge they cannot resist. OC engagement is not, therefore, a synonym for work intensity.

OC engagement can therefore be considered a distinct and unique construct that consists of cognitive, emotional and behavioural components that are associated with individual role performance. Furthermore, OC engagement is distinguishable from several related constructs, most notably job satisfaction, organizational commitment, organizational citizenship behaviour, job involvement, flow and workaholism.

Summary

In this chapter we have highlighted a number of theories applicable to OC engagement including JD-R, COR and Social Exchange Theory. Such theories provide an overarching framework for understanding the nature, development and consequences of OC engagement. Since OC engagement forms part of the social exchange that takes place within an organization, the Social Exchange Theory is a good theoretical foundation for understanding the concept of OC engagement, since OC engagement is relational. OC engagement is also a different construct from job performance and citizenship behaviours, job involvement, job satisfaction, workaholism and flow. While these are important constructs with meaningful implications for human resource management, they differ from OC engagement. Despite the fact that a potential partial overlap is observed between OC engagement and OCB and commitment, the concept of OC engagement cannot be reduced to either of these. OC engagement is a unique and valuable construct which deserves the same theoretical and practical attention as other more established organizational constructs.

Implications

There are a number of practical implications that arise from the discussion in this chapter.

- Define what OC engagement is and what it looks like within the organization. Review whether and how you define and communicate a valid and appealing purpose for change and its linkage to the vision, values and strategy for change. Differentiate between OC engagement and other constructs in order to be able to identify what will influence it.
- Invest time in OC engagement. Engagement with change is very delicate and fragile. Individuals are constantly looking for signals about what change means for them, whether their engagement with OC matters and how safe they are

to engage. If the signs are positive individuals will engage, if the signs look negative then they will disengage with change immediately which is the fragility of engagement. Managers need to learn to dismantle the obstacles to engagement and create social interactions with and amongst employees. How can you do this better?

Part 2

Dilemmas and drivers of OC engagement

Chapter 5

The dilemma of OC engagement

Learning outcomes

After reading this chapter you will be able to:

- consider whether engagement is a fad or fashion;
- critically examine the concept of OC engagement;
- discuss the ethical implications of OC engagement;
- identify the cross-cultural perspectives of OC engagement.

Introduction

OC engagement is fundamentally important to the effectiveness of organizations, however, debate has raged, particularly in academia, about whether or not it is a sound construct for organizational effectiveness as well as about its applicability across cultures and sectors. In this chapter we turn our attention to the more critical views of OC engagement and examine the dilemma of whether or not OC engagement is a viable construct across the globe. Such critiques of the topic are to be encouraged, since it is only through subjecting OC engagement to critical and analytical scrutiny through a range of lenses that the field can progress. In the first part of the chapter we review whether or not OC engagement is just another consultancy fad or if it has validity. In the second part of the chapter the focus is on cross-cultural perspectives of OC engagement and whether or not it is a construct which is applicable across borders.

Engagement – fad or fashion?

Since its inception engagement has been critically evaluated, particularly in academic circles, as to whether it is a fad or fashion and if it will follow the path of the faded stars or become more firmly established at the heart of continuing good management practice. Keenoy (2014) critiques the notion of engagement as a fad developed and operationalized by policy makers, consultants and practitioners. According to Gibson and Tesone (2001) such a fad will either evolve into new management practices or be abandoned as a failure. In an article specifically considering whether employee engagement is a management fad, Wefald and Downey (2009) distinguish between fads, fashions and folderol. They view fads as short-term ideas that soon disappear and folderol as useless ideas, often based on the repackaging of old ideas while fashions are viewed more positively as approaches that become established as normal behaviour. These definitions reveal an absence of a clear consensus about what we mean by management fad or fashion and, therefore, whether or not engagement fits the category of one or the other. However, there is the implication in each of the definitions that there may be superficial innovations or ideas that are commonly described as passing fads and there are fashions that may be transitory or become an established part of management practice. There is evidence to show an attempt to fit engagement into the latter definition. For instance in the UK a government-sponsored movement has attempted to promote engagement which has led to the publication of a report entitled *Engaging for Success*. The authors of the report, MacLeod and Clarke (2009), have also launched a range of activities to raise awareness of engagement including conferences and workshops, a so-called 'guru' group, a web page, Twitter account and a series of case studies. All these have helped to market the idea of engagement as a good thing and advocate the need for it. The Engaging for Success movement has also produced a report entitled 'Nailing the evidence' (Rayton et al., 2012) which reviews a body of evidence that purports to explore the causal relationship between employee engagement and a wide range of performance outcomes. The report is designed to convince managers, as well as sceptics in the academic community, that engagement is more than just a fad. Unfortunately, it does not offer a convincing definition of employee engagement and much of the academic research cited in the report addresses commitment, job satisfaction and other widely researched variables. It, therefore, risks reinforcing the scepticism about the utility and discriminant validity of engagement.

In an attempt to validate its utility, a plethora of meta-analysis studies have been conducted into the concept, although to date there is little longitudinal research. This is not the place for a full review of the literature but much of the relevant research is summarized in a meta-analysis by Christian and colleagues (2011) of 90 studies which found a strong association between engagement and both task and contextual performance. However, we need to be cautious about concluding that this analysis offers clear rational support for engagement since only a small proportion of the studies measured performance and a majority used self-rated performance. Moreover, most were also cross-sectional, raising questions about causality. On this basis, critics argue that the results are encouraging but not yet convincing. Critics also point out that many of the studies are conducted at the individual level and while they address relevant outcomes such as organizational citizenship behaviour and turnover, these are more proximal measures than the kind of financial and performance benefits at the organizational level that are often claimed for employee engagement.

Although the academic literature on engagement has accumulated a sufficient body of evidence to suggest that it does indeed represent something conceptually and statistically different from what has gone before, critics do, however, express more significant reservations about the consultancy perspective on engagement, and note that the measures for engagement developed so far are problematic, concluding that the longevity of the consultancy version of engagement is difficult to assess (Guest, 2014).

Keenoy (2014) raises the concern that the engagement agenda risks being hijacked by consultants and others aware of the potentially lucrative nature of the engagement industry. Similarly, Guest (2014) suggests that the popularity of engagement is due more to effective marketing by consultants than to sound theory and evidence. Such critics warn that if engagement is driven by consultants, it can be expected to thrive as long as it provides a basis for competitive advantage and consultancy fees. When this changes, and more particularly if something comes along to take its place as the latest focus for improving engagement, then Guest (2014) predicts that it may experience a swift decline. This is supported by Clinton and Woollard (2012) who say that the first sign of a decline in initiatives to promote employee engagement is evident. Despite this supposed decline there is a belief among practitioners and even academics that engagement is important, deserves continued attention and is a topic worth studying. After closer examination of the concept some critics have begun to concede that there is a case for claiming that engagement has become an established area of academic interest and research rather than a passing fad. Moreover it can be argued that the academic form of engagement appears to have achieved a respectable degree of longevity and cannot reasonably be described as a passing fad.

The paradox of OC engagement

The debate about whether engagement is a fad or fashion has also led to concerns about the dark side of engagement, the idea that perhaps engagement is not always a good thing. Although research has shown the benefits of engagement (such as Karatepe, 2013) which are generally considered good for an organization, critics warn that taken to an extreme they may become negative. Masson and colleagues (2008) raise the question of whether the potential benefits of engagement have overshadowed the possible downsides while Macey and colleagues (2009) go as far as to caution that too much of an engagement culture can also have bad consequences, including burnout, disengagement and other negative and psychological and behavioural outcomes, such as not adapting to the changes required for the company to succeed. Similarly, Bates (2004) also warns against trying to boost engagement due to the negative repercussions it can have on retention, claiming that one of the paradoxes that many organizations discover when boosting engagement is that the kind of training that gives workers higher feelings of engagement also gives them more opportunities to leave the organization. This supports the findings of a study (Britt, 2003) of US Army rangers which indicates that those rangers who are the most engaged with their work also report being the most demoralized when they are faced with obstacles to high performance and, as a result, are more prone to leave the organization.

   Critics of engagement also question whether employees can become too engaged (such as van Beek et al., 2011). For example, employees who are engaged in their current jobs and projects may become so committed to the project that their commitment becomes so rigid that changes become unacceptable. Siegrist and colleagues (2004) propose that over engagement occurs when employees seek high job demands and extend their work efforts beyond what is expected of the organization, all in an effort to obtain approval. Too much engagement has also been cited as leading to disengagement (Macey et al., 2009). That is, employees who are given too much challenge at work, too much autonomy, too much support for engagement, and their work becoming too meaningful will become disengaged, distancing them from work. Macey and colleagues (2009) base this assertion on the idea that engagement is like other constructs that when too much is present it results in an overload of the psychological system. In contrast, the managerial perspective on engagement tends to ignore the implications of over engagement for those so engaged and/or paint an overly rosy picture of high engagement which fails to consider the reality that many employees actually face.

Impact on well-being

Continuous OC engagement may come at a cost to the health of individuals and organizations. People cannot expend their energy at the highest level all the time, as they need time for recovery to ensure their well-being. If this does not happen then it may lead to depletion or the 'dark side' of engagement where employees, who try to enact all of their roles, experience burnout, health problems and disengagement. The core roles which an engaged employee is expected to contribute to include: job holder; innovator; team member; and an organizational member (Caza, 2012). These are all areas where employees are expected to exercise their discretionary behaviour which leads Welbourne (2011: 94) to ask, "can leaders expect employees to do more of the non-core job roles and still keep doing more of the core job role? . . . Are organizations asking employees to be super people who go above and beyond in everything?" This raises the potential concern that when OC is added to an individual's role it will drive work intensification with employers coming to expect employees to 'go the extra mile' as a matter of course with overtime becoming normalized (Rees et al., 2013). Macey and colleagues (2009) point out the paradox that this creates with those who are most engaged being the most likely to suffer from burnout. Thus an overload of OC engagement may result in exhaustion and disengagement.

Change overload

There appears to be an implicit perspective that change initiated by management is typically good and that the proper outcome of change is that employees support it. This may not always be the case. There may be times when a proposed change is not the right thing to do. It may be that the costs outweigh benefits, that the politics of change, even if successful, could have long-term damaging effects, or that the organization is suffering from an overload of change; so called change fatigue.

Change fatigue or overload occurs when employees have too much OC to cope with in the time available for its completion. Although OC has the potential to raise expectations and enhance engagement, there may come a point where demands from OC can overwhelm individuals' capacity and trigger negative emotions, such as fear, anxiety or anger, that make them feel unable to adequately deal with these demands and less capable of having the physical, cognitive and emotional energy available to invest in OC. Empirical research provides support for this reasoning; for example, a study of blue and white collar workers indicates that workers who feel overloaded have decreased levels of engagement (Korunka et al., 2009). Thus, while engaging with OC can be beneficial for employees, it can also overwhelm the capacity of the individual. This is illustrated in a survey carried out by Moorhouse Consulting (2012) into Financial Services organizations entitled *Too Much Change?* The study highlights that there is concern among managers about the ability of staff to cope with the volume and complexity of change with nearly half (48 per cent) of respondents saying that front-line staff are not coping well with change. The survey concludes that workers in the financial sector are struggling with an overload of change. Similar signs of change fatigue are evident in the pharmaceutical industry where many employees are suffering from too much change due to decades of transformations such as restructuring (Gyurjyan et al., 2014), which can increase levels of stress.

Stress is perceived to be the opposite of well-being and is defined as a particular relationship between an individual and their environment that is appraised by the individual as taxing or exceeding their resources and endangering their well-being. So for example, an individual will use their cognitive appraisal process to determine if OC is a challenge, threat or non-threat. This appraisal process depends on an individual's perceptions, expectations, interpretations and coping mechanisms (Yahaya et al., 2012). Too much change can lead to disengagement which can affect employees' well-being at work and ultimately can cause stress.

So, should we therefore expect employees to be fully engaged all the time with change or can too much engagement be a bad thing? At the extremes the answer is probably 'yes'. For people cannot expend their energy at the highest level all the time as there is a need for recovery to ensure continued well-being. High levels of continuous OC engagement may have negative individual and organizational consequences such as exhaustion and loss of creativity. Under conditions of ambiguity, uncertainty and the need for creative solutions, sustained conscious OC engagement may have detrimental effects, whereas alternative levels of high and low levels of OC engagement may lead to more desirable outcomes (George, 2010). Hence the need to recognize OC engagement as a transient concept and be cognisant of the ethical issues of OC overload.

The ethics of OC engagement

The pursuit of OC engagement may involve work intensification or over engagement that can actually diminish employee well-being and result in stress and disengagement thus raising ethical issues. Ethics are the agreed standards and constraints that determine what is and what is not acceptable action and behaviour. Whether or not a company behaves ethically is essentially the result of the decisions and actions of individual people taken every day. Ethical behaviour is the mutual understanding of the responsibilities that individuals have for one another. Organizational ethics identify this responsibility in relation to the individuals within an organization. They form the basis of the relationship between the individual and the organization and as such determine the extent to which an environment of trust is created.

Ethics is key to the enactment of OC. When engaging with change an individual, as part of an organization, has a role to fulfil. However, they must not be in the position where they are either being asked to operate outside their areas of competence or feel that the duty of care to individuals or groups is being compromised. Ethical issues can occur, for example when employees are expected to participate in cost-saving exercises that may ultimately affect their jobs, and are expected to contribute more, for no greater personal reward. Ethical issues are, therefore, raised when the OC engagement agenda relegates employees to a passive role when OC engagement initiatives are perceived to be driven by the organization and done *to* rather than *with* employees.

From a critical standpoint, Overell (2008) warns that the ethics of employers drawing on engagement by eliciting employees' discretionary effort can appear less a concern for mutuality between employers and employees and more like a corporate takeover of psychological space. Critics argue that engagement seems to imply that employees should have super-human levels of energy and performance that may be unrealistic (Purcell, 2013). This has been condemned as producing 'willing slaves' who must progressively face the 'specter of uselessness' if they can no longer keep up with the pace or the working conditions (Overell, 2008).

So is it really beneficial to have everyone engaged, all the time, at the highest intensity level? There is concern that employees who are engaged frequently, over long periods of time, or at very high levels of intensity, may eventually become burned out and that high levels of engagement interfere with conscious decision-making and problem-solving processes (Halbesleben et al., 2009). Specifically, it is suggested that when an employee is in a state of high engagement, problem-solving is limited because conscious thinking cannot access as much information as the non-conscious mind (George, 2010). People who work at intense levels of concentration for consecutive periods, with little rest in-between, have been found to suffer from emotional exhaustion and mental fatigue (Schaufeli et al., 2006b). Moreover, George (2010) concludes that high levels of engagement may be dysfunctional in decision-making, creative work and complex problem-solving, and consequently too much engagement can be detrimental to an organization. However, other researchers have argued that rather than engagement leading to such negative outcomes, when employees work obsessively and to their own detriment, they are no longer demonstrating engagement, but rather they are demonstrating workaholism (Schaufeli et al, 2006b) thus suggesting that workaholism is different from engagement or disengagement.

Since ethics forms a key part of the fluid nature of OC engagement there is a need to recognize where ethical issues need to be examined, raised and addressed and to have mechanisms in place to enable this to happen. Ethical standards and behaviour are, thus, central to the actions associated with OC engagement.

OC engagement across cultures

OC engagement in different sectors

As a concept there is debate about the validity of engagement across cultures and sectors. Research shows that across industries, engagement has been found to be substantially higher in the third sector than in other sectors (Towers Perrin, 2003). This would appear logical, given that people tend to be drawn to the third sector through a sense of mission, rather than from any prospect of high pay or wealth accumulation (Hodges & Howieson, 2017). This is also consistent with the numerous definitions and views surrounding engagement in the third sector, which identify a 'passion for work' as being a key component factor (Holbeche & Springett, 2004). Indeed, the fact that the third sector is traditionally not a high-paying one emphasises that it is not possible to buy engagement in the conventional sense by offering higher rewards. Conversely, in a study comparing the public and private sectors, Truss and colleagues (2006) found that employees in the public sector had a more negative experience of work and were less satisfied with the opportunities they had to use their abilities and consequently were less inclined to engage. This reinforces the findings of previous studies and underlines the scale of the challenge facing public sector managers in particular, and the potential negative impact on their levels of engagement.

OC engagement across countries

The concept of OC engagement in different national contexts is important to understand for at least two reasons. First, contextualization is a necessary, although often ignored, part of OC initiatives, whereby context is broadly defined as a set of factors surrounding a phenomenon that exerts some direct or indirect influence on it (Whetten, 2009). Context effects such as national culture are central to understanding organizational phenomena such as OC. Research (Hofstede, 1979) has shown that organizations must adapt to different cultural values and norms when it comes to attracting, motivating and retaining staff, so this may well be extended to include OC engagement. Second, understanding whether OC engagement has found relevance in different national contexts provides practical knowledge for managers and human resource professionals who work in multi-national organizations since employees bring to the workplace diverse cultural backgrounds and varied skillsets derived from an eclectic array of personal histories.

Multinational corporations (MNCs) which are considering OC engagement across their operations are faced with the question of whether OC engagement is a universal concept, similar across the globe, or whether its meaning, and the factors that influence it, differ in the different parts of the world in which they operate. MNCs need to consider whether OC engagement can be compared in a meaningful way across their multi-national operations, and whether similar policies and practices are likely to influence levels of OC engagement similarly in different national contexts.

Most research on engagement has been conducted in either North America or Europe with much of the available international evidence coming from the Gallup organization, which has conducted employee engagement surveys in several countries. The focus of research in North America and Europe is not surprising given that two of the main theoretical models on engagement were developed by Kahn (1990) in the USA and Schaufeli and colleagues (2006a) in Europe. This is beginning to change, for instance Kelliher and colleagues (2012) conducted research on MNCs operating across the globe, which examined whether the meanings and antecedents of engagement varied in different national contexts. The findings from the study suggest that the drivers of engagement that are common across the different national contexts and across employee groups are the importance of communication between the large corporate entity and the local units in different countries, and the critical role of line managers. All other drivers are dependent on cultural contexts. This suggests that it may be difficult to achieve a standardized approach to OC engagement across an organization's workforce.

To customize their approach, leaders and managers need to understand the interaction of discrete cultural factors and the contextual meaning of OC engagement. For example, in Australia, workplace initiatives such as employee involvement, learning and development, role clarity, and teamwork have been shown to increase engagement (Parkes & Langford, 2008). In a UK study by Alfes and colleagues (2010), positive working conditions, experiences of HRM practices, perceived organizational support and the quality of interactions with line managers have been found to be essential for promoting engagement. Studies done in North America have found that employees are likely to be engaged when they find their workplace culture to be positive and when they can derive meaning from their work (Fairlie, 2011; Kernaghan, 2011). Among the French police Gillet and colleagues (2013) found that perceived organizational support (POS) encourages engagement. Similarly, in Germany and Sweden, research has found that it is necessary to provide social support and autonomy in order to increase engagement (Taipale et al., 2011; Vincent-Höper et al., 2012). Providing relevant resources to challenging job demands (De Braine & Roodt, 2011) and organizational support (Mostert & Rathbone, 2007) are also necessary to encourage greater engagement in South Africa. Hong Kong employees are more likely to engage when holistic care is provided to help them to reduce their levels of stress and burnout (Fong & Ng, 2012), while with Japanese employees organizations should pay attention to group harmony and employee support (Shimazu et al., 2008; Inoue et al., 2010). Whereas, in the Philippines, strategies for engaging employees need to include the use of performance management systems and the provision of competitive employee benefits (Resurreccion, 2012). Such studies show that the cultural context has to be unpacked to fully understand OC engagement. Cross-national comparisons of levels of employee engagement should, however, be treated with some caution due to cultural and definitional differences. Consideration should, therefore, be given as to whether or not the same OC engagement techniques work for employees in countries with different economies and cultures or if there is a need to customize them for local cultures.

In sum, what do these findings mean for MNCs considering OC engagement across their operations? Cultural and sectoral differences are likely to have implications for OC engagement in relation to the factors which influence and contribute to levels of OC engagement. The national context in relation to culture, institutions and economic circumstances are, therefore, important determinants of the factors influencing OC engagement. This is illustrated in the following case (Box 5.1) of change in a stockbroking company in Mauritius, which highlights that an approach to engagement in a company in one sector may not be transferable to a company in a different sector.

Box 5.1 Creating an environment for engagement with change in a stockbroking company in Mauritius

Written by Roshan Ramoly,
Customer Experience Trainer and Strategist, LinearArc Solutions

When I was asked to take up the challenge of heading the stockbroking arm of the group of companies that I was working in, I accepted the assignment with a degree of apprehension. The company was the largest stockbroking firm in Mauritius and I was coming from the head office with a background in strategy and little knowledge of the stockbroking industry. Quite understandably, my arrival was welcomed with an equal degree of apprehension from both team members as well as clients. My predecessor was a well-respected thought leader in the industry having spent more than 15 years as a stockbroker, and was also the Vice-Chair of the Stock Exchange of Mauritius. So, I had some big shoes to fill and in case I did not grasp the full extent of this, I was quickly made to realize it through my first interactions with the team, where they expressed their expectations of me, and also through some challenging meetings with clients who wanted to test my capabilities.

I began by meeting the team members and top clients in order to try and understand what made the company successful, as it is part of an industry that functions in a competitive market, whereby the shares purchased through one broker are identical to those bought through another broker. My initial assessment indicated that there was a culture of service within the team and the members valued the customer who trusted their advice. Moreover, it was felt that the company would not wish to make a deal at all costs. However, upon digging deeper, I also found that the organization was run with a sense of control from the top while the team members were provided with little information on strategy, lagging or lead indicators of performance. The company was also run in a very strict manner whereby each member had specific tasks to perform and had to deliver them by the end of the day. It was more of an operations culture than the desired service orientated culture. Furthermore, there was little room for taking initiatives as the senior management, which had been running the company for 15–20 years, had more experience and so employees were expected to trust their way of doing things without questioning it.

Even though the team was fairly small, it operated in silos, namely: trading; operations; and research. The relatively tough work environment made the three individual teams work like family units with a high degree of trust and mutual support. This, I realized, was in fact the biggest asset of the company along with the very good individual capabilities of the team members. On the other hand, operating in a fiercely competitive market, the focus was too often on being reactive rather than proactive to competition, and there was a lack of focus on the company's capabilities and strategy. Over time, a lot of the processes had also become heavy and time-consuming. A good day for the company would mean that it would be a bad day for the employees who had to work longer hours to catch up on backlogs and administrative work that followed a hectic trading session.

There were a number of things that I quickly identified as needing to be changed in order to address the issues identified. I started by exploring the dependency on senior leadership to provide direction and make decisions. I realized that if I wanted to leverage on the capabilities of the team, I would have to fully empower them. However, this required a lot of unlearning, as they were used to be being closely managed. Therefore, after discussing with the leadership team and providing this reassurance to the team that empowering would not mean that I would not stand by them if they took bad decisions, I decided to take a plunge and empower fully the heads of departments. The premise was that they knew their line of work better than I did and my role was as an enabler to make things happen for them. I encouraged new ways of doing things and allowed the team to take decisions. Giving staff autonomy meant that we had some events that backfired but standing by the team in such situations and continuing to pursue this direction only increased the level of trust that they had in me and it provided the team with a stronger sense of responsibility to avoid such mistakes again. At the same time, we worked on creating a better work atmosphere by renovating the offices and changing the mood into a more fun approach to work by celebrating deals and little successes. The small surprise parties with cakes or ice-cream even became a trademark of the company and we got into the habit of celebrating; which was critical to changing the mind-set from one of working to achieving.

To help generate engagement with the change the teams were tasked to review processes and streamline them as much as possible. They addressed the issue of the heavy administrative work by continuously challenging what was being done. Inevitably, there was a high degree of internal resistance from some people who were wary of doing the wrong things and being out of line with the regulatory framework of the industry. This stemmed from the previous style of management which had created a sense of conservatism, and even though I had adopted a more inclusive style of management I realized that it would take time for the team to unlearn their previous ways of working. I therefore needed to allow time and provide the necessary environment for the team to rebuild their confidence through regular conversations while highlighting all the good work that had been covered. Moreover, the initial restructuring and proposed changes were only done after obtaining the blessing of the regulatory authorities in order to provide the necessary reassurance to the team. The result was that we reduced the time taken for a number of lengthy processes from 2–3 hours down to only 15 minutes. This was achieved by involving the teams in the decisions about what should be done differently, by reviewing the processes and suggesting improvement, and also through the use of improved technologies which sometimes entailed financial costs, but which we saw as investments. The immediate benefit was that the team members would have more time for strategic reflection at work as well as an improved work-life balance since they were able to reduce the amount of overtime they were working.

Personally, I am driven by purpose and have a strong conviction that people will work best if their personal purpose is in line with that of the company. I therefore decided to meet every staff member one-to-one for regular informal chats to find out what motivated them at work. The discussions during these conversations often had little to do with the company, but more with their individual needs. This helped me understand individual perspectives better and also ensure that employees could align their personal purpose with that of the company. This was important because the main asset of the company was the spirit of togetherness and this had to be safeguarded.

One of the difficult times I faced was in dismissing a staff member who was creating a lot of disruption which was impacting on staff morale. While the team member's work was satisfactory, her presence was disruptive in terms of her behaviour which made the general mood of the workplace very gloomy, especially during her regular outbursts and conflict with other team members. Another people issue which had to be addressed was recruiting new staff. We had to ensure that not only did we recruit good technical people but also people who would fit in with the culture. To engage staff in this process we took the decision to let the peers of the potential recruit do the preliminary selection before recommending the top three names to the head of department, who would make the final decision. As the head of the company, I merely gave advice, supported the decision and respected the choice of the team. The result was that the team recruited individuals who were the best fit for the culture and their team and who were also able to learn the systems and processes quickly.

Being the largest stockbroker in the industry, we wanted our team members to feel part of a winning team, so we changed the culture of withholding information to one where there was transparency. This involved information being shared regularly, such as: statistics on budget; market share; revenues; costs and profits. Moreover, any deviation on costs was explained to the team who, as a result, started feeling part of the bigger picture. In fact I recall, when we were renovating the office, some team members felt that too much was being spent on it and wanted me to reconsider how much was being spent. They took some convincing, but it was interesting to note that the team had developed a sense of responsibility towards the company and wanted to ensure that every cost was justified in the same way that they would for their personal expenses.

After two years of the change process, we started noticing a marked improvement across the company. The staff morale was high, with the participation of all staff members at company events. Our market share increased as the team was allowed to do what they did best, and this translated directly into excellent financial results. Our research was being quoted on Bloomberg and Reuters, we would be asked to speak at regional conferences, and the head of research was even being called for quarterly interviews on CNBC. The efficiency of the administrative team had also improved, with accounts being released just a day after month-end and client accounts managed more adequately and efficiently. It was a proud moment when the team won an award for outstanding work within the group that we belonged to.

After four years of working in the stockbroking industry, I decided to test new waters and moved to a large multinational bank as the head of strategy, thinking that I had the magic formula for success. Unfortunately, I quickly realized that what works for smaller companies does not necessarily work in larger ones – especially multinational organizations. The main difference was that in my previous role I had more latitude to create the space to work with my team in an autonomous manner while I handled the 'heat' from the top. In a multinational, my experience was very different. The team members have various reporting lines and the latitude provided to a head of function is limited. The matrix organization with multiple reporting lines of the team members to persons who were often more senior than myself, allowed them to leverage their power bases, making it difficult to manage.

After spending a lot of energy re-aligning power bases by establishing my credibility with the various persons with whom my team members had 'dotted' reporting lines and even parting ways with a person who was the disruptor, the team was then ready to work in a different way. It was then that I adapted and applied the following five principles, which had been a successful approach in the stockbroking firm, to engage staff in changes:

1 Build trust by connecting with the individuals;
2 Ensure that the individual purpose meets that of the group;
3 Create a sense of autonomy and freedom of action;
4 Change the role of the leader from directing to being an enabler; and
5 Provide visibility on the bigger picture.

This approach started to reap benefits and started to change the environment of the department. Although I did find that it was important to adapt these principles to the context of the situation in which I was working.

Summary

Despite its critics there is a case for claiming that engagement has become an established area of academic interest and research rather than a passing fad, as well as a serious area of focus for organizations. OC engagement appears to have the potential to be seen as having longevity and cannot therefore be described as a passing fad. There is, however, a need to recognize that ethics form a key part of the fluid nature of OC engagement and ethical issues need to be examined, raised and addressed. Ethical standards and behaviour are, thus, central to OC engagement.

To date much of the debate about engagement has been explored in a Western context and relatively little is known about what OC engagement may mean and what factors are likely to influence it elsewhere. Cultural and institutional differences are likely to have implications for the meaning of OC engagement and the factors which influence it. Hence this raises the question of whether OC engagement is a universal concept or simply a Western concept and whether strategies to promote higher levels of OC engagement can be used across operations in different countries. Despite limited research it is likely that due to different cultural contexts OC engagement might take different forms around the world and should be considered in order to understand what influences OC engagement.

Implications

There are a number of practical implications which arise from the discussion in this chapter.

- Demonstrate the value of OC engagement. Review to what extent you know and share the value of OC engagement and whether and how you identify and personally display, promote and reinforce the value that informs and supports it. In identifying the value consider the ethical principles or standards that are considered to be important or beneficial in leading change efforts and, in particular, those that are deemed to be 'good' or 'bad' or 'right' as opposed to 'wrong'. How can you better ensure you accurately know and personally display, promote and reinforce behaviours that inform and support the importance and value of OC engagement?
- Appreciate the advantages and disadvantages of OC engagement. Understand that OC engagement brings with it risks and a potential 'dark side'. However, these risks also bring with them something positive, namely the opportunity to learn, improve and develop. Review your own experiences of OC engagement and ask yourself what you could improve upon.
- Ethics needs to be part of the dialogue within organizations that characterize OC engagement. OC engagement may involve work intensification or over engagement that can actually diminish employee well-being and result in stress and disengagement. This raises ethical questions about how far employees can be expected to participate in activities that save costs for the organization at the expense of jobs. Review how you identify the ethical issues of engaging people with change.
- Take into account cultural differences. Recognize that the implementation of practices intended to enhance OC engagement levels must take account of the national and organizational cultures and be adapted locally.

Chapter 6

Antecedents and outcomes of OC engagement

Learning outcomes

After reading this chapter you will be able to:

- differentiate between the different antecedents of OC engagement;
- appreciate the impact of the drivers of OC engagement;
- outline the levels of OC engagement;
- identify the outcomes of OC engagement.

Introduction

Much of the appeal of OC engagement derives from its competitive advantages for organizations in terms of the potential for effective and successful change. Consequently, researchers and managers naturally want to know what key drivers can be leveraged to bring about increases in OC engagement. It is not, however, easy to identify a definitive list because just as there are different views on what engagement is, there are even more arguments about what influences engagement. In this chapter we will explore the thinking and evidence on what drives OC engagement and draw out some common themes to propose a model of the principal antecedents and outcomes of OC engagement. We begin by considering what OC engagement looks like.

What does OC engagement look like?

What OC engagement looks like may vary from individual to individual and organization to organization, apart from the fact that it means people working hard and caring about what they do. When individuals are engaged with OC they tend to feel optimistic about it and are more receptive to the need for OC. They are also focused and physically present in being involved and invest a lot of their energy in participating with the change. Descriptions of engaged employees include how they deliver improved business performance, go the extra mile, as well as their higher productivity, innovation, higher quality discretionary efforts, energy, enthusiasm, and ability to solve more problems than disengaged employees. Engaged employees transform non-meaningful change into something meaningful and devote discretionary effort to it willingly, even eagerly. Conversely, when people are disengaged, they are only physically present. They have little or no emotional attachment to change, do not care about the rationale for the change or its goals, and rarely participate actively in the change process. Disengaged individuals are more likely to feel apathetic, cynical or detached and perform tasks in a robotic manner without putting in any effort, and they will tend to be negative about the change. When employees are engaged in change they can observe the influence of their contributions so everyone is invested in its success. Conversely, when change is imposed and employees feel unable to influence change within the organization, this may lead to them withdrawing which can then result in a decrease in their engagement with OC. A key differentiator between an engaged and a non-engaged employee is thus the degree of personal investment they have in OC. So what drives individuals to engage with OC?

Antecedents

There is debate in the literature around what influences engagement and what potential antecedents matter the most. Like many researchers, in terms of prognosis, Saks (2006) believes that the consequences of engagement are largely positive, but the important thing to find out is what causes it. In an attempt to address this, consultants have provided lists of a variety of factors that can play a part in affecting engagement. Such checklists can be helpful but are essentially generic and lack any substantial evidence or detail about what influences OC engagement.

To identify potential antecedents it is helpful to look at the results of meta-analysis studies. Meta-analyses use advanced statistical procedures to combine the results of individual studies and arrive at an overall best determination of the strength and direction of relationships between constructs of interest. Halbesleben's (2010) meta-analysis study which is consistent with the JD-R theory suggests that feedback, autonomy, social support and organizational climate, as well as personal resources, such as self-efficacy and optimism, are consistently associated with engagement. Similarly, Mauno and colleagues (2010) show that increases in employee experiences of job control and support at work consistently predict an increase in engagement over time. Robinson (2006) also suggests that organizational, personal and job characteristics, as well as employee experiences, all influence engagement. By implication, if these features of work are promoted, then the outcome will be enhanced OC engagement.

Such studies show that although engagement is a personal attitude of individual employees, it does not occur in isolation. So when considering the sources and consequences of OC engagement we need to go beyond the individual dynamics and also consider the organizational context and processes. Based on this premise and existing research we propose that the main antecedents of OC engagement are context, process and individual. These are key factors which influence the generation and sustaining of OC engagement and are illustrated in Figure 6.1.

Contextual antecedents

OC engagement happens within a context and some contexts are likely to be more conducive than others to the development of OC engagement. The contextual antecedents of OC engagement include: the organizational culture; trust; the history of change; nature of OC; and change readiness. By their nature, such contextual

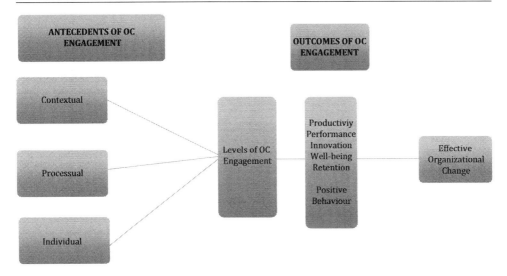

Figure 6.1 Antecedents and outcomes of OC engagement

antecedents are more distal determinants of OC engagement. That is, they set the stage for, and interact with, the proximal (process) influences. Contextual factors tend to develop relatively slowly and their influence is more subtle, and as a result, they are not easily modified and do not serve as effective short-term levers for OC engagement. For example, trust in management is crucial for OC engagement but trust is earned over the long term and cannot simply be switched on when the need arises. Since contextual factors are not easily modified in the short term, they must be managed carefully even during times of continuity and stability.

Organizational culture

The organizational culture, or a shared system of beliefs, values and assumptions (Schein, 1997), guides the activities of an organization and its members. It provides employees with a common understanding that unites them, helps them to understand how they fit in and what is valued, appropriate and inappropriate. Employees' experience of organizational culture tells them what to believe about the workplace, how to behave at work, what they will be rewarded for, the organization's values, as well as the extent to which they can become connected to the organization and its members (Schneider, 1990). The culture shapes the experience that employees have of OC and can drive employees towards becoming engaged with change, or else it can push employees towards disengagement.

Within an organizational culture there are a number of linkages or bonds which need to be established between an individual and the organization (Sparrow & Balain, 2010) which affect OC engagement. At the individual level, four bonds appear to be important. First, people need to have a motivation and incentive to bond that is a reason and a desire for social membership with the organization, which includes feelings and beliefs regarding the reason why they want to maintain a relationship with, or their membership of, the organization. Second, there needs to be organizational identification; which is the degree to which an employee defines themselves by the same attributes that they believe define the organization. The notion of identification involves a "significant psychological linkage between the individual and the organization whereby the individual feels a deep, self-defining affective and cognitive bond with the organization as a social identity" (Edwards, 2005: 209). People tend to identify with their organization when they perceive synergy between their own goals and values and those of the organization. They are motivated to build identification with the organization because they want to feel involved and to have challenging jobs through which they can experience personal growth and the chance to achieve something worthwhile (Holbeche, 2017). Individuals create identities through social interactions with others. This interactionist approach is known as Social identity theory (Tajfel & Turner, 1986). Wherever possible people at work look for something beyond their job, such as a sense of purpose or redemption, a source of challenge or enjoyment, or the ability of the work to confer or reinforce social identity or identities (Baldry et al., 2007). Employees will engage most energetically, creatively and enthusiastically when they believe they are contributing to a purpose that is bigger than themselves. Third, there has to be a process of internalization that is the personal learning, internal recognition and personal adoption of the values and goals of the organization. Fourth, there needs to be a sense of psychological ownership which is an attitudinal state of mind involving feelings of being psychologically tied to an object along with a sense of responsibility and obligation that comes from this feeling of ownership. Collectively these bonds create two conditions: job engagement (specific to the role an employee is principally hired to perform) and organizational engagement (Saks, 2006). Hameed and colleagues (2013) show empirically that the psychological bonding between an individual and their organization has a positive effect on OC. This is consistent with the arguments of Cherim (2002) who suggests that in order to facilitate effective change an organization should focus on developing a strong attachment with its employees. So establishing such bonds through the culture of the organization can have an impact on OC engagement.

Organizational cultures can also negatively influence OC engagement. For instance, cultures that stifle innovation and creativity may lead to employees feeling trapped by their work as opposed to energized by it, leading them to psychologically, if not physically, withdraw and therefore disengage. A culture of broken promises and unmet expectations during previous changes can also lead to disengagement with future changes. If the organizational culture is not conducive to change, and employees do not maintain the motivation to change throughout the intervention, change is unlikely to happen (Nielsen et al., 2010). In contrast, organizations that establish a culture of trust maximize the probability that their employees will be engaged with change.

Trust

A culture of trust is necessary for employees to feel and act engaged. Trust refers to an individual's willingness to be vulnerable to the actions of another party based on the expectation that the latter will perform a particular action (Schoorman et al., 2007) and is an attitude that is referent focused, such that an individual can trust, that is, be willing to be vulnerable to their co-workers, line manager and the organization (Dirks & Ferrin, 2001). Trust in co-workers creates safety and reduces the need for self-protection; while trust in line management increases employees' willingness to share sensitive information and be more vulnerable to criticism. Research has found a direct relationship between trust in managers or leaders and employee engagement (Wang & Hsieh, 2013). Employees will be more willing to engage with change that is initiated by a management team they trust than one they do not. Trust is composed of four dimensions: (i) concern for employees' best interests; (ii) management's strategic competence; (iii) management reliability; and (iv) openness and honesty (Mishra & Spreitzer, 1998). Management trustworthiness in each dimension reduces employees uncertainty related to change. For example, a belief that management is concerned for employee well-being implies that management will consider the implications of change for employees. Trust in management competence fosters the belief that change-related decisions and outcomes will be of a high quality and in the organization's and employees' best interests. Management's reliability gives employees confidence that what is said will be done. Finally, openness and honesty helps employees feel in control so that they understand the need for change and how it will affect them.

Trust is fundamentally a judgement of confidence in either a person or an organization. Employees who perceive their leader as being able to lead change effectively, who perceive their manager as trustworthy and supportive and who feel respected are likely to be more willing to accept and support change. In a survey carried out by the Work Foundation (Tamkin et al., 2010) into what leaders themselves believe leadership to be and how they practise it, trust was identified as one of the most important aspects. Good leaders, the survey found, have trust as a personal value but outstanding leaders understand how to use trust to create the conditions for exceptional employee engagement.

Trust in management and leadership makes a big difference in employees' perception of OC and their ability to carry out change activities. People will often judge whether someone is to be trusted based on three key dimensions: (i) ability – the ability to reliably and effectively meet goals – employees who trust their organization believe its leaders are competent and will take the organization in a direction that is beneficial; (ii) benevolence – how effectively care and concern for the well-being of its staff is demonstrated; and (iii) integrity – how effective leaders and managers are at consistently adhering to moral principles and a code of conduct acceptable to its employees. Moreover, trust concerns the degree to which people feel safe around others and in the organization as a whole in that they feel: others will not act opportunistically in ways that might harm them and that investing their energy towards OC will yield positive outcomes (Sousa-Lima et al., 2013). Trust is also a necessary condition for vulnerability, in which employees and other stakeholders demonstrate a belief in each other's dependability, reliability and competency and an emotional feeling of mutual caring. People trust others when they are willing to reciprocate the care and consideration they receive from others and also when they feel that the others with whom they interact have ability, benevolence and integrity (Madhok, 2006). Trust is revealed when individuals are willing to cooperate with others and when they behave in free and open ways with others rather than in restrained ways. People will therefore engage in cooperating in change with leaders and managers who they trust.

Employees who trust their organization perceive a social exchange relationship with the organization and have positive expectations about the organization's concern for their well-being. As discussed in Chapter 4, Social Exchange Theory provides a foundation for OC engagement as it suggests that employees are obligated to reciprocate to a leader or manager who offers something of value, such as support. The social exchange relationship is predicated on trust, in which the organization trusts the employee to reciprocate and the employee trusts the organization to continue in this relationship once obligations are fulfilled.

Trust thus constitutes a key antecedent required for OC engagement to flourish. A lack of trust within an organization will inhibit individuals becoming engaged in change. Trust in leadership and management is essential for employees to feel a willingness and safety to invest in OC.

History of change in the organization

OC engagement can be influenced by both an organization's history of change, which is the frequency and success of previous changes, and also by an individual's personal experience of change in the organization.

The social information processing theory (Salancik & Pfeffer, 1978) suggests that employees draw on past behaviour and what others around them think, to form their own attitudes, behaviours and beliefs to adapt to their current situation, as well as to create the reality of their own past behaviour and situations. Thus, individuals are constantly adapting and absorbing from the information in the environment. Social information processing theory applied to OC suggests that employees form opinions about change in the organization through processing the information and social environment around them, including previous changes.

The history of change in an organization can shape employees' attitudes towards future change and their behavioural responses to it. As Bordia and colleagues (2011: 25) say:

> . . . as when driving a car, changing the direction of an organization should involve a 'rear view' inspection of the change management history. We recommend that leaders pay attention to employee change beliefs arising from the history of change in the organization.

Studies indicate the importance of looking in the rear view mirror of change. For instance, Rafferty and Restubog (2010) found that among organizations going through a merger, those who report having experienced a poor history of change have lower levels of OC engagement than those who have experienced a successful history of OC. This suggests that past experiences of change can influence current and future OC engagement. Ignoring the impact of previous changes, particularly if they failed, can cause negative attitudes towards OC. This can result in a vicious cycle, whereby employees will avoid engaging in change and consequently prejudice the success of future changes due to their perceptions and experience of past changes. The personal experiences of individual employees can have either positive or negative effects on their willingness to engage with a change. Those who have experienced success might be more likely to commit, whereas those who have experienced failure might become cynical about the motives for change and/or sceptical about their ability to manage it (Stanley et al., 2005). So the history and experience of change can influence levels of OC engagement.

Nature of OC

The scale, pattern as well as the pace or time urgency of change can influence OC engagement. Time urgency refers to the processing speed required for employees to complete tasks. Pressure to complete change within a given time frame can tax employees' energy and capabilities, but it can also focus their attention and effort such that by coping with this demand they experience a sense of personal accomplishment (LePine et al., 2005). Time urgency can increase a person's focus on OC because it helps to eliminate distractions that would otherwise occupy their time and attention. Empirical evidence supports the assumption that time urgency is associated with increased engagement but also with increased strain. For example, Schaufeli and colleagues (2008) found that having to work very fast creates engagement as well as exhaustion. Similarly, the type of change (such as incremental, transformational, planned or emergent) and the pattern of change (for example, gradualist) will have an impact on OC engagement (see Chapter 3 for further discussion on the nature of change). The nature of change is therefore a potential antecedent of OC engagement.

Readiness for change

Readiness for change is a predisposition to OC engagement. Readiness for change refers to "organizational members' beliefs, attitudes, and intentions regarding the extent to which changes are needed and the organization's capacity to successfully make those changes" (Armenakis et al., 1993: 681). Underpinning an individual's change readiness, Armenakis and Harris (2002) say, are five beliefs: (i) discrepancy – the belief that change is needed; (ii) appropriate – the belief that the proposed change is an appropriate response; (iii) efficacy – the individual's perceived capability to implement the change; (iv) principal support – the belief that the organization will provide resources and information; and (v) valence – the individual's evaluation of the personal costs and benefits. In addition to these beliefs, Rafferty and colleagues (2013) propose that affective states such as hope and optimism, as well as cognitive components, must also be considered when identifying if individuals are ready for OC. An individual's readiness to engage is therefore dependent on behavioural, affective and cognitive states.

Change readiness may vary at different levels – individual, team and organization-wide. At an individual level the self-perceived readiness for change is a function of an individual's beliefs that change is needed, that they have the capacity to undertake change successfully and that the change will have positive outcomes for their job. At a team and organizational level, change readiness is a function of the shared beliefs and emotional responses of individuals. Team members who are ready to engage with OC will exhibit a proactive and positive attitude towards change, which can be translated into willingness to support and own the change. Readiness depends on whether at each of these levels the benefits of change are perceived as outweighing the anticipated risks (Hodges, 2016). Each person will perceive the significance of change differently and as a result, the readiness level may vary on the basis of what employees perceive as the balance between the costs and benefits of the status quo and the costs and benefits of change. Readiness to engage with OC encompasses the extent to which employees are open and receptive to the need for change and believe that OC has positive implications for themselves and the wider organization.

In sum, the contextual antecedents of OC engagement – organizational culture, trust, the nature of change and readiness for change – influence OC engagement in various ways. A culture of OC engagement, particularly if based on trust, strengthens the probability that stakeholders will engage with change, while a lack of trust will inhibit OC engagement. The nature of the change will also include the extent to which individuals engage or not. Change that happens too suddenly, and without warning, or is forced upon people, will negatively affect levels of engagement. Similarly, readiness (or lack of) for change will influence whether or not stakeholders will engage in OC practices. These contextual factors are also supported by processual antecedents which impact on OC engagement.

Processual antecedents

The processual antecedents of OC engagement include: fairness; justice; relationships; and support.

Fairness and justice

The perception by employees about whether or not change is fair or unfair is based on their assessment of fairness, using observations of their own and others' experiences (Konovsky, 2000). The fairness of OC is evaluated based on the following types of justice: distributive; procedural; interactional; interpersonal; and informational (Saunders & Thornhill, 2003). *Distributive justice* refers to judgements about the degree to which the outcomes of OC are fair. This may relate, for example, to the roles which are being made redundant, to redeployment or to training and development opportunities. *Procedural justice* concerns the way in which decisions about OC are taken, the information collected, the openness of the process and the extent to which people's views are taken into account during, for example, a restructuring exercise. Judgements about "procedural justice play a major role in shaping people's reactions to their personal experience . . . in particular about being treated with respect" (Tyler & Blader, 2003: 350). Procedural justice is linked to *interactional justice*, which is an employee's assessment of the fairness of the interpersonal treatment they receive when procedures for OC are being planned and implemented and refers specifically to the relationship between senior management and those subject to their decisions. The following rules are postulated as underlying interactional justice: truthfulness (openness and honesty when implementing procedures); justification (adequate explanations); respect (sincerity and dignity in treatment); and propriety (appropriateness of statements). Interactional justice is split further into interpersonal and informational justice. *Interpersonal justice* is the interpersonal treatment individuals receive from managers and leaders as the way in which individuals are treated can have a significant impact on their perceptions of fairness. This is not only about the process of how the need for change is discussed and agreed but also about the ethical obligations to treat everyone fairly that underpins the process. If managers and leaders treat employees with dignity, respect, politeness and honesty there is more likely to be a positive reaction from individuals. *Informational justice* is based on the communication individuals receive about OC since communication builds trust and can address fears and uncertainty, as well as help develop positive attitudes and a sense of fairness among individuals. Perceptions of informational justice during OC are shaped through accounts and explanations provided by leaders and managers about the reasons why change is needed (Fuchs & Edwards, 2012). Links between these various types of justice and engagement are evident in the research since, for example, Saks (2006) has found that both distributive and procedural justice perceptions are positively linked to engagement.

Similarly, research by Inoue and colleagues (2010) indicates that procedural and interactional justice perceptions are positively associated with engagement. This is supported in a study by Siltaloppi and colleagues (2009) which indicates that interactional justice perceptions are positively associated with engagement. Perceptions of fairness and justice are, therefore, important drivers of OC engagement.

The ways in which organizations treat other stakeholders also influences OC engagement. For example, a meta-analysis by Colquitt and colleagues (2001) of the academic literature on justice shows that an individual's engagement depends, in part, on perceptions of whether the organization treats other employees fairly. This is supported by research which demonstrates that employee perceptions of the socially responsible activities of their employers towards external stakeholders such as customers, taxpayers and charities, are also important determinants of engagement (Brammer et al., 2006). Furthermore, when management supports change in ways that go beyond merely selling the need for it or its benefits by visibly caring about what is required for it to be effective, research shows that employees tend to perceive the fairness of change more favourably (Liu et al., 2012).

Perceptions of fairness and justice are also more likely to reduce individuals' appraisal of the threat of OC and cause them to feel obliged to be fair in how they perform their roles by giving more of themselves to change initiatives through greater levels of engagement. On the other hand, low perceptions of fairness are likely to cause employees to withdraw and disengage themselves from OC. Fairness and justice thus appear to be important antecedents of OC engagement.

Relationships

Relationships can shape the extent to which people engage with change since organizations are defined by the sets of relationships among people who coordinate their activities in the service of tasks, goals and missions. Relationships are, metaphorically, the nervous system of the organization, the source of complex social interactions, the coordination of systems and the integrated processing of concurrent signals. Research using Social Exchange Theory (Alfes et al., 2010) indicates that social relationships at the workplace are reciprocal, and Saks (2006), in particular, has established that employee engagement develops through a model of social exchange. Relationships affect how OC gets done and how individuals and teams coordinate, share knowledge and accomplish change initiatives.

Employees get meaning from the relationships that they create with one another at work. Colleagues can provide help to do the work and make sense of ambiguous situations, as well as provide personal support and mentoring. Individuals' work lives matter more when individuals feel connected to others at work and less when they feel isolated and alone (Dutton & Heaphy, 2003). Moreover, good working relationships at work foster creativity, innovation, productivity and OC engagement. Relationships deepen and affirm the meaningfulness of OC engagement partly through a process of social identification, in which people's preferred identities, that is how they wish to see themselves, are reflected and confirmed by their participation in desirable relationships (Bartel, 2001). Social identification not only provides positive confirmation of a preferred identity, it also enables people to feel a sense of belongingness. When people are part of desirable teams or groups with whom they identify, and which affirm their own preferred identities, they experience a sense of shared fate or humanity with others. Belongingness occurs not simply through the mechanism of social identification but more familiarly through interpersonal connectedness, generated in certain interactions through which people feel supported (Rosso et al., 2010).

High-quality connections are crucial to building and sustaining OC engagement. In support of this, Dutton (2003) identifies what he calls 'respectful engagement', which refers to being present to others, affirming them, and communicating and listening in a way that communicates regard and an appreciation of another's worth, as central to creating relationships that connect and energize individuals at work. All organization members are embedded in relational networks of some sort and thus are influenced by the restorative or draining nature of those networks. When those relationships are positive people can think and solve problems more quickly (Baker et al., 2003), have more physical energy (Heaphy & Dutton, 2008) than when embedded in relationships in which they need to make themselves less available.

The relational antecedent of OC engagement is crucial. Indeed, OC engagement cannot be cleanly separated from work relationships. When organizational members are engaged with change, either by themselves or with others, their choices about how to perform change activities are shaped by their relationships. In the context of those relationships, individuals may feel more fully engaged as they join with and attach to others to work on change together. It is the nature of those relationships and the behaviours and experiences that they enable that matters most in terms of OC engagement or disengagement. Individuals who experience relationships positively at work may be able to engage themselves more fully with change: saying what they think and feel in order to make the change better; working enthusiastically and energetically; and seeking to provide and receive feedback, in order to learn as much as possible to implement and sustain OC.

Social support

Social support received from management and colleagues is a key part of effective relationships at work. Social support refers to employees' perceptions concerning the degree to which the organization values their contributions and is concerned and committed to their well-being (Rhoades & Eisenberger, 2002). Social support from line managers and co-workers has been positively linked to engagement in several studies. Schaufeli and Bakker (2004), for example, found that social support from supervisory relationships was positively related to engagement. Research shows that support fosters feelings of safety because it gives employees the flexibility to take risks and perhaps fail without fearing negative consequences (Kahn, 1990). It also fosters in employees a feeling of obligation to care about the organization's welfare and help the organization reach its objectives (Rhoades et al., 2001). In a study of neonatal intensive care units, Nembhard and Edmondson (2006) found that units whose supervisors actively invited and appreciated employees' contributions reported increased levels of engagement. Providing support can make individuals feel valued and involved. Studies reveal that employees who feel valued by the organization are more likely to engage. For example, support has been found to help create engagement among teachers (Bakker et al., 2007), dentists (Gorter et al., 2008), fast-food workers (Xanthopoulou et al., 2009) and hotel staff (Salanova et al., 2005). Positive support is important for OC engagement as it gives employees confidence that they are valued and can create reciprocal mutuality and build trust.

In sum, the processual antecedents of fairness, justice, relations and support are associated with increased OC engagement because they contribute to more fair, supportive, predictable and non-threatening situations in which individuals perceive they can try and perhaps fail with change without fearing negative consequences. To the extent that individuals perceive fairness and support as providing protective guarantees for their self-investments, they may become more willing to take the risks involved in engaging in OC. So individuals who engage with OC will do so because of the continuation of favourable reciprocal exchanges. As a result, individuals who are more engaged are likely to be in more trusting and high-quality relationships with their employer.

The following case about change in a public sector organization illustrates the impact of a lack of contextual and processual antecedents on engagement.

Box 6.1 Engagement – the right and wrong way within a public sector organization

Written by Andy Davies,
Head of people first Professional Services Enablement

A few years ago I was involved with the transformation of the training provision for a large organization. The aim of the project was to bring together the dispersed training resources and centralize the delivery of training for both internal and external customers. This change was driven by the need for efficiencies across the organization and for significant cost savings. The organization was dealing with cuts to previously reliable revenue streams and was looking at reducing costs whilst increasing revenue through new ventures. This was being considered through many channels including the commercialization of services, including the training provision, before then floating them off to third parties. The main impact for the training departments would be an increasing commercial focus, reduction in numbers of courses delivered in order to focus on high value courses and increasing their target audience to public, private and charitable sectors.

Training in the organization was provided within each department by their own teams and across various locations. Each training team had their own processes which meant that across the organization people were performing many of the same functions but in a different way. There was also a lack of technology driven systems and processes which necessitated the need for teams of administrative staff to manually support the training.

The training provision was a key area where efficiencies could be made. I was brought in to help the strategic HR team and had been asked to lead the review into the current training arrangements, before developing a strategy for the future delivery of training. I presented a proposal for centralizing the training teams and reducing the overall physical footprint at several scrutiny meetings and was also grilled by the Board about it. My proposal included a stakeholder assessment that encompassed employees, contractors, suppliers, leadership teams, internal customers, external customers and crucially Trade Unions.

Engagement involved many hours of individually briefing Directors and understanding their needs for future training provision. This individual approach reflected the cautious nature of the organization and even the day before the announcement to the people who had been identified as part of the review was made, I was not sure that the change would progress. There was so little support for the centralization of the training teams from some of the leadership team that for a month before the consultation started, there was a delay in discussing the project while the Board debated the proposed changes. The impact of this delay was only realized mid-way through the consultation period.

As part of the initial review, I identified all the people who delivered or supported training within the organization and whose roles would be affected by the change – these people formed the consultation group. The estimates of costs and potential savings were calculated from the overall cost of the employment of this group. The inclusion of these people and their jobs within the consultation group was ratified by the Board.

When clearance to proceed with the project was finally given, engagement with stakeholders focussed on 'town hall' meetings and individual meetings which I had with every person within the consultation group. I would have preferred a more technology based forum where we would post updates and people could ask questions which we could then release as anonymized FAQs, since this would have provided a more transparent way of publishing FAQs and would have enabled quicker communication across the consultation group. The ability to share documents with everyone would have greatly reduced the time to prepare for many of the meetings and would have acted as a central information source. However, this was not available and on reflection, I am not sure that this would have been supported by the stakeholders as this would have been too much of a leap forward from the way that transformations were usually dealt with. For many, change was something that happened to other people and for many stakeholders this was the first time they had experienced such transformational change.

Some of the employees required a high level of support, as they resisted the necessity for the organization to change. This stemmed from their belief that they had a job for life and that the organization did not have the right to vary/remove their job in any way. Each one had a story from previous consultations and restructures where other colleagues had been offered retirement packages or generous relocation packages (none of this was substantiated or evidenced in the formal offers made through other consultations and was an organizational myth based on a mis-representation of the individual circumstances of other people). Or, they were in a state of complete denial and refused to engage in any form of discussion. One person walked past me in the car park only 30 minutes before we were due to discuss their forthcoming redundancy and then did not turn up for the meeting. It was evident that this person had withdrawn from the process.

During the project, we held three 'town hall' meetings and frequently met with teams and individuals to discuss what the project meant for them and what the future would hold. For some people, it was an opportunity to look closely at their career and to either forge ahead or to have a change of direction. Others took the opportunity to retire early or look for a new job elsewhere.

Redeploying some people enabled new stakeholders to become involved who had not been considered during the initial stakeholder mapping. As vacancies throughout every organization can be fluid, some departments were not included in the stakeholder assessment that I had presented to the Board during the initial stages of the project. This mapping had looked at the influence and interest of each stakeholder so as to consider which to keep informed, keep satisfied, monitor or manage closely. The additional stakeholders who eventually had vacancies which were relevant for the 'at risk' people would have been classed as 'keep informed' as they had little power in the overall restructure but had a high interest in the outcome of the consultation and the pool of talent that would be available to them.

Although the consultation group had been agreed by the Board before the commencement of the consultation process, many people felt that HR was simply imposing the change on them centrally, and that their Directorate had not been engaged in the decision making. I soon found that, while it was important that I met everyone in the consultation group individually, it was also beneficial to arrange team meetings where we could all discuss the future structure of training in the organization, changes to processes, implementation of new software, closure of buildings and the increased use of existing resources, including printing, transport and IT. This helped teams within the consultation group and within the organization to explore how they would work together in the new structure. New working relationships needed to be established and new processes, that complied with the central governance requirements, had to be adopted.

The engagement of line managers could have been handled more effectively. Whilst leaders had been advised to release details of the new training unit to line managers within the affected teams, those managers only found out the details of changes at the same time as their staff. As a consequence, the managers were unable to properly prepare themselves and their teams for the change. The managers were trying to deal with their own reaction to the news of this transformational change whilst at the same time seeing their colleagues and friends facing an uncertain future. Understandably, some managers simply withdrew and focused on self-preservation. Others, who were keen to remain in a job in the new structure, made efforts to provide support for their team members, but were not able to answer the myriad of questions they asked. The only advice they could offer was to direct the questions to me and their Directors. The reasoning behind this lack of transparency was to speed up the process and reduce the risk of any blockers to the change process. This was based on previous change were people across the organization had reacted by creating as much noise as possible in an attempt to maintain the status quo which had led to the failure of some changes. In reality, the lack of manager engagement slowed down the adoption of the new structure for many managers as they 'recovered' from the shock of this approach. Contractor and supplier engagement could also have been improved. Once the transformation to a single training unit had taken place, the newly appointed management team began to review the processes required by the new training team. This included the adoption of technology to streamline the booking and management of all training for internal and external stakeholders. For some contractors and suppliers, it was only during this process that they discovered the changes had taken place and what this meant for them. Much like the managers, the contractors and suppliers had been deliberately kept at arm's length during the consultation period so we could focus on the staff and not invite any further complications. Had we engaged the managers, contractors and suppliers at an earlier stage, it is possible that we could have made the business case stronger and eased the transition to the new structure. New processes could have been co-designed to ensure a future-proofing of the training service.

Once it was clear that the changes would take place regardless of resistance, some political battling ensued between the Directors, with people being added in and taken out of the consultation group. There was some resistance from some Directors who had not fully raised their concerns before the start of the consultation process and who only became fully involved once the roles of colleagues/friends had been placed at risk of redundancy. These Directors had previously agreed that these roles should be included in the review but were now raising concerns about making them redundant. They claimed that their department would not be able to function without some individuals, which appeared to be based on emotion rather than a real business requirement.

This instability challenged the trust between the project team and many of the stakeholders. The managers, customers and consultation group saw this activity as undermining what confidence they had in the new structure and for some 'at risk' people gave a false impression that they could ask their Director for protection. This could have been avoided if there had been more engagement from senior leadership stakeholders to brief their teams on the reasons for the restructure and how this would bring long-term benefits to the organization. Attending the town-halls and standing at the front to show that senior leadership were involved in the processes would have given some reassurance to people that this was not a centrally imposed change, but in fact driven by their own departments who retained an interest in the new structure. Furthermore they could have opened their doors and held discussions with individuals and teams and providing support.

Working with the Trade Unions enabled the project team to clarify points of confusion very quickly. I built up a rapport with the Trade Union Representatives who provided an excellent level of support for their members. This was achieved through a weekly meeting where I would discuss any questions I had received and any further details I had disseminated to their members. This open channel of communication allowed the Trade Unions to raise concerns quickly and, on some occasions, helped to convey messages to people who were struggling with a level of change they were not used to.

Engagement at an earlier opportunity with the consultation group could have avoided some of the difficult discussions with many people since their roles were de-scoped by some Directors in the later stages of the consultation. A more visible presence of the leadership teams to help with stakeholder engagement throughout the project could have also helped to ease the transition. Additionally, engaging the Trade Unions prior to the announcements would have also provided a better level of support to those affected by the transformation and potentially given more time to plan for extra support to be available.

What did not work was expecting the manager and leaders to provide adequate support to their people so that they could be fully on-board with the change. They should have informed their staff that they had been involved in the discussions about the project, and explained to the consultation group the reason for the change.

My lessons learnt from this project are:

- Discuss changes with stakeholders as early as possible to provide time for discussions.
- Where possible release information to key stakeholders at an appropriate time so they feel part of the project and are able to field questions.
- Small team discussions help to clarify future team roles and individual discussions help staff to understand changes to individual roles.
- Be wary of starting a project unless all of the senior leaders have been bought into the change.

Individual antecedents

OC engagement is generated by the contextual and processual aspects of an organization and is also something that an individual brings to the workplace through their own perceptions, personality and emotions which shape and direct their attitudes and intentions towards how engaged they will be with change.

Individual *perceptions* are a key factor in individual behaviour. Buchanan and Huczynski (2017) define perception as the dynamic psychological process responsible for attending to, organizing and interpreting sensory data. To a large extent, perception relates to the way in which individuals make sense of their environment and interpret and respond to the events and people around them. Equally, it is important to emphasize that each individual receives information differently. This is because individuals do not receive information about what is happening around them passively and dispassionately or in the same way as others. Individuals categorize and make sense of events and situations according to their own unique and personal frame of reference, which reflects their personality, past experiences, knowledge, expectations and current needs, priorities and interests.

A key influence on the process of perception is *personality*. Bowditch and colleagues (2001) describe personality as acting as a kind of perceptual filter or frame of reference which influences an individual's view of the world. It is an individual's personal perception of their social and physical environment that shapes and directs how engaged they are, rather than some objective understanding of an external reality. Employees engage with change when they feel that, on balance, it matters to do so. This is partly about self-interest as individuals are more likely to engage with change when it is in their interest to do so. Consequently, individual differences shape a person's ability and willingness to engage with OC. For example, when people consider change as potentially a risk, it is a matter of individual difference which coping strategies they deploy, and the extent to which they engage or disengage. Moreover, it is argued that individual differences play a vital role in determining an employee's potential level of engagement. Studies that have considered such factors are based on the premise that different people respond differently to any given situation, and that such differences in reactions stem from factors within the individual that predispose them to react in a certain way (Robinson, 2006). These characteristics can be divided into: (i) dispositions; (ii) coping styles; and (iii) personal resources.

Personal dispositions

Dispositions are personality characteristics or general tendencies to experience affective (emotional) states (Macey & Schneider, 2008). In relation to engagement, the most frequently studied dispositions include: conscientiousness; positive and negative affectivity; and locus of control. Conscientiousness refers to behavioural tendencies towards achievement striving, dependability, orderliness, duty and deliberation (Barrick et al., 2001). Halbesleben and colleagues (2009) found that conscientious individuals exhibit significant positive relationships with engagement. Studies have also found links with conscientiousness and engagement among police personnel (Mostert & Rothmann, 2006) and sandwich shop employees (Kim et al., 2009). Positive affectivity is an individual's dispositional tendency to feel enthusiastic, active and alert which builds an individual's physical, cognitive and emotional resources (Fredrickson, 2001). In contrast, negative affectivity is the dispositional tendency to feel anger, disgust, guilt, fear and nervousness which hinders the mobilization of cognitive resources and behavioural options (Bledow et al., 2011). Studies examining negative affect have found it is associated with decreased levels of engagement (for example, Sonnentag et al., 2010). So, whereas positive affect is associated with increased engagement, negative affect is associated with decreased engagement.

The disposition which has been most frequently considered to influence employees' engagement with change is locus of control. This trait has to do with the explanations individuals give to the events that occur in their lives (Rotter, 1966). Individuals with an internal locus of control tend to perceive themselves as responsible for what happens to them, whereas those with an external locus of control attribute what happens to them as resulting from outside forces. Relationships have been found between locus of control and employees' reactions to change (Holt et al., 2007). In their study Chen and Wang (2007) found that internal locus of control was positively associated with engagement to change among Chinese customer service staff. Overall, an internal locus of control tends to correspond with more positive reactions to OC. For example, an internal locus of control is positively associated with employees' emotional adjustment, and negatively associated with distress, including mental health complaints, job-induced tension and job dissatisfaction (Näswall et al., 2005). So people who are open to engaging with OC tend to be individuals who exercise influence over events that affect them.

Coping styles

How people cope with OC will determine their engagement with it. Two main coping styles are problem-focused and emotion-focused coping (Fugate et al., 2002). Problem-focused coping involves directly addressing the problem, whereas emotion-focused coping is aimed at alleviating the discomforting symptoms, rather than their actual source. In the context of OC, a problem-focused coping style has typically been shown to involve a more positive reaction to the change since individuals with a problem-focused coping style report greater readiness for OC, increased participation in the change process and a greater engagement with it (Cunningham et al., 2002). In a study of a merger, problem-focused coping was found to be positively related to identification with the newly merged organization (Amiot et al., 2006). Contrarily, emotion-based coping styles involve the use of maladaptive defence mechanisms, such as denial, dissociation and isolation and yield greater behavioural resistance to change in comparison with the use of adaptive mechanisms, such as humour and anticipation (Bovey & Hede, 2001).

Personal resources

Personal resources are positive self-evaluations and refer to an individual's sense of their ability to control and impact upon their environment successfully and thus influence their engagement (Halbesleben, 2010). The personal resources which demonstrate positive organizational behaviour (POB) are: hope, efficacy, resilience and optimism (summarized using the acronym: HERO) (Youssef-Morgan & Bockorny, 2013). Hope is a positive motivational state that is based on an interactively derived sense of successful agency (goal-directed energy) and pathways (planning to meet goals). In order to achieve hope, an individual must have the agency or determination to reach a goal, as well as the pathway to achieve the goal. Hope is considered a requirement for engagement, especially as it is tied to vigour and dedication (Sweetman & Luthans, 2010). When a hopeful employee is working towards OC goals, they will harness more energy and cognitive resources to their work.

Efficacy is conceptualized as "the belief in one's capabilities to organize and execute the courses of action required to manage prospective situations" (Bandura, 1995: 2). High levels of self-efficacy are related to greater acceptance of change (Wanberg &

Banas, 2000), readiness to change and engagement in change (Cunningham et al., 2002). For example, Bakker and colleagues (2006) report that female school principals high in self-efficacy are more engaged. Efficacy can promote engagement in a number of ways. First, when employees perceive that their personal abilities and resources match the challenges of change, this can lead to higher levels of OC engagement. Second, efficacy can promote the critical engagement dimension of energy as an efficacious individual energetically and persistently pursues OC goals. Third, efficacy is recognized as developing over time through the distinct mechanisms of: task mastery; vicarious learning (learning from relevant role models); social persuasion and encouragement; and physiological and psychological arousal (Bandura, 1995). Each of these factors impacts on OC engagement in various ways: a sense of mastery can provide confidence to engage in OC; the interpersonal dimensions of vicarious learning and social persuasion can increase dedication to OC; and the physiological and psychological arousal mechanisms can help promote energy, making available more physical, cognitive and affective resources for active involvement in change. Employees who feel capable of meeting the demands of change, those with higher self-efficacy, will develop a greater willingness to engage with it.

Resilience is the capacity to bounce back from adversity, uncertainty, conflict or failure and the ability to continue moving forward (Luthans, 2002). As setbacks are experienced, resilient employees will regain their confidence and try again. They will endure and remain engaged during OC, whereas less resilient individuals may give up. Masten (2001) explains two criteria that must be present for an individual to be considered resilient. First, an individual must experience some type of threat; if an individual has never experienced a threat or risk, it will be hard to determine how this individual would handle this type of situation. Second, the way in which an individual handles the threat or risk has to be deemed positive. For the individual to simply cope is not being resilient. Overcoming and growing through the event characterizes resilient individuals. Resilience can be a valuable personal resource that can help employees facilitate the necessary balance with job demands and OC demands, especially when faced with obstacles and setbacks.

Optimism is a combination of a general positive outlook and a positive explanatory style of events. An optimistic individual attributes success to internal strengths, as well as permanent and pervasive causes. The optimist also attributes failures to external circumstances that are only temporary in nature. As a result, optimists recognize that they are in control of their lives, take credit for the good fortune they have created and believe that positive things will come to them and that they can carry this good fortune into the future and control their own destiny (Carver et al., 2009). Optimism can increase energy and enthusiasm for change. Thus the HERO constructs provide resources which can positively influence OC engagement.

Research on positive organizational behaviour (POB) has also shown that there can be a dark side to the HERO constructs. For example, research has found that high self-esteem can lead to an underestimation of the time that is necessary for achieving OC goals and that unrealistic optimism can harm individuals and organizations by promoting inappropriate persistence (Armor & Taylor, 1998). Furthermore, overconfidence has been found to hinder subsequent performance (Vancouver et al., 2002), and creativity which may lead to frustration (Ford & Sullivan, 2004). In order to overcome such issues there is a need to consider the underlying mechanism which links the constituent resources of HERO which is a positive cognitive, agentic, developmental capacity that promotes "positive appraisal of circumstances and probability for success based on motivated effort and perseverance" (Luthans et al., 2007: 550) known as Psychological capital (PsyCap). PsyCap is an individual's positive psychological state of development that is characterized by (i) having confidence (efficacy) to take on and put in the necessary effort to succeed at challenging tasks; (ii) making a positive attribution (optimism) about succeeding now and in the future; (iii) persevering towards goals and, when necessary, redirecting paths to goals (hope) in order to succeed; and (iv) when beset by problems and adversity, sustaining and bouncing back and even beyond to attain success (Luthans et al., 2015). According to Sweetman and Luthans (2010), employees high in PsyCap are characterized by their tenacity and persistence and driven by their belief in future success. Additionally, they continue to provide hope for goal achievement, even in the face of new challenges, and expect good things to happen to them. PsyCap, as well as each of its constituent resources, has been shown to be measurable, open to development and management in the workplace, and able to yield a wide range of tangible performance outcomes (Avey et al., 2011).

Personal resources positively impact OC engagement so that employees who are, for example, more self-efficacious and who find their work meaningful are better able to mobilize their own job resources and become more engaged (Albrecht, 2013). Individuals who perceive themselves as having the prerequisite abilities to fulfil OC demands will derive a sense of competence, meaningfulness and self-worth from OC and thus be more willing and able to fully engage and give themselves to their role. In contrast, employees who perceive that they do not have the necessary abilities are likely to experience stress or boredom from perceiving that the OC is not sufficiently challenging; both of which reduce the likelihood that they will engage with changes. Personal resources are, thus, a necessary prerequisite for OC engagement.

Emotions

OC engagement is influenced by individuals' emotional experiences. Emotions are a natural feature of people's psychological make-up and affect not only individuals' personal lives but also their behaviour with OC. As Wilson (2004: 99) says:

> feelings connect us with our realities and provide internal feedback on how we are doing, what we want and what we might do next . . . Being in organisations involves us in worry, envy, hurt, sadness, boredom, excitement and other emotions.

Emotional factors are linked to an individual's personal satisfaction and the sense of inspiration and affirmation they get from OC. This is grounded in the Affective events theory (AET) – a theory of affect in the workplace – which posits that emotions flow from discrete affective occurrences such as job and task characteristics/design, reward systems and performance feedback (Weiss & Cropanzano, 1996). For example, employees can feel frustrated about not succeeding with a project, or proud about the feedback they receive from their supervisor.

Being able to appreciate the effect of emotions on OC engagement is important. As Lockwood (2007) suggests that the key lever for engagement, and ultimately effective performance, is an employee's emotional commitment to the organization and the job, that is the "extent to which the employee derives enjoyment, meaning, pride and inspiration from something or someone in the organization" (p. 4). Emotions provide the affective colour of employees' experience of OC and have been found to predict employee engagement with change (Smollan & Sayers, 2009) especially when the change is emergent, complex and/or radical (Liu & Perrewe, 2005). Empirical studies such as that of Barsade and O'Neill (2016) show the significant impact of emotions on how people perform on tasks, how engaged and creative they are, how committed they are to their organizations and how they make decisions. Research has also substantiated the impact of negative emotions. For instance, Kiefer (2005) found that perceptions of future insecurity, inadequate working conditions and inadequate treatment were associated with negative emotions for employees in merged companies.

OC engagement is more likely to develop when employees are experiencing positive, rather than negative, emotions because positive emotions create the cognitive space, emotional safety, mental energy and resources necessary for employees to experience the vigour, dedication and absorption dimensions of engagement (Schaufeli et al., 2002). Positive emotions and reactions signal that things are going well (George & Zhou, 2007) whereas negative emotions and reactions to change are important signals that indicate that there are problems that need to be addressed. There is a tendency in the change management literature to focus on the benefits of positive emotions and improve or repair negative ones; however, negative emotions often occur because there are real problems and these reactions are focusing attention on the problems and the need to make improvements in the workplace. While no one likes to feel badly, in organizations negative emotions are likely to be experienced nonetheless when individuals see problems with proposed change. For instance, having change forced upon them or just being told what will change without any explanation of the reasons why or without opportunities to discuss options and views can be very destabilizing for individuals and make them feel threatened, vulnerable or angry and so they may react negatively. Thus emotional reactions may affect OC engagement.

Autonomy and control

Employees will often thrive best in situations where they have autonomy and control over their work. Research (Kahn, 1990) shows that the job characteristics of control and autonomy are a key antecedent of engagement.

CONTROL

Control refers to the extent to which an employee is able to act in a proactive way to attain OC goals (Menon, 2001). In any organization individuals need to be able to contribute at their discretion and perceptions of control may influence engagement with change. In cases where employees have been given some control over how they implement OC, positive benefits have appeared to emerge. For example, research carried out on factory workers and the number of injuries they reported, given the differing levels of control over their work, found that after the workers were given the training and freedom to make repairs to their own equipment rather than having to call a supervisor every time they experienced a problem, they reported fewer occupational injuries (Beardwell & Claydon, 2007). This would suggest that workers who feel they have some discretion over OC are likely to be more focused and engaged. Being able to take control of aspects of change may also satisfy individuals' basic need for autonomy.

AUTONOMY

Before employees can engage with OC, they must perceive that they have the opportunity to make changes and be able to engage without fear of negative consequences. This refers to the sense of autonomy employees have in what they do and how they do it. Employees with decision-making power may feel a heightened sense of ownership of OC because they will feel personally responsible for how the change is achieved. A front-line manager who is allowed to use their judgement to solve problems is likely to feel a sense of ownership over the solutions. In contrast, a lack of autonomy might result in feelings of frustration and disengagement. Research (CIPD, 2011) supports this premise that autonomy evokes high levels of engagement. For instance, when organizations give employees autonomy to choose which change projects they will work on, people are likely to focus their energies on what they care about most. This is practised in the gaming software company Valve which gives employees desks on wheels and encourages them to join projects that seem interesting and rewarding. Employees are still held accountable for their work, expectations being agreed when employees join a new project, and 360-degree evaluations are done when projects wrap up, so that individual contributions are evaluated and recognized. As in the case of Valve, employees will often be more willing to engage in change where they have autonomy over aspects of it.

In sum, the individual antecedents of OC engagement include perceptions, personality and emotions, as well as the amount of autonomy and control individuals perceive that they have with regard to changes in the workplace.

Levels of engagement

OC can range from relatively simple incremental alterations to highly complex transformations and will manifest itself at different levels. Consequently, the most beneficial way of thinking about OC engagement is to see it as an individual, team or organizational concept, rather than something to be managed merely at one of these levels. However, most organizations still think about OC engagement at the individual level and see it as gaining the "hearts and minds" of their employees. Indeed this is one part of OC engagement but it also manifests itself at a team level which is a collective engagement based on team dynamics and identities. OC engagement can also manifest at an organizational level. The antecedents of OC engagement will therefore affect engagement at an individual, team and organizational level and the impact of engagement at each of these levels will in turn affect the outcomes of OC engagement.

Outcomes of OC engagement

OC engagement is a unique construct associated with specific positive outcomes. As Harter and colleagues (2002: 272) confirm, engagement is "related to meaningful business outcomes at a magnitude that is important to many organisations". OC engagement levels can be linked to outcomes, such as performance, productivity, innovation, well-being, decrease in absenteeism and turnover. Through these outcomes OC engagement can create organizational effectiveness

Productivity and performance related outcomes

OC engagement can have an impact on productivity and performance. The academic and practitioner support for this view is evident, and research investigating the relationship between engagement and performance continues to expand the understanding of this important longitudinal relationship. Consultancy firms claim that a positive association exists between the engagement and business success. For example, research from Gallup reveals that levels of engagement are positively related to indicators of business unit performance, such as customer satisfaction and loyalty, profitability, productivity, turnover and safety (Harter et al., 2009). Similarly, a global longitudinal study by Towers Perrin (2006) based on data gathered from opinion surveys of over 664,000 employees from more than 50 companies shows that companies with a highly engaged workforce improved their operating income by 19.2 per cent over a 12 month period, compared to those companies with low engagement scores which saw operating income decline by 32.7 per cent over the same period. Furthermore, companies with high engagement scores demonstrated a 13.7 per cent improvement in net income growth compared to a decline of 3.8 per cent in low engagement companies. This would suggest, as Bill Blasé, Head of Human Resources at AT&T says, that "the company with the most highly engaged workforces can earn three times more than those with less" (cited in Friedman, 2016: 215). Several academic studies have investigated exactly this issue, providing a large amount of evidence of the links between engagement and performance at business unit and organizational levels (such as Winkler et al., 2012). Academic meta-analytic evidence supports the view that engagement is linked to a wide variety of performance measures (for example, Halbesleben, 2010). Studies report relationships between engagement and organizational metrics such as profitability, revenue growth and earnings per share (Rayton et al., 2012), better employee performance (Bakker & Bal, 2010), financial performance (Farndale et al., 2014) and customer satisfaction (Harter et al., 2002). Research also indicates that levels of engagement of front-line staff in hotels and restaurants are positively associated with a high quality of service rated by customers (Salanova et al., 2005). Moreover, a diary study among staff at a fast-food company found that on days when employees were more engaged, the financial turnover of the restaurant was higher. The more engaged the employees of a particular work shift were, the more food was sold (Xanthopoulou et al., 2009). This suggests that OC engagement can have a positive impact on productivity and performance.

Engagement can also be a source of competitive advantage. Macey and colleagues (2009), for example, report substantial differences between organizations in the top quartile of average engagement from those in the bottom quartile with respect to return on assets, profitability and market value. The impact of OC engagement on productivity has the potential to increase, at least in part, because engaged employees are more involved and socially connected with change.

Innovation

Innovation is high on the agenda of many organizations as they strive to differentiate themselves from their competitors and peers in an increasingly competitive global environment. The link between engagement and organizational innovation is compelling since research shows that engaged employees are more likely to foster an innovative environment. For example, using longitudinal data, Hakanen and colleagues (2008) found that engagement plays a central role in promoting innovative work behaviour. Studies also show that engagement leads to more innovative behaviour at a team level (Hakanen et al., 2008). So an outcome of OC engagement is a likely increase in innovation.

In the following case, Duncan Sperry outlines how he has effectively engaged a team in creating innovative solutions.

Box 6.2 Harnessing forces of change and innovation

Written by Duncan Sperry,
Chairman and CEO Aurora Transact

Arguably, achieving and sustaining competitive edge in business has never been harder. Proactive and sustained innovation within organizations is fundamental to survival. Forces for change such as Blockchain and cryptocurrencies are changing the way companies do business, in turn changing the operating environment for banks and other trusted third parties to the extent that disintermediation is for the first time a real and evolving threat: intermediaries must adapt to a new operating paradigm or atrophy; or even disappear as a business model. Business-as-usual is simply not a strategic option.

I am developing a start-up company utilizing the Blockchain to solve the problem of cross-border and cross-industry business-to-business trade without the need for intermediaries and so-called trusted third parties. In other words, by establishing mutual trust in business networks where mutual distrust is ordinarily the default state. It did not start out like that though: in 2015 I became aware of the underlying technology of cryptocurrencies as a technology in its own right and its concomitant power of a global, agnostic, immutable, distributed ledger. For nearly two years, I researched the possibilities in depth: talking to technologists, evangelists and protagonists within the UK and beyond; reading every industry white paper possible in order not only to understand the technology, but more importantly its disruptive potential in all its dimensions. Recognizing that a community of like-minded innovators was already established, I proactively expanded my business network into this new arena through digital networking media. This, for me, is an important principle: you will not create a new vision of your organization's future in isolation. Diversity of thinking and expansion of perspectives is key. One has to be willing to reach out beyond one's existing circle and be prepared to share ideas in order to gain the breadth of perspective and depth of insight required. In doing so, the innovation team becomes extra-organizational. Collaboration (based on mutual confidentiality) is expanded and run on a virtual platform of collaboration and on-line story-boarding software. Such a level of collaboration quickly takes on a life of its own: cross-fertilization of ideas and insights create a dynamic environment for innovation, thought experiments and rapid prototyping.

After several months, I was able to map potential scenarios for future business and applications. Developing these scenarios into likely business models inductively (what could it possibly look like) and deductively (how could I execute) took a long time. Gradually, a broad perspective and an in-depth insight were developed, and one model emerged as a likely winner.

Drawing on my experience of global payments and financial technology (Fintech), it became clear that creating a technology platform for facilitating global trusted trade was possible, yet by no means a certainty, given the conceptual and practical challenges. But underpinning my assumptions with in-depth research and robust critical thinking, reinforcing that by testing premises and notions with potential clients, and then referencing so-called Industry Use Cases, the vision began to crystallize, becoming both credible and believable in the process. Clarity and purpose became manifest: in other words, the Vision (now with a capital V) became *compelling*. A clear, though by no means fully formed, vision emerged as a result of this process. Along the way, I gathered together a small team of like-minded souls who bought into this early Vision. Without this brilliant small team of highly motivated and capable individuals, the concept simply would not have left the scenario planning stage.

The vision began to crystallize in the form of a series of internal Pink Papers (drafted for internal or wider stakeholder use only: a rigorous process which creates discipline of mind and clarity of thought), fully articulating why, how and by what means the Vision could and would become reality. This disciplined approach not only formed and crystallized our foundation thinking but provided the repository of informed thought from which we could formulate our business strategies, core value propositions and business model.

Any vision needs at its heart a core team of innovators and entrepreneurs to forge the vision into something real and tangible. Such a team is effective, in my view, if it shares the same core values and a collective will, yet has diverse backgrounds, culture, age, perspectives, attitudes and, specifically, gender. This diversity of thought, different cultural perspectives and attitudes is for me a fundamental ingredient to success. Such diversity leads to rich and potent dialogue which challenges pre-conceived notions and assumptions, and which can make for more than a few uncomfortable moments. Strong and compassionate leadership is required to prevent fragmentation.

I was fortunate in being able to test my notions and assumptions with potential clients. This had the effect of accelerating the innovation cycle and producing a solution that solves real-world business problems. All too often, corporate innovation creates solutions to non-existent problems.

In my experience, approaching existing or potential clients to collaborate in innovation is received very positively, and clients rise to the occasion. Clear bounds of intellectual property rights need to be delineated but this is not usually a problem, especially when a clear, bounded relationship exists. Bringing clients into the fold also has the effect of 'pre-selling' the concept to them. In the case of our platform development, a key potential client was involved in the specification of the functionality; they formally signed off the Minimum Viable Product specification as being appropriate to their use; and then signed a Memorandum of Understanding that 'Aurora' was their platform of choice in complex project transaction management. Collaboration at this level engenders trust and accelerates time-to-market.

All great things are forged, moulded or crafted and it is the same with the implementation of a vision. It is forged and implemented over a period of time in the crucible of endeavour, sweat, and perhaps a few tears along the way. A key factor for me therefore is to build sufficient space and time into the forging process. Rather like the Japanese concept of *Ma*, this allows time for individual and collective reflection, induction, and in due course, internalization – the way in which members of a group take on the beliefs, perspectives and values held by the remainder of the group. In other words, time and space are as essential for success as the practical and material ingredients. Also key to success is flexibility, or the absence of a dogmatic approach, for continual adjustments are often needed along the way in order to navigate to one's final objective.

In summary, to achieve innovation from engagement my views are to cast broad and go deep and to:

- Look at all likely scenarios dispassionately and apply both inductive and deductive techniques to scenario planning;
- Test likely scenarios with critical thinking and in-depth research and do not be afraid of scale;
- Create leverage, by building a community of collaborators, utilizing collaboration and storyboarding software;
- Reach out beyond your organization and existing networks; be generous with your thoughts; you will receive the same in return from quite unexpected sources;
- Share your ideas, but protect your intellectual property;
- Create a vision that is compelling in its clarity, breadth of perspective and depth of insight;
- Form an innovation crucible which has at its heart a small, diverse but passionate and highly capable innovation team. They will be the evangelists for the vison, who will attract new members, stakeholders, partners and potential clients;
- Involve potential clients at the earliest opportunity and you will accelerate the innovation cycle, speed up time to market and have a better chance of early success;
- Maintain strength through flexibility, adjusting your navigation on your way to your overall objective.

And above all, enjoy the process.

Well-being

Employee well-being is an outcome of OC engagement. Research on well-being is derived from two general perspectives: (i) the hedonic approach, which focuses on happiness and defines well-being in terms of pleasure attainment and pain ; and (ii) the eudaimonic approach, which focuses on meaning and self-realization and defines well-being in terms of the degree to which a person is fully functioning (Seligman, 2002). The World Health Organization (WHO)[1] defines employee well-being as: ". . . a state of well-being in which every individual realizes his or her own potential, can cope with the normal stresses of life, can work productively and fruitfully, and is able to make a contribution to her or his community." This holistic definition converges on the core dimensions of well-being: psychological, physical and social, identified by Grant and colleagues (2007). The psychological dimension includes satisfaction, self-respect and capabilities. The physical dimension includes nourishment, shelter, health care, clothing and mobility; and the social dimension includes participating in the community, being accepted in public and helping others. These dimensions are valued as ends in and of themselves rather than as means to other ends.

Engaged employees report positive health outcomes and well-being. Alfes and colleagues (2010) found that those who were engaged in their work were almost three times as likely to have key positive emotions at work, such as enthusiasm, cheerfulness, optimism, contentment, feeling calm and relaxed, rather than negative ones, such as feeling miserable, worried, depressed, gloomy, tense or uneasy. Studies show that engaged workers in Dutch service organizations suffer less from headaches, cardiovascular problems and stomach aches (Schaufeli & Bakker, 2004), engaged Finnish teachers report good health (Hakanen et al., 2006), and engaged Swedish health care workers have fewer back pain and neck pain problems, and lower anxiety and depression (Peterson et al., 2008).

Surveys by consultants also confirm the positive relationship between engagement and well-being. Among these, a Gallup survey (Witters & Agrawal, 2015) shows that employees who are engaged and have high levels of well-being are more likely to evaluate their overall lives highly, to report excellent performance in their own work, to report excellent performance by their organization and to report high levels of adaptability. Evidence indicates that employee well-being has a significant impact on the performance and survival of organizations by affecting costs related to illness and health care and discretionary effort (Spector, 1997), which in turn leads to improvements in organizational performance, higher productivity, customer satisfaction and lower turnover, sickness and absence. There is evidence that people with higher levels of well-being are healthier (mentally and physically), have happier lives and live longer (Cartwright & Cooper, 2008), but importantly, research also shows that they are likely to take a more positive approach to their work and their relationships with colleagues. People with higher levels of well-being are less likely to see ambiguous events such as OC as threatening (Seidlitz & Diener, 1993). Research findings thus confirm the positive link between employee engagement and employee well-being; engaged employees have a greater sense of well-being. The benefits of this are that people with higher levels of well-being, learn and problem-solve more effectively, are more enthusiastic about change, relate to others more positively and accept change more readily.

Retention

Research indicates that engaged employees are significantly more likely to want to stay with their organization compared with those who are less engaged (Alfes et al., 2010). For example, a survey by Gallup (Harter et al., 2009) demonstrates a link between lower engagement scores and higher employee turnover both for organizations with historically high turnovers and those with much lower turnovers. In looking at those firms with 60 per cent or higher annualized employee turnover, those in the bottom quartile ranked by employee engagement had 31 per cent higher employee turnover than those in the top quartile of engagement scores. For firms with annualized turnover of 40 per cent or lower the results indicate that those in the bottom quartile had 51 per cent higher annualized turnover. These findings are reinforced by Wellins and colleagues (2005) with evidence from a Fortune 100 manufacturing company where turnover in teams where engagement was low averaged 14.5 per cent, compared with only 4.8 per cent in teams with high engagement.

An individual's expressed intention to leave their organization is generally regarded as an important measure of how they are feeling about their work. As noted by Schaufeli and Bakker (2004), engaged employees are likely to have a greater attachment to their organization and a lower tendency to quit. Research by Truss and colleagues (2006) supports this and concludes that engaged employees are less likely to leave their employer. So research suggests that the scope of an individual's engagement will vary from change to change supporting the proposition that OC engagement is transient.

Positive behaviour

OC engagement can have a positive impact on the behaviour and attitudes of individuals (Karatepe, 2013). Fleck and Inceoglu (2010) identify three behavioural outcomes of engagement – (i) effort; (ii) extra-role; and (iii) advocacy:

i) Effort. Employees who are engaged are likely to exert a lot of effort in their change tasks
ii) Extra-role. Engaged employees are more likely to demonstrate organizational citizenship behaviours (OCBs) that go beyond the requirements of their job, such as taking the initiative to solve problems, or offering help to co-workers before being asked for it. Research (Sulea et al., 2012) indicates that engaged employees exhibited more OCBs and less counterproductive work behaviours than their less engaged colleagues.
iii) Advocacy. Engaged employees are more likely to act as positive advocates for OC when interacting with people external to the organization.

An engaged employee is, therefore, more likely to exhibit positive energy towards change and a consistent commitment to the quality and implementation of the change.

The return on OC engagement (ROCE) is, therefore, productivity, performance, innovation, a more healthy workforce with greater intention to stay, employees who are willing to exert discretionary effort and are more enthusiastic. So ultimately through these outcomes OC engagement can create effective OC.

Summary

Although what influences OC engagement will vary according to circumstances it is suggested in this chapter that the main antecedents can be categorized as contextual, processual and individual factors. The organization's change history, its leadership and its approach to change are all important as well as people's perceptions of how they are treated, either fairly and justly as adults or as expendable chattels. There is also a connection between the antecedents, levels of OC engagement and various outcomes. Engaged employees will perform better and more vigorously, offer innovative suggestions, and pursue the objectives of OC in the face of obstacles. An organization's specific context and conditions will determine, to some extent, the antecedents and outcomes. At an individual level engagement can be influenced by personal factors which can distract and deplete energy, or in the case of positive events, result in people being more enthusiastic. An individual's level of engagement may also be affected by the characteristics of the person, such as generally being very energetic, as well as physical, emotional and psychological resources available at a given moment. Team engagement can be fostered through collective efficacy that is people's shared beliefs in their collective power to produce desired change. This is not simply the sum of efficacy beliefs of individuals but as an emergent team-led activity (Francis & Reddington, 2012) and this forms a collective engagement based on team dynamics and identities. By understanding the potential antecedents, levels and outcomes of OC engagement, leadership and management can play a crucial role in enhancing OC engagement. We explore these roles in the next chapter.

Implications

There are a number of practical implications which arise from the discussion in this chapter:

- Identify what drives OC engagement. Review whether and how you build and sustain key drivers of OC engagement. To what extent do you know each of your team members, both collectively and individually, in respect of what influences their engagement with change? How can you do all this better?
- Build a culture of OC engagement. Leaders need to be mindful of how they contribute (or not) to building a culture of OC engagement. Review whether and how you define and communicate a valid and appealing purpose for a change and its linkage to the vision, values and strategy for change. How can you do this better?
- Build and maintain trust. To encourage engagement with OC, trust needs to be built and maintained and conversely those actions that erode trust need to be avoided. Trust is two-way; employees not only must have trust in others and the organization to feel safe to engage with change as well as feel that they are trusted by their managers and the organization. How can you build relationships based on fairness and justice in order to help to make employees feel valued and respected?
- Identify what influences readiness for change. Managers and leaders need to be aware of what influences employees' readiness for change, such as existing organizational conditions, the nature of the change and an individual's belief in their ability to engage with change. Creating readiness involves proactive attempts by leaders and managers to influence the beliefs, attitudes, intentions and ultimately the behaviour of employees. How can you improve upon this?

Note

1 www.who.int/features/factfiles/mental_health/en/

Part 3

OC in practice

Chapter 7

Creating an environment for OC engagement

Learning outcomes

After reading this chapter you will be able to:

- appreciate the roles of leaders and managers in OC engagement;
- evaluate different theoretical perspectives of leadership within the context of OC engagement;
- recognize how OC engagement can be mismanaged;
- discuss the role of the individual in OC engagement.

Introduction

As discussed in the previous chapter, OC engagement is influenced by contextual, processual and individual factors. These antecedents can be affected by leadership and management which shape the culture of an organization as well as individuals' affective reactions. Leaders and managers should not, therefore, be complacent about OC engagement, yet, research shows evidence of an engagement deficit among UK senior executives (MacLeod & Clarke, 2009) and it is questionable whether the UK is the only country where this is prevalent. In some cases it may be because leaders and managers are unaware of the need for OC engagement or do not understand its importance. In other cases, leaders may understand its importance but lack the capabilities to implement OC engagement strategies, especially if these might challenge their power base. Whatever the reason it is evident that leadership and management play a vital part in influencing the antecedents of OC engagement.

The purpose of this chapter is to explore the roles of leadership and management in creating an environment in which employees and other stakeholders can engage with OC. Although a distinction will be made between the different roles, we emphasize that both leadership and management are needed to effectively create OC engagement. For, while it must be managed, OC engagement also requires effective leadership. The chapter begins by examining the type of leadership required for OC engagement and goes on to explore the differences and similarities between the role of management and leadership in the OC engagement process. Attention is also paid to the impact of effective and ineffective management. Since OC engagement is a shared and mutual responsibility, consideration is also given to the role of the individual in OC engagement, which is important because the focus of change is usually from the perspectives of leaders and managers rather than its recipients.

Importance of leadership

Leadership is an essential component of OC engagement. A report by the CBI and IPA (2011) provides several case studies and makes a compelling case for leadership being essential for engagement. This is supported by findings from the Kenexa Research Institute (2010), which surveyed 29,000 employees in 21 countries, and found that employee engagement was five times higher in businesses with effective leadership. In particular, research (for example, Aryee et al., 2012) highlights that leadership that demonstrates interpersonal characteristics, such as personally recognizing employees' efforts, being caring and showing an appreciation for employees, is positively associated with high levels of engagement. Although such research recognizes that leadership is important to the success of OC the question of "what type of leadership is effective for OC engagement?" needs further exploration. In an attempt to answer this question we begin by clarifying what is meant by leadership within the context of OC engagement.

In spite of a plethora of studies, still little is known about the defining characteristics of leadership with OC engagement. Indeed, as critics point out, as a scientific concept leadership is a mess (Augier & Teece, 2005) which has been conceptualized in many different ways. Researchers tend to define it according to their individual perspectives and the aspect of leadership that is of most interest to them; which means that there is no universally agreed definition. A popular approach is to see leadership as being about "capturing attention and motivating people to follow your way – your vision and your dreams" (Augier & Teece, 2005: 116). This provides a simplistic view which has spawned numerous "I did it my way" biographical tomes on leadership.

Of the many definitions on offer, the one which is probably the most comprehensive and succinct within the context of OC is that: "Leadership is a process whereby an individual influences a group of individuals to achieve a common goal" (Northouse, 2012: 9). This is similar to Gary Yukl's (2006) definition of leadership as the process of influencing others to understand and agree what needs to be done and how to do it, and the process of facilitating individual and collective efforts to accomplish shared objectives. Such definitions suggest several components central to the leadership of OC engagement, which are that: leadership is a process; leadership involves influencing others; leadership happens within the context of a group or team; leadership involves achieving change goals; and these goals are shared by leaders and individuals. The very act of defining leadership as a process suggests that leadership is not a characteristic or trait with which only a few certain people are endowed at birth, but instead something that can be developed.

The element that is missing in the definition of leadership as a process of influence is the emphasis on the relational aspect, since leadership is inherently a mutual relational process (Fairhurst & Uhl-Bien, 2012). As the norm of reciprocity suggests, individuals feel empowered in the light of a strong relationship with their leader and this builds a sense of obligation to reciprocate through high levels of effort and engagement (Graen & Uhl-Bien, 1995). Building on this, leadership effectiveness can be viewed as the success in mobilizing and motivating stakeholder efforts for OC goals based on mutuality. Leadership is not, therefore, the sole responsibility of a single individual, rather, it is an inherently shared relational process which infers that what matters most in the role of leadership is what they convey to stakeholders.

Viewing leadership as a relational process which influences OC engagement stresses that it is a two-way, interactive event between leaders and individuals, rather than a linear, one-way event in which the leader affects individuals only. It means that leaders affect and are affected by their employees' OC engagement, either positively or negatively. More importantly, it means that leadership is not restricted to just the one person in a team, department or organization, who has positional power (usually the formally appointed leader) but instead makes it available to people throughout the organization. It is the process that translates into acts of leadership that can be enacted by individuals at different levels to influence OC engagement. The leadership of OC engagement is, therefore, a relational process involving mutual responsibility.

Theoretical perspectives on leadership

Although much is written and talked about the leadership of OC, the reality is that empirical evidence about it is rare, inconsistent and virtually impossible to integrate into a coherent set of conclusions and recommendations. As a result, critics point out that what is said about the leadership of OC borders on the mythology and romance of hero worship (By et al., 2016) with the majority of OC leadership research focusing on the individual leader as the source of change outcomes (Ford & Ford, 2012). This perspective mirrors a traditional leadership research assumption that leadership is a personal possession of the leader and that leadership is bestowed upon followers who are recipients of that bestowal, rather than all being partners in the co-creation of change outcomes. Instead the effectiveness of the individual leader is seen as the key to change success. This is evident in traditional approaches such as transformational leadership theories.

Transformational leadership

Transformational leaders motivate followers to transcend immediate self-interests to work for goals that benefit the team and/or the organization (Burns, 1978). Transformational leaders, Bass and Avolio (1994) say, inspire those around them by providing meaning and challenge to their followers' work by inspirational motivation, intellectual stimulation, individualized consideration and idealized influence. Through the use of inspirational motivation and intellectual stimulation, transformational leaders encourage individuals to re-examine assumptions, look at problems in new ways and think innovatively to challenge traditional ways of doing things. This view is supported by empirical research. For example, in their study of employees from two insurance companies in Pakistan, Ali and colleagues (2010) found that transformational leaders encourage individuals to feel free to explore and to express their ideas, thus enabling creativity. Through individualized consideration, transformational leaders look for the unique potential in each individual and spend time listening and coaching individuals to encourage them to reach their potential and through idealized influence, transformational leaders model high levels of moral and ethical standards showing that what is right and good to do is important. These factors encourage employees to try new things and think differently rather than fearing that they may be punished or reprimanded for doing so. In this way transformational leadership is concerned with transforming the way people feel about themselves and raising their motivation in order to improve their performance beyond previous expectations.

Although studies of transformational leadership and OC are limited, those that do exist show that transformational leadership impacts positively on engagement. For example, transformational leadership has been found to exhibit a positive relationship with reported levels of engagement for telecommunications employees in China (Aryee et al., 2012). In particular, the combined effects of idealized influence, inspirational motivation, individualized consideration and intellectual stimulation increase overall engagement through unleashing inspired effort focused on achieving individual and organizational goals (Tims et al., 2011). Transformational leaders have also been found to promote employees' feelings of self-efficacy (Lester et al., 2011), which results in them feeling that they have what they need to carry out OC and do it well. Such leadership also appears to encourage autonomy and trust (Bono & Judge, 2003) – key antecedents of OC engagement. So if it is assumed that employees become engaged under a transformational leader, then increasing transformational leadership behaviours would seem to be a logical approach in comparison to other types of leadership such as transactional leadership.

Transactional leadership

In contrast to transformational leadership, transactional leadership focuses on establishing and communicating goals and performance standards, then consistently and objectively rewarding individuals using contingent rewards (Bass, 1997). At the ineffective and passive end of the transactional leadership model are potentially negative aspects of leadership: active management by exception (error monitoring), passive management by exception (dealing with errors when brought to the leader's attention) and laissez faire leadership (withdrawal from leadership responsibilities). Although not mutually exclusive, research shows that transformational leadership is significantly more effective than transactional leadership and yields a unique set of positive work outcomes (Avolio, 2011), whereas findings suggest that transactional leadership is negatively correlated with OC engagement (Conway & Monks, 2008). In contrast the positive forms of transactional leadership highlighted in the research (Bass, 1997) may be necessary for OC engagement, but need to be combined with transformational leadership to be effective.

Critics of transformational leadership

Following decades of corporate scandals, the behaviour, role and impact of so-called transformational leaders have been severely questioned (Hodges, 2011). Critics question whether or not the traditional forms of leadership are really necessary for engagement. Khurana (2002) is scathing in his assessment of transformational leaders, pointing out that they go beyond the boundaries of their influence and control, exploit the irrational desires of their followers and often deliberately destabilize their organizations to foster revitalization. Likewise, Joseph Nye Jr, a political scientist and former Dean of the John F. Kennedy School of Government at Harvard University, cautions about extolling the virtues of transformational leadership:

> . . . theoretical expectations that transformational leaders make all the difference and incremental/transactional leaders are simply routine managers greatly mis-states the roles of leaders. Exaggerating the importance of transformational leadership is not necessarily the best way to understand . . . the leadership needs in the 21st century.
>
> (Nye, 2014: 124)

In support of this view Hüttermann and Boerner (2011) advise against blind enthusiasm for transformational leadership as it may encourage excessive dependency on the leader in resolving problems. Morgan (2001: 3) condemns the "larger than life leaders and their grand strategies", arguing for "a quieter, more evolutionary approach to change, one that relies on employee motivation instead of directives from on high". This is consistent with the views of Huy (2001) who dismisses the role of visionary leadership, arguing that it is middle managers who achieve the balance between change and continuity, and that radical change imposed from the top makes this difficult. In other words, organizations should lose the notion that you need heroic leaders in order to have meaningful OC engagement.

Attempts to link transformational leadership to effective OC have produced mixed discussions with some indicating that it is possible that such leadership may facilitate and/or present major risks for change programs (Herold et al., 2008). For instance, it has been suggested that individuals may be reluctant to disagree with a transformational leader, given his or her personal influence on them, which can be a barrier to engaging organizational members with OC (Edmondson et al., 2015). Employees may also become angry or frustrated when they realize that the change vision created by transformational leaders may not be feasible, which may lead employees to feel betrayed and become cynical. Due to such risks, Bass and Steidlmeier (1999) argue that transformational leadership needs to be sharply questioned in terms of its morality as it can be unethical due to leaders making egocentric decisions. For example, a leader may hide some evidence of risk or failure during a change process in order to prevent losing their credibility and their idealized influence on individuals. Consequently, in the place of traditional models of leadership must come more collaborative and distributed ways of leading.

Distributed leadership

Distributed or shared leadership is based on the idea that the leadership of an organization should not rest with a single individual, but should be shared or 'distributed' among those with the relevant skills (Gronn, 2000). A distributed leadership perspective recognizes that there are multiple leaders at different levels of an organization and that leadership activities are widely shared within and between organizations. It focuses upon the interactions, rather than the actions, of those in formal and informal leadership roles (Spillane, 2006) and is about connecting people up, down and across the organization. Distributed leadership has been shown to be a complement to and, in some cases, a more powerful predictor of change outcomes than transformational leadership (Pearce & Sims, 2002). Distributed leadership acknowledges that change in organizations can be led from the top, the line or the bottom of organizations and that it is the work of all individuals who contribute to leadership practice, whether or not they are formally designated or defined as leaders.

Within the context of OC, distributed leadership is the sharing of power and influence among a group of individuals rather than centralizing it in the hands of a single person. Meyerson (2001) describes this as behind-the-scenes and below the radar leadership, while Badaracco (2002) calls it a quiet approach to leadership emphasizing careful moves, and controlled and measured effort. This means that in the appropriate situations, individuals with the motivation and capabilities can lead and implement change, just as effectively as transformational leaders.

One of the issues with distributed leadership is that the capabilities and contributions of those who are involved may not be recognized. These are the 'unsung heroes' who take personal responsibility, and risk, for driving change without formal reward or recognition. The idea that change outcomes are the product of an individual leader is especially questionable in transformational or complex changes. It is much more likely that effective leadership for generating OC engagement is distributed and collaborative.

Collaborative leadership

Similar to distributed leadership, collaborative leadership is aimed at encouraging employees to engage with OC (Hodges & Howieson, 2017). In his book *Collaborative Leadership: Developing Effective Partnerships for Communities and Schools*, Rubin (2009) defines collaboration as a purposeful relationship in which all parties strategically choose to cooperate in order to accomplish a shared outcome. This definition is built upon by Archer and Cameron (2009) in their book *Collaborative Leadership: How to Succeed in an Interconnected World*. The authors identify that getting value from difference is at the heart of the collaborative leader's task and that they have to learn to share control and to trust others to deliver. In other words, acting collaboratively is about creating a purposeful relationship in which all parties choose to cooperate in order to accomplish a shared outcome and deliver results. Research shows that the collaborations that are most successful include both experienced people and newcomers and bring together people who have not worked with one another before (Ibarra & Hansen, 2011). The leadership of OC engagement is about making concerted efforts to promote this mix. Collaborative leaders must be able to harness ideas, people and resources from across boundaries and build strong connections both inside and outside the organizations. To get all the disparate stakeholders to work together effectively, they also need to know when to wield influence, rather than authority, to move things forward, and when to halt unproductive discussions. Differences in convictions, cultural values and operating norms inevitably add complexity to collaborative efforts but they also make them richer, more innovative and more valuable. Getting that value is the heart of collaborative leadership.

Forms of leadership, variously described as distributed and collaborative, reflect the socially constructed nature of OC in which people can make sense of what is happening and are enabled to make necessary changes at the right level. This means employees need to be willing and able to seize opportunities without constant checking from higher up. Therefore, when leaders enable stakeholders to become more active developers, and not merely recipients of OC, the results are likely to include greater engagement with change. These forms of leadership can also influence engagement through influencing individuals' hope, efficacy, resilience and optimism (HOPE – see Chapter 5) which in turn increases employees energy and focus for engagement with change.

For effective OC engagement there is a need to reframe leadership. As Gratton (2014) points out we are in the midst of a transition from the old order, signalled by powerful leadership, supported by legions of PR-speak, to a new, emerging order, where the hierarchies are becoming dismantled and individuals are becoming more demanding. This transition is by no means complete; however, in a time of accelerating change there is a need for leadership that is distributive and collaborative and more pertinent to OC engagement than traditional theories of leadership, particularly as they offer the potential to involve stakeholders as partners in the co-creation of OC.

In sum, the leadership of OC engagement is complex and the perspective dominant in traditional leadership literature fails to consider that leaders enact multiple functions that are likely to be distributed among multiple people based on their knowledge and expertise, rather than concentrated in a single individual or position.

Stakeholder relationships

The success of OC engagement depends on stakeholder relationships. According to stakeholder theory, "managers must develop relationships, inspire stakeholders and create communities where people strive to give their best to make good on the firm's promise and manage the relationships with its stakeholders in an action-oriented way" (Freeman et al., 2004: 364). This involves knowing which groups and individuals internal and external to the organization will affect, or be affected by, the change including employees, shareholders, customers, trade unions, suppliers, partners and distributors, as well as local communities, government and non-governmental organizations.

Stakeholder management

The development and management of stakeholder relations requires the identification of the relevant stakeholders which can be conducted through a stakeholder mapping exercise. This involves addressing questions such as: Who are the current and potential stakeholders? What are their interests/rights in OC? How does each stakeholder affect the OC? How will the OC affect each stakeholder? Auster and Ruebottom (2013) suggest the following stakeholder mapping process that can be tailored to particular contexts: (i) map the political landscape of who will be affected by change; (ii) identify the key influencers – those who have the skills and interest to influence and convince others of the benefits of change – within each stakeholder group; (iii) assess influencers' receptiveness to change; (iv) mobilize influential sponsors and promoters – those who have the skills, connections and insights to champion change; and (v) engage influential positive and negative sceptics. Missing from such generic processes is how to engage stakeholders and manage conflicts of interest. This requires orchestrated stakeholder dialogue through which organizations use the expertise of stakeholders in order to build innovative change interventions.

Management's role is to engage in dialogue with a range of stakeholders, managing any conflicts of interest as they do so. Inevitably, with OC there will be tensions and conflicts between individual stakeholders and stakeholder groups at different times during OC. As change progresses, its scope may alter and some stakeholders will become less relevant, they may lose interest, new stakeholders may emerge and old ones may leave the organization or move to another job where they are no longer involved or impacted by the change. The needs of these different stakeholder groups are often in tension and managers may find themselves in the middle of dilemmas arising from such tensions. Management's task is to address and seek to resolve potential conflicts, which is where a set of principles, such as those outlined in Box 7.1 for stakeholder management, can be helpful.

Box 7.1 Principles of stakeholder management

- Acknowledge and actively monitor the concerns of all legitimate stakeholders, and take their interests appropriately into account in decision-making about OC.
- Listen to, and openly communicate with, stakeholders about their respective concerns and contributions to OC.
- Adopt processes and modes of behaviour that are sensitive to the concerns and capabilities of each stakeholder group.
- Recognize the interdependence of efforts and rewards among stakeholders, and attempt to achieve a fair distribution of the benefits and challenges of OC among them, taking into account their respective risks and vulnerabilities.
- Work collaboratively to ensure that risks arising from OC activities are minimized and, where they cannot be avoided, appropriately mitigated.
- Avoid activities that might jeopardize ethics or give rise to risks which, if clearly understood, would be patently unacceptable to relevant stakeholders.
- Managers need to acknowledge the potential conflicts between their own role as organizational stakeholders in OC, and their legal and ethical responsibilities for the interests of all other stakeholders, and should address such conflicts through communication, appropriate reporting and incentive systems and, where necessary, third party review.

Developing stakeholder relations provides management with an approach for identifying and engaging a diverse set of stakeholders in OC in mutually rewarding ways, especially those who can and will exercise their power and political means, in covert and overt ways, that have the potential to subvert any change. The management of stakeholders therefore needs to be an on-going and dynamic activity.

Power and politics

The process of building relationships and engaging stakeholders with OC usually involves power and politics, so to effectively engage stakeholders with OC, leaders and managers need to understand the power and politics within the organization, especially as power and politics can be used to impact on change either positively or negatively. As Dawson notes, in managing transitions practitioners need to be aware of:

> the importance of power politics within organizations as a determinant of the speed, direction and character of change; the enabling and constraining properties of the type and scale of change being introduced; and the influence of the internal and external context on the pathways and outcomes of change on new work arrangements.
>
> (Dawson, 1994: 180–82)

In line with this argument, Pugh (1993: 109) points out that since organizations are political and occupational systems as well as rational resource allocation ones,

> every reaction to a change proposal must be interpreted not only in terms of rational arguments of what is best for the firm . . . The reaction must also be understood in relation to the occupational system . . . and the political system (how will it affect the power, status, and prestige of the group?)

In particular, transformational change provides opportunities for gaining, keeping or increasing power or indeed of losing it. Consequently, leaders and managers can be very power conscious during OC resulting in what Mast and colleagues (2010: 460) term "power motivation" – the motivation to keep and increase their power. Power is, however, not just a matter of an individual's formal position in the organization but also their personal characteristics and experience. People are more likely to enthusiastically accept and commit to an individual whom they admire or whose expertise they respect, rather than someone who solely relies on their positional power. Leaders and managers who use their expertise, knowledge, skills and capabilities to engage stakeholders with OC are more likely to gain their commitment, rather than those who wield their power to coerce and threaten them.

Power

There are two sides to power in OC. On the one hand there is a positive side, as Kanter (1997: 322) explains:

> When managers are in powerful situations, it is easier for them to accomplish more. Because the tools are there, they are likely to be highly motivated and, in turn, be able to motivate subordinates . . . They gain respect and cooperation that attributed power brings.

Kanter's view assumes that power is wielded for benevolent means. On the other hand, there is a negative side to power. This is illustrated in an article by Rosenthal and Pittinsky (2006: 629) on narcissistic leadership which highlights that some leaders are "principally motivated by their own egomaniacal needs and beliefs, superseding the needs and interests of the constituents they lead." Rosenthal and Pittinsky (2006) draw a line between charismatic leadership which seeks to motivate people and narcissistic leadership which seeks to exploit people in order to gather more power for themselves, be it the referent power that comes with reputation, or actual mental and physical control over people or both. So depending on how it is used, power can be seen as either negative or positive. Mary Beard (2017), a Professor of Classics at Cambridge University, proposes that we think about power differently. Beard (2017: 87) says that, "It means, above all, thinking about power as an attribute or even a verb ('to power'), not as a possession." This means thinking collaboratively about the power of stakeholders not just of leaders. Translated into OC engagement this suggests the ability of stakeholders to be effective, to make a difference and the right to be taken seriously, together as much as individually. It is this type of power that many stakeholders often feel they do not have with OC but that they need in order to engage effectively with it. The challenges of understanding the power of stakeholders are illustrated in the following case (Box 7.2).

Box 7.2 Stakeholder management for success

Written by Greg Longley,
Senior Independent Consultant

During my time as an independent consultant, across numerous organisations and in varying sectors, one stark observation of mine is how badly stakeholder management is often done, or rather how it isn't even done at all.

Business is all about people, and people mean relationships. Just like a profit and loss account, an HR system, or an operation more generally they also need to be managed and managed well.

Managing stakeholders and building relationships are key to the success of any operation, project or change initiative. Discount the importance of this at your peril! Stakeholder management and, more importantly, good stakeholder management will probably be the most important thing that you do.

In order to offer more granular insight, we can review a bad example and a good example of stakeholder management. Following that, some general principles based on lived experience will be offered.

At a global technology company I worked as part of the management information, reporting and analysis function of the European sales operation. This role was quite early on in my career post university, but it was an important position and one that provided many challenges. One of my main tasks was to develop and regularly publish a management information pack detailing operational performance, key metrics, commission to staff, sales figures and many other data. I had a fairly loose brief from my line manager and created what I considered to be a comprehensive and strong management information pack, which would be sent out to internal customers from Director level downwards. I sent the first edition out feeling pretty pleased with myself. Not long after I had clicked the send button on my e-mail, one of my internal 'customers' mailed me saying that it did not give him what he needed. I was disappointed and a bit cross to be honest. How on earth did it not give him what he needed? It was 60 pages long! I had every metric under the sun in there. I replied to his e-mail in a tone that probably showed my immaturity and asked him how this could be the case, and didn't he find it comprehensive enough? And so, an e-mail tit-for-tat began. His requirements and my ability to listen and understand somehow got lost in the cacophony of e-mails where we both fought our corner.

This was not ideal, and in all honesty, it was my fault. I'll explain. What I should have done before even creating the first pack was understand stakeholders' requirements. I should have identified who the receivers of this management information pack were, plotted them on a stakeholder matrix of power and influence, ideally spoken to them face-to-face (or at least by phone) and gathered what data points they would like to see in any pack. Then depending on resource, ability and importance of the stakeholder I could have defined a final list of data points that would have gone into the pack. Once that final list was done, I should then have had a conversation with those stakeholders who would not have their requirements incorporated explaining the reasons why. I tried to salvage something out of the situation by sending yet another e-mail but trying to get back to understanding this particular stakeholder's requirements – which he then duly sent. I began re-drafting the pack based on my interpretation of his requirements and sent it to him. I was still some way off according to him. I was frustrated and tried again, about four times. In the end, I concluded that this was not a good use of my time or his. I decided I would go and speak with him face-to-face. This was the best thing I could have done.

I was nervous, as he was more senior, and I had not delivered against his expectations. We sat down together, and I asked him to talk me through his operation, what the key metrics were, what metrics he needed from me and why they were important. The dysfunctional relationship we had over e-mail disintegrated almost immediately. He could see that I genuinely wanted to do a good job, and I could see that he was not just awkward. I had also gained some context around his requirements.

I went back to my desk and produced the management information he needed. It was a success. He was pleased that he now had the visibility of performance he was looking for. A lesson had been learned, by me. Going forwards in the role I made sure that I did not make the same mistake again, with him or others. I later found out that this stakeholder became one of my biggest advocates amongst senior management.

During my time working for a global bank I took on a consultancy role as senior change lead for a global implementation programme. There were many stakeholders across different continents. The programme had been working hard to finalise the agreed deliverables in order to get them ready for sign off by key stakeholders. But one of the stakeholders was not positive in supporting the work done and was making noises that they would not sign off the deliverables in all of our programme update conference calls.

I decided to address the issue and picked up the phone to talk with the stakeholder concerned. We talked for some time about her frustration that the rest of the business was not listening to her, or her business unit, about the importance of some other external deliveries and activities that were connected to the deliverables of the programme. This had left them frustrated that they did not have a voice within our programme and that other people's opinion seemed to matter more. I tried to reassure her that this was not the case, and then talked through the list of concerns about activities one by one. I shared the opinion that this would have some influence on what the programme was delivering and asked her to try and see that the good work the programme had done should not be ruined by the issue. I also asked what could be done to put her mind at ease about the deliverables.

I was almost taken aback when she said that she had no problem with the deliverables, and that they were very good pieces of work. Her standpoint of saying that she would not sign off the deliverables was solely based on the fact that she reluctantly considered that others would not listen unless she threatened this. Nobody knew the real reasons and assumed that it was due to unhappiness with the deliverables.

I promised I would raise these concerns as agenda items in our next meeting with key stakeholders, make sure that her concerns were officially minuted and that we were all aligned in supporting any subsequent actions. This led to her supporting the programme's deliverables and signing them off, even adding that she was pleased with the end result. This not only led to the start of a positive working relationship, but it also developed an ally for me cemented in trust and a willingness to listen. As I had taken the time to understand and address the issue in a supportive manner, I had moved the interaction from a negative one to that of positive support for the programme.

With those examples in mind, and to expand further, there are some practices that are useful to adhere to when managing stakeholders:

- Step away from the e-mail. E-mail has made our personal and working lives easier in so many ways, but it can also be the scourge of building relationships. Wherever you can, try and speak to people face-to-face. If you can't do this, then pick up the phone. Also, if you think you are about to get into an e-mail tit-for-tat, don't. Instead have a chat face-to-face or pick up the phone/Skype or Facetime.
- Stakeholders are human. This is true of even the most challenging ones. Honest. We all have bad days. Maybe your stakeholder has had some bad news or an argument with their partner. Try and understand the human side of stakeholders when building and managing relationships. Sharing something personal about yourself can often lead to others opening up as well, even something as simple as a hobby or love of a sports team. This is really important in helping to build stakeholder relationships. You will often find that you have at least one thing in common. Use this to try and build your relationship.
- Listen. Active listening is essential. Make sure you listen to and understand what your stakeholders are telling you, and in some instances not telling you. Do you fully comprehend the opinions of stakeholders? If in doubt, take the time to double-check. Rather that than going down a rabbit warren to nowhere.
- Address bad behaviour quickly. It is not OK for anyone to shout and swear at you, and that includes stakeholders. I have tackled bad and aggressive behaviour on numerous occasions, often with those who are more senior. You need to address it calmly and professionally, outlining why you are not happy with a stakeholder's tone or approach. In all instances where I have dealt with this immediately it has not recurred. If trying to deal with this yourself is not helpful, then escalate it to your line manager.
- Gather requirements. Make sure you accurately gather the requirements of all necessary stakeholders that you are intending to engage and whose expectations you need to manage. You do not want to be in a position towards the end of a large programme delivery where a key stakeholder e-mails the Director of the programme saying that they have not been engaged effectively. This can create delay as well as reputational damage to you and/or the change.
- Understand the influence and power of the stakeholders. Plot your stakeholders on a graphical axis according to 'power' (y axis) and 'influence' (x axis) split into four quadrants as illustrated in Figure 7.1. This can help develop your approach on

how you might engage people and what level of effort you need to employ in doing that.

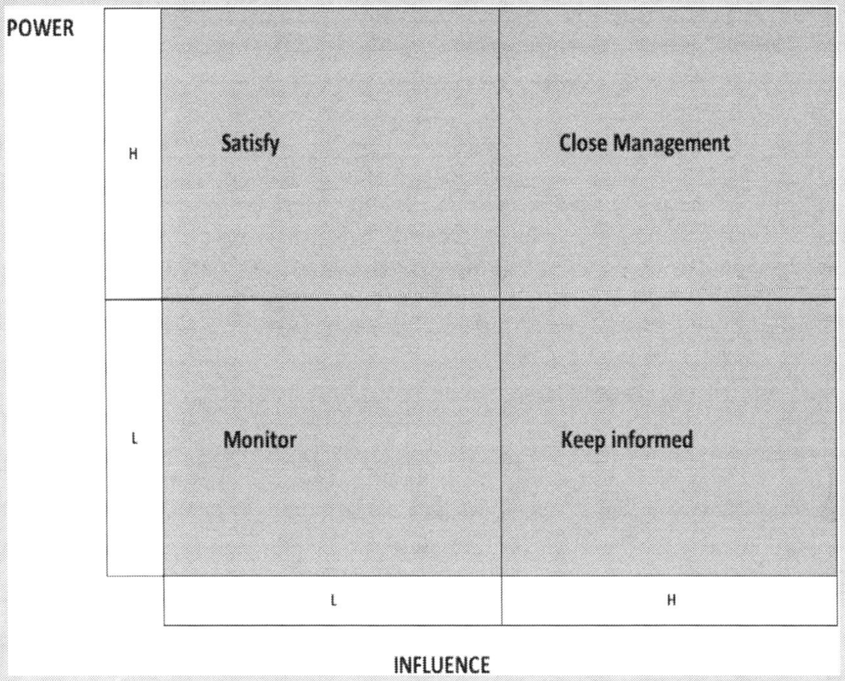

POWER

	H	**Satisfy**	**Close Management**
	L	**Monitor**	**Keep informed**
		L	H

INFLUENCE

Figure 7.1 Power and influence of stakeholders

- Show you are competent and do it quickly. Building confidence in your competence is key to building relationships with stakeholders. It may seem obvious, but stakeholders need to feel happy that you know what you are talking about. If you have a meeting with a stakeholder and are presenting something to them, make sure you prepare and rehearse in advance. This is particularly true for initial meetings as these first impressions do last. It is always a good idea to try and find things out about that stakeholder's world. Understanding things like their role, business area structure, strategy and challenges will help show that you at least have a working knowledge of the things that shape and influence their decisions and day-to-day activity.
- Thanks, and appreciation. Almost everyone likes to be thanked for their support and commitment. The same applies to stakeholders. Where it is appropriate take the time to recognise positive behaviour. It can make people feel valued and help build and sustain those relationships

Silent veto

The one kind of power that is universal, held by every person in every role in every organization, is silent veto power. People can exercise this type of power by ignoring change and by denying that it requires that they do anything different from what they are already doing, or they can disclaim any responsibility for it. Unless people have a compelling reason to cooperate, they can use the power of silent veto to disengage from OC. The power of silent veto along with the abuse of power can impede engagement with OC and heighten organizational politics.

Politics

Politics are a natural occurrence during OC and are described as a turf game involving a competition of ideas (Buchanan & Badham, 2008). There are two different perspectives on organizational politics: one views politics as a negative process that actively inhibits the effective running of an organization; the other sees politics in a more positive light. The former view focuses on the waste of time and energy and the damage that politics can cause. In support of this, Ward (1994: 143) warns that:

> To ignore organizational politics when managing change is to fail. What then is the alternative? Should one be political? The short answer is no. If you do become political, then professional integrity is sacrificed. You are just another silver-tongued hustler parading your wares while seeking to manipulate. This is the road to disaster. Politics does not add value.

This negative side of politics is also referred to by Ferris and Kacmar (1992: 113) as "characterized by destructive opportunism and dysfunctional game playing". This supports Ferris and King (1991) who describe politicized decision-making as "a walk on the dark side", which is echoed in Egan's (1994) book, *Working the Shadow Side: A guide to positive behind-the-scenes management*. Chanlat (1997) goes as far as describing politics as a 'social disease', which is often associated with high levels of stress, depression and other undesirable individual and corporate outcomes. This negative interpretation is, however, widely challenged by proponents who have a positive perspective of organizational politics. Kumar and Thibodeaux (1990), for instance, acknowledge and indeed advocate the use of political strategies in planned change. In support of their argument they identify three levels of change: first-level change, which involves improving unit or department effectiveness; second-level change, which involves introducing new perspectives to organizational subsystems; and third-level change, which concerns organization-wide shifts in values and ways of working. While first-level and second-level changes require political awareness and political facilitation respectively, third-level change entails political intervention. In other words, the more widespread the implications of OC, the greater the political involvement required by leaders and managers.

Advocates point out that organizational politics can provide the stimulating force for change, and political forces can generate the energy and creativity for OC (Hardy & Clegg, 1996). As Pettigrew (1977) points out, politics concerns the creation of legitimacy for certain ideas, values and demands. Likewise while agreeing that the costs of eliminating politics are high, Pfeffer (1992) also observes that the quality of debate in a politics free organization is likely to be poor.

In sum, OC can trigger and intensify political behaviour since it may threaten to push individuals out of their comfort zone, as well as jeopardize existing practices and routines, status hierarchies, information flows, resource allocation and power bases. Political behaviour can also be triggered by a diversity of opinion, values, beliefs and interpretations of change. Stakeholders who believe that they will lose out in some way or who feel that there are better ways to achieve the same result or better results, may oppose proposed changes. If their voices are not heard, and the issues are important, some people may demonstrate their opposition through covert, political means. So since politics is a natural and necessary aspect of OC this highlights the need for leaders and managers to intervene in the political system of the organization in order to legitimize the rationale for change, particularly when they are faced with opposition to it, in order to create conditions for OC engagement.

Role of leaders and managers

Leadership and management are complementary, but research tends to focus on leadership over management. This is confounded by locating leadership in the people who occupy positions of authority, and thus overstating the role of leadership while understating that of management. To have a full appreciation for the role and contribution of leadership in successful OC engagement, we need to take into account the role and contribution of management and to differentiate the distinct contributions of leadership and management.

Leadership and management play important but distinctly different roles in OC engagement. The differences between the roles are highlighted by Caldwell (2003: 291): "Leaders . . . envision, initiate or sponsor strategic change of a far-reaching or transformational nature. In contrast, managers . . . carry forward and build support for change within business units and key functions . . ."

The difference in the roles is defined further by Stoughton and Ludema (2012) who propose that leaders provide a framework for OC by communicating their commitment to it, adopting reporting systems and prioritizing issues for attention, while managers adopt the new ways of thinking and behaving to translate the organization's vision for OC into action. Nahavandi (2000: 13) agrees with this distinction and emphasizes the difference in the long- and short-term approaches of leaders and managers:

> Whereas leaders have long term and future-orientated perspectives and provide a vision for followers that looks beyond their immediate surroundings, managers have short term perspectives and focus on routine issues within their own immediate departments and groups.

These definitions assume that leadership is about creating a vision for change, while management is about translating the vision into agendas and actions. Although these differences do exist between leadership and management, the two constructs also overlap. Both are needed to ensure that people are engaged with change, in order to effectively embed it in an organization.

Leadership signals

Effective leadership creates the conditions for people to be motivated and even inspired – to be engaged *with* OC. A passive lack of leadership or active instigation and promulgation of poor practices is the obverse of effective leadership (Soane, 2014). Research shows that leadership is positively related to engagement and that ineffective leadership, or lack of leadership, is likely to inhibit or prevent employees from becoming engaged (Aryee et al., 2012).

Leaders profoundly influence OC engagement since they are highly visible and keenly watched by employees and other stakeholders to see which way they turn and what they give priority to. Consequently, leaders are considered as constantly required to adopt impression management behaviours to deal with this visibility (Bolino et al., 2016). Individuals look to leaders, whether or not they want to, to see what they reward and what they sanction, and what they themselves do. Employees look for signals about what is accepted and what is not. In every interaction – meetings, corridor conversations, emails – employees are looking for their leaders' signals, for their answers to those unspoken questions. This can determine the extent to which employees consider engaging or not with OC since they are looking around constantly for signals about whether their engagement matters, how safe they are and whether leaders truly wish to know their opinions and welcome their participation with OC. If the signals are good, they might move towards engaging in change. If the signals are not so good, they will step back and if the signals look bad, then they will disengage. As Joseph M. Tucci, CEO of EMC – the US-based information storage business – says, "every move leaders make, everything they say, is visible to all, therefore the best approach is to lead by example" (cited by Aitken & Scott, 2007). Yet research by McKinsey (Boaz & Fox, 2014) suggests that half of all efforts to transform organizational performance fail because leaders do not act as role models for change but instead they give out the wrong signals.

Difficulties arise when leaders believe, often mistakenly, that they already are the change. They commit themselves to personally role modelling the desired behaviours but, in practice, nothing significant changes. The reason for this, according to Aitken and Keller (2009), is that most leaders do not count themselves among the ones who need to change. Yet a challenge for leaders is knowing what they need to change at a personal level, which will only occur when they recognize that they must change. This is illustrated by the founder of Infosys, N.R. Narayan Murthy, who proposes that leaders have to sacrifice themselves first for a transformation before they can ask others to do the same (cited in Aitken & Keller, 2007). Therefore, leaders need to take actions that role model the desired change and demonstrate that they are also engaged with it. This needs to be done authentically and for mutual gains rather than for merely impression management.

Authentic leaders

Authenticity is defined as the extent to which an individual is true to themself by emphasizing their core values, and acting accordingly (Gardner et al., 2011). Authentic leadership is "a process that draws from both positive psychological capacities and a highly developed organizational context, which results in both greater self-awareness and self-regulated positive behaviours on the part of leaders . . ., fostering positive self-development" (Luthans & Avolio, 2003: 243). This type of leadership comprises: self-awareness (an understanding of one's strengths and weaknesses); internalized moral perspective (self-regulation that is based on internalized moral values); balanced processing (objective evaluation of information before making a decision); and relational transparency (being true to one's values and expressing this to others) (Walumbwa et al., 2008). Authentic leadership has been found to be significantly predictive of outcomes, such as satisfaction, commitment, organizational citizenship behaviours and performance (Walumbwa et al., 2008). In addition, it is considered particularly important for leading emergent change (Alavi & Gill, 2017). Authenticity is crucial in how leaders engage others in change as well as how they themselves enact OC engagement.

Engaged leaders

It is not only the people who will be affected by OC who need to be engaged with it, but leaders themselves also need to be engaged and to proactively maintain their engagement until the change is embedded. Yet in reality this is not always the case. In their 'Barometer on Change' the Moorhouse Consulting (2014) highlights that almost half (47 per cent) of senior leaders are not engaged at all, or only partially committed at most, to change initiatives. This lack of engagement from leaders can lead to a boomerang effect, where initial changes start to fade when leaders lose interest or stop paying attention to a change initiative.

A lack of OC engagement from leaders is shown in different ways such as by: a lack of acceptance of ownership and responsibility for the change initiative; a lack of eagerness to be involved; an unwillingness to invest in resources; a reluctance to take tough decisions when required; a lack of awareness of the impact of their own behaviour; inconsistent messages; and no regular reviews held to discuss progress. When leaders withdraw their proactive support or refocus their attention on other priorities, this can result in a lack of dedicated effort, conflict and resistance to change from others in the organization, and employees at all levels reverting back to old ways of working and behaving. Leaders need to proactively maintain their own engagement with change in order to develop and sustain a culture of OC engagement.

Creating a culture for OC engagement

Leadership profoundly affects the culture of OC engagement, indeed as Schein (1997) points out that leadership and culture are two sides of the same coin, since leaders exert extraordinary influence on culture and vice versa. Organizational culture is, however, complex and can have a positive, neutral or negative impact on OC engagement. Haudan (2008) observes that too often employees are so overwhelmed by complex work cultures that they are pushed onto the back foot and so reacting stops engagement. In contrast, by eliminating needless tasks and promoting simplification, Haudan (2008) says that leadership can help increase OC engagement by providing employees with greater clarity and simplicity of purpose. Not only does this help people connect the dots but the people have fewer dots to connect. In other words, leadership plays a key role in building cultures conducive to OC engagement. Microsoft is a case in point. Since being appointed as CEO, Satya Nadella has been credited with transforming Microsoft's cautious, insular culture to one of risk taking and exploration. Nadella has achieved this through listening, learning and analyzing. His idea of how to engage employees is not by making a speech but rather by leading a company-wide hackathon, and empowering employees to work on projects they are passionate about. This approach to engagement has helped drive Microsoft's expansion into cloud services and AI (Nadella, 2017). As is evident in the case of Microsoft, creating a culture of OC engagement requires more than completing an annual employee survey and then leaving managers on their own, hoping that they will learn something from the survey results that will change their daily behaviour. Instead it needs leadership to develop a culture that enables OC engagement.

This requires leaders to: create meaningful change; create and share a strategic narrative; make and build sense of change; and provide proactive leadership and energy. Each of these critical leadership enablers of OC engagement is discussed next.

Leadership enablers of OC engagement

Creating meaningful change

US President John F. Kennedy once met an employee mopping the floors at NASA headquarters long after normal hours and asked, "Why are you working so late?" The employee replied, "because I'm not mopping the floors, I'm putting a man on the moon." This story offers an important lesson in people finding meaning in their work and consequently in OC. Classical theories of motivation, such as Maslow (1968), propose that people need work that is meaningful and purposeful. Individuals seek meaning through personal accomplishments by associating their existence with something bigger or something that is perceived as more significant than themselves and by fulfilling purpose, value, efficacy and self-worth (Baumeister, 1991). People need to feel that they matter and their contributions have meaning.

Stakeholders need to understand the need for change, to feel as though it will make a difference and that the change is important for them and for others. A perception that the change has a clear rationale, purpose and meaning provides connection to others, and allows an individual to feel a part of something.

Meaning is not just derived from the recognition that the organization can give but from an individual feeling that what they are doing is making an important contribution and that what they will gain is worthwhile and relative to the cost of their effort. Employees who perceive a fit between themselves and proposed change are more likely to find meaning in OC. This is illustrated in the self-concept-based theory of motivation proposed by Shamir (1991) to explain why people seek meaning and ultimately become engaged at work. Self-concept–job fit refers to congruence between an individual's feelings of their self-perception as derived from their work performance and their ideal self. Their performance on the job creates a self-perception of how they are doing, what their knowledge, skills and abilities are in performing the job. If this self-perception matches or is consistent with their identity or self-concept of how they should be able to perform on the job, they have self-concept–job fit and lack of congruence is a lack of self-concept–job fit. Scroggins (2008) found self-concept–job fit was positively related to meaningful change. So when individuals feel that they have self-concept fit with OC then the change is meaningful to them. This perspective suggests that OC engagement comes from within the employee, and can be encouraged through an organizational culture that enables and helps employees align their behaviour with their self-concept.

Empirical support for the relationship between meaningful change and engagement is shown in a study of earthquake survivors in China (Wang et al., 2011). Survivors from the earthquake reported that their efforts in providing post-quake relief and reconstruction was meaningful work, which gave them energy (they explicitly reported not being exhausted by this) and made them feel engaged. Such findings are supportive of the subjective definitions of meaning, where deriving meaning from OC is about having purpose or direction (Park, 2010) that may result from an individual seeing their contribution to the achievement of changes. Employees who work for organizations that do not consider employees' need for meaning about OC will inhibit their employees' ability to become engaged (Chalofsky & Krishna, 2009). Failing to provide a clear purpose or justifying the need for the change may result in employees struggling to understand what makes the change meaningful to them and lead to disengagement.

Leaders can influence stakeholder perceptions of meaningful change. To do so they need to create a shared sense of purpose and direction that provides meaning for employees and other stakeholders. This involves engaging employees and other stakeholders internally and externally around a common purpose – which answers the need for change and enables individuals to internalize what it will mean for them. This is highlighted by Tamkin and colleagues (2010: 4) who say:

> what is clear is that outstanding leaders have great clarity on how to do things, of how to translate what is on the inside to create impact on the outside. They have a toolkit to create change and plug away at it understanding that growing individual and team capability takes time and effort.

To create a credible and authentic purpose of OC involves developing a strategic narrative and case for change.

Strategic narrative

A strategic narrative is a key leadership enabler of OC engagement since it creates clarity about the need for OC and how stakeholders can contribute to it. This means providing "a strong strategic narrative which has widespread ownership and commitment from managers and employees at all levels" (MacLeod & Clarke, 2009: 75). To create the narrative for change and bring the narrative into reality involves crafting strategies and ensuring that people are able to collaborate in the alignment and adaptability of this process; something which Hooper and Potter (2000) call emotional alignment. The importance of such alignment is emphasized in a report by the World Economic Forum which notes that alignment galvanizes people around the aspirations and objectives of change. The report goes on to say that adaptability is needed alongside alignment for "alignment without adaptability results in bureaucratic, sclerotic organizations that can't get out of their own way . . . Adaptability without alignment results in chaos and resources wasted on duplicate and conflicting efforts" (Hooper & Potter, 2000: 10). A key element required for the alignment and adaptability of the strategic narrative is clarity. Clarity ensures that the purpose is clear for stakeholders since they need to understand what is being proposed, how they can influence it and how it will affect them. As Proctor & Gamble (P&G) CEO Alan G. Lafley says, clarity is important because employees have so many things going on in the operation of their daily business that they do not always take the time to stop, think and internalize (cited in Aitken & Keller, 2007).

In sum, leaders need to create a strategic narrative about OC to help stakeholders to understand what it means. Without a strategic narrative, particularly at the start, transformations can stall or fail to gain traction. A strategic narrative also helps people sustain their energy throughout a transition since it gives them the resolve to continue moving forward, rather than return to the status quo. The more people share and understand the purpose early in the initial development of a transformation, the better. This means that leaders need to share the strategic narrative, believe in it and get other individuals involved in creating it, so that it has clarity which helps stakeholders to make sense of it.

Sense-making

A key enabler for leadership in developing OC engagement is to understand the way in which individuals make sense of change. Theorists adopting this perspective suggest that the world does not consist of events that are meaningful by themselves, rather, organizational members interact with and affirm the existence of events, casting them in a particular light through the process of sense-making (Dutton, 2003). Weick (2000) describes how engaging in sense-making involves constructing, filtering, framing, creating facticity and rendering the subjective into something more tangible. Sense-making is a process where people give meaning to experience. It is a retrospective process that uses evidence from past events to construct a storyline that makes sense in the present. In other words, individuals will refer to their past experiences of OC to make sense of proposed OC initiatives.

An individual's interpretation of change is unique and is affected by the way they process information about it. The brain can only absorb a limited amount of detail through the senses in any one moment so to avoid becoming overwhelmed, the brain filters information, in effect taking mental shortcuts to process information which can lead to biased thinking about OC. Such biases comprise confirmation, status quo, availability and bandwagon effect (Sidhu, 2015):

- *Confirmation bias* is a tendency for people to pay attention only to information that confirms their beliefs and to ignore evidence that indicates otherwise. This may lead people to argue against the need for change.
- *Status quo bias* is a preference to keep things the way they are and to avoid change. People with this bias will not agree that the change is needed, or they may say that they agree but show inertia and take little action to make the change happen.
- *Availability bias* is a tendency to perceive the more memorable or easily available information as the most significant. For example, instances of changes not going so well, or failing and being negative about future changes.
- *Bandwagon effect* refers to the fact that the more people come to believe something, the more others want to hop on the bandwagon. For instance, teams who oppose change or are cynical about it start to influence others and opposition or cynicism will spread.

The uncertainty and complexity of OC requires individuals to be able to make sense of it. This involves the complex interactions between different entities being carefully addressed in a coordinated and collaborative setting. Issues do not always present themselves with black and white solutions, nor are they always amenable to rational and overly logical thinking. Instead they come as complex, interrelated sets of factors in which action in one sphere is likely to lead to unintended consequences in another. Individuals will look to leaders to help them make sense of the need for change and to help them engage in a purposeful way. This requires proactive leadership.

Proactive leadership

Leaders need to enable stakeholders to make sense of the complexity and uncertainty of OC by enacting proactive leadership. Leaders often start out enthusiastic and full of bold promises about how they will lead OC and engage people with it, but their enthusiasm can often fade when something more urgent, glamorous or susceptible to quick wins comes along. This may be a rather cynical view, but it is a reality that other issues may well take precedence over OC engagement. To avoid a lack of on-going OC engagement, proactive leadership needs to be prevalent not only at the start of a transformation but throughout its implementation until it becomes a sustainable part of how the organization operates. Activities that make proactive leadership effective are varied. This is evident in research by the Kenexa Research Institute (2008), which investigated engagement in various countries including Australia, Brazil, Canada, China, India, the Netherlands, Russia, Saudi Arabia and the United Kingdom. The research suggests that employees are engaged by leaders who: inspire confidence in the future; respect and appreciate their employees; and display a genuine responsibility to employees. In other words, they need proactive leadership.

In my book on *Sustaining Change in Organizations* (Hodges & Gill, 2014), the activities of proactive leadership are defined as entailing: envisioning and communicating a desirable future as a result of the change; promoting a clear rationale for the need for change; providing intelligent strategies for the change effort; enabling those involved in managing change to be able to do what needs to be done, and engaging all those concerned to want to do what needs to be done. Such activities are visible signs of on-going proactive leadership that can help to build OC engagement.

Role of management

Along with leadership, management is at the heart of OC engagement because while OC engagement must be well led, it must also be effectively managed. However, the literature on OC is often positioned from the point of view of leaders and ignores the perspective of those who are directly affected by the decision to change, have to implement it, and have to manage others through it. Line managers are, however, of vital importance to OC engagement. This assertion is supported by a number of studies. For example, research by Judge and colleagues (2001) indicates that individual engagement and performance is closely tied to how satisfied employees are with their line manager. So although leadership is important, it is not alone a sufficient condition for successful OC engagement.

In general, there are two approaches to the management of OC engagement: the conscious and the unconscious. Both may involve the application of any of the conventional approaches to managing engagement with change. The conscious approach can be seen as continuous, proactive and driven by awareness, choice and decision. Such an approach should not merely concern one individual manager's approach to OC engagement, but rather form the foundation of the organization's management approach to OC engagement. Alternatively, the unconscious approach can be perceived as discontinuous, reactive and driven by organizational crisis, fear and chance. For instance, people may argue that, 'a lot of the change efforts we see have a feeling of despair'. The initiators of unconscious OC engagement often know it is not going to work, that it is too late but are trying to do something about the situation. Owing to the nature of these two different approaches, it may be suggested that the former approach provides a greater probability of successful OC engagement because active management enables employees to be psychologically ready for change, while the latter provides greater probability of failure, because by the time change is initiated it is already too late to engage stakeholders. Consequently, management needs to be ready to generate and nurture OC engagement as and when required.

So how can managers respond to the OC engagement challenge? Traditional approaches highlight the need for OC engagement to be managed – it must be defined, planned, organized, directed, implemented, monitored, controlled and measured. Along with this there is the need to focus on the behaviours required from people and to create the work environment to foster those behaviours. None of this can be done in isolation, managers need to link in with leaders in order to engage others in the change.

The interaction between leaders and managers is important for creating strategic alignment for OC engagement. While leaders define the purpose and set the direction for change, managers must translate the purpose of OC into something that is more tangible and personal for individuals and address the issues that might prevent or inhibit individuals from engaging with the change. The role of managers is critical in connecting the purpose of the change at the organizational level to the reality that people have to change at the local operational level, such as departmental and/or team. Yet managers are often brought in to work on change initiatives once the business case has been approved and implementation is about to start, or when it has already started but in order to ensure participation and build support, the involvement of managers should commence well before the start of any transformation is confirmed. They should be involved in developing the business case for the change, so that they can provide their views on which ideas will work in practice, and the feasibility of different approaches. If this is not possible, then at the very least, managers should be informed about the work that is being done on the change and what they will need to support and implement it. Inevitably, this must all be done whilst managers maintain performance standards and business as usual.

The challenges of managing and motivating staff to engage with OC can be made more difficult by a lack of management capacity, particularly due to wide spans of control and widely distributed workforces. This often means that there is less time for managers to get to know individuals and to find out what makes them engage with OC. There may also be capability issues if line managers lack effective people management skills; particularly if individuals are relatively new to management then they may not have experience or knowledge of how to engage others with change. There is a need, therefore, to develop the capabilities and capacity required for managers to effectively manage OC engagement.

Effective management of OC engagement

The effective management of OC engagement is about making it happen. This involves managing OC engagement at three levels: (i) self, (ii) others, and (iii) organization. For each level managers need to ask the following key questions:

(i)   Self: How do I engage with change? What do I find challenging about change? What do I need to do differently? How does my behaviour impact on the engagement of those around me? How do I ensure we have the capability for engaging with change throughout the organization?

(ii) Others: How can I help others to engage with change? How should I acknowledge and respond to the different feelings and reactions people have to change? How do I build relationships and persuade stakeholders to support the changes I am managing?

(iii) Organization: How do I engage internal and external stakeholders? How do I manage engagement with change in the context of the power and politics of the organizational culture?

Line managers need to be able to engage with each of these three levels effectively as they are responsible for making the people they manage feel comfortable with OC and encourage them and other stakeholders to engage with it. The likelihood of a manager being able to implement and manage change successfully without people engaging with the change is arguably like a toddler trying to walk before they are able to crawl – possible for some but impossible for most.

Ineffective management of OC engagement

The root of OC disengagement is poor management, whereby employees do not have good working relationships with their managers and are denied the opportunity to communicate and have some involvement in decision-making, let alone receive information about changes from their managers. As Bardwick (2007) rightly says, when people work for a manager who does not care about people as individuals, focuses on their weaknesses and not on their strengths and does not communicate or listen to their input, then employees will be neither committed nor engaged. They are much more likely to feel resentful, frustrated or under-valued.

To avoid this, traditional methods of management for OC engagement may be considered, however they are increasingly open to question. There is growing awareness that command and control management methods are counterproductive and that other conventional methods of motivation, such as pay for performance, are becoming exhausted or even ineffectual. As Holbeche and Matthews (2012) point out, many managers struggle to rise to the challenge of getting employees to deliver just that bit more for the organization. This has led to criticism of traditional management technique. Hamel and Breen (2007) are not alone in suggesting that management is out of date and that a paradigm shift is needed. Goffee and Jones (2009) also argue that with the dependence of organizations for their success on workers, traditional approaches will not work. 'Old' styles of management, based on a convention of low trust and high control, fit uncomfortably against a paradigm of workers who are expected to be accountable and empowered, and willing and able to engage in OC. So as with leadership there is a need to reframe management within the context of OC engagement.

Engaging managers with OC

Organizations are in need of effective managers who care and who are seen to be committed to engaging their staff with OC. Only then can managers encourage employees into putting discretionary effort into changes at work. However, managers themselves also need to be engaged before they can engage their staff, for there are many change initiatives that have "crashed upon the rocks of line management" (Lawrence, 2014: 110). Managers must be engaged with OC in order to be able to positively influence the engagement of others.

The engagement of line managers is important because they are usually the recipients as well as the purveyors of change. For example, structural changes such as downsizing and delayering often mean that line management are asked to exercise greater spans of control and do more work, while at the same time they may be experiencing greater uncertainty about their own job. If the leadership team fails to engage line managers in change, then managers may exercise their power by cooperating to the minimum extent they feel they can get away with, focusing instead on protecting themselves and their own job and team (Thomas & Hardy, 2011). This can result in what Lawrence (2014) calls the 'frozen line' where managers disengage from OC for various reasons such as: they feel that they do not have the skills to successfully implement the strategy; they doubt the potential effectiveness of the change; or they may perceive a conflict between the goals of OC and their own personal goals. As a result they might not support the changes and procrastinate in communicating and implementing decisions or even directly sabotage and build opposition against the decisions made. If managers aren't engaged, it's unlikely that employees will respond to any efforts to engage them. In order to create a highly engaged environment managers must be engaged. They need to be able to understand the rationale for OC and be able to communicate it to employees. If line management is involved in discussions about OC from its inception, then they have the potential to act as advocates and facilitators of change.

They must know how to develop and motivate their staff to engage with change and understand the needs of different staff, such as older as well as younger generations. Managers need to be able to create a positive working environment. Unless managers do these things they will struggle to build relationships with their staff and engage them in OC.

Building relationships and providing support

The quality of the relationship that an employee has with their immediate manager is an influential factor driving OC engagement. Research demonstrates that engagement is a reciprocal construct which reflects the state of the employment relationship between employees and their manager (Blizzard, 2003). Reciprocity theory lends support to the fact that the way in which line managers perceive their working conditions and themselves may influence how they behave towards their staff. This is illustrated in a study by Winslow and colleagues (2009) which indicates that the degree to which line managers receive support from their peers predicts the degree to which their employees experience receiving support from their line managers. In other words, the degree to which line managers feel supported themselves is related to the support their staff experience receiving from them.

Employees have been found to be most engaged when they have good relationships at work. Research by Zak (2017) indicates that when people intentionally build social ties at work, their performance improves. A study of software engineers in Silicon Valley found that those who connected with others and helped them with their projects not only earned the respect and trust of their peers but were also more productive themselves. It is important, therefore, for managers not to have a purely transactional relationship between themselves and their employees, based on the fulfilment of agreed standards, but to supplement this with a supportive and relational style of management. A supportive environment fostered by managers encourages individuals to feel safer to engage themselves more fully in OC, try out innovative ways of doing things and discuss ideas and issues. Providing support, so that individuals feel valued and involved, can create reciprocal mutuality and build trust.

Building and maintaining trust

Trust is a critical element of the social exchange relationship and an antecedent of OC engagement (see Chapter 6 for further discussion on antecedents). Trust develops through a social exchange in which employees interpret the actions of management and reciprocate in kind. According to Blau (1964: 315), ". . . the gradual expansion of the exchange permits the partners to prove their trustworthiness to each other. Processes of social exchange, consequently, generate trust". However, in some organizations there is a growing trust deficit between people at the bottom and the top of the hierarchy creating what Saks (2006) calls an engagement gap. Where there is no trust, there can be no OC engagement. People are unlikely to engage or surface their concerns about proposed change in a context where they do not trust leadership or management. O'Toole and Bennis (2009) suggest that there is potential for catastrophic consequences when employees possess critical knowledge but fail to bring that knowledge forward due to a lack of trust. People are more likely to provide information to people they trust. Not only are they likely to be more motivated to share and discuss information, they are also more likely to contribute information through formal communication channels if they trust that the information will not be distorted, or misused. Trust can, therefore, influence the quality of decisions about OC by increasing the amount and accuracy of information that is available.

To generate OC engagement, trust has to be built which involves not only leaders and managers keeping promises, but also keeping appropriate boundaries and being sensitive to social and cultural cues. Trustworthy managers are fair, for instance, preventing 'change creep' which results in engaged employees who show discretionary effort ending up having to do more and more work related to OC. Building trust involves managers having the ability to ethically do the right or best thing; being guided by some principles of benevolence or well-meaning, especially in treating people with respect; having integrity and honesty; and being predicable (Hope-Hailey et al., 2012). When a CEO breaks a promise, as in the case of Kraft's Irene Rosenfeld when she reneged on her pre-merger pledge not to close Cadbury's chocolate factory in Somerdale, UK, trust takes a beating. Trust is fragile and can be difficult to re-build so leaders and managers need to constantly work at engendering it in order to encourage OC engagement.

Role of employees

While leadership and management have the primary responsibility for creating OC engagement, employees too have their part to play as OC engagement flows up, down and across an organization. Although much organizational effort appears to be based on the belief that employees are not responsible adults and they need to be 'managed' into OC engagement, we disagree with this view. Instead we support the organizational effectiveness view that highlights the importance of adult-to-adult employment relationships characterized by inclusivity and equity, both of which are discussed further in Chapter 8.

Instead of aligning people to the organization by shaping them to organizational requirements, while treating them as expendable resources, organizational effectiveness focuses on building trust and enablement with the employee deal tailored as much as possible to the needs of individuals. This means a shift to inclusivity and mutuality with change OC. It also means that the leadership for OC engagement is not just at the top of the organization but more distributed and collaborative across the organization.

Employees are active agents in the OC engagement process. Engagement with change does not just happen to employees, but rather employees actively create engagement experiences. As Grant and Ashford (2008: 3) say, "employees do not just let life happen to them. Rather, they try to affect, shape, curtail, expand, and temper what happens in their lives." This highlights that employees are by no means passive actors in organizations but instead employees may be proactive in mobilizing their own job challenges and job resources. One way of doing this is for employees to actively design the tasks and social interactions comprising their work.

Job crafting

The practice of employees shaping their jobs is referred to as job crafting which is defined as an action where "the physical and cognitive changes individuals make in the task or relational boundaries of their work" alters employees' work identities and meanings, that is, understanding of the purpose of work (Wrzesniewski & Dutton, 2001: 179). In this definition, physical changes refer to changes in the form, scope or number of job tasks, whereas cognitive changes refer to changing how an individual sees their job. For instance, a maintenance technician may craft the scope of their job by taking on additional tasks such as proactively helping newcomers to learn the job. Changing task boundaries refers to making amendments to the tasks of the job whereas changing relational boundaries refers to exercising discretion over which colleagues employees interact with while doing their job. By changing the nature of relationships, people can reframe the purpose, and experience, of their work so that it is more meaningful. The meaningfulness of their work is thus a product of their relations with both those who benefit from that work and those who confirm its importance. Studies have framed job crafting within the Job Demands-Resources (JD-R) theory suggesting that employees craft their jobs by regulating the level of job demands and job resources, depending on their needs (for example, Tims & Bakker, 2010).

Job crafting behaviours have been found to have favourable effects on engagement in changing environments (Petrou et al., 2012). Importantly job crafting has been found to relate to openness to OC that is the willingness to accept specific changes (Wanberg & Banas, 2000). Research also suggests that employees who job craft to modify their job resources, for example increase social support by interacting more with co-workers socially and restructure job tasks to increase autonomy, variety, and opportunities for development, do report higher levels of engagement (Tims et al., 2013). In a study of Greek employees, Demerouti and colleagues (2017) found that employees who are able to craft their jobs and to 'fit' their jobs to their strengths, skills and preferences are likely to feel better despite the overall negative climate, and consequently are more willing to adapt and be more open to change. In contrast, empirical studies indicate that individuals who refrain from using proactive strategies, like job crafting, experience more distress and health problems (Torkelson & Muhonen, 2003), implying that they may be less open to engage with change. Through the proactive behaviours of job crafting, individuals may become more open to OC and adapt more successfully to these changes and therefore engage with them.

Job crafting is not, however, a panacea since it is not always effective and requires attention to whether those in the job are ready for the change and whether the change is best for those in the job. That is, job crafting is appropriate sometimes but not always. Crafting jobs does, however, challenge employees, increase their motivation and stimulate learning and development. It can be seen as a positive action that employees take, with the support from HR, to develop and sustain their OC engagement. Such proactive approaches capture the importance of employees taking the initiative to anticipate and create changes in how work is performed and plays a key role in OC engagement since engaged workers can transfer their engagement to others, especially in their immediate environment.

The important role played by HR in facilitating employee engagement is further illustrated in the following case (Box 7.3).

Box 7.3 HR change management in Hitachi

Written by Stephen Pierce,
Deputy Managing Director and Chief HR Officer, Hitachi Europe

Hitachi is a company with a strong culture and values developed from its origins more than 100 years ago in Japan. Today it is one of the world's biggest corporations with over 300,000 staff and a focus on social innovation with a wide range of products and services from trains to power stations, financial services to consulting, information technologies to construction machinery, all underpinned by expertise in IoT and data analytics.

For many decades the business was concentrated in Japan but to compete with other global companies it was essential to grow revenues outside Japan. This growth needed to be underpinned by transformation of processes, practices and systems and HR has led this global management challenge to change a company with Japanese traditions and a culture of diverse, autonomous businesses.

The start point for the journey in 2011 was developing an HR database – not perhaps the most attractive and compelling start point but we realised that until we knew who works for us, where they work, what they do and their background and expertise, we could not build a talent strategy and change our organisation. Up until that point we had headcount data but we could not report to our executives on the information that would help underpin decision-making and develop our ambitious HR agenda for change. We had no systematic way of tracking employees, evaluating performance or identifying future leaders – but today we do.

The database was the first step on a roadmap to identify the changes required which would create a clear competitive edge for Hitachi in talent management. It started with the basics that already existed in many of the group companies where there were some leading edge processes and practices but which were inconsistently applied across the group. There was plenty to work on to develop new, best practice approaches but it soon became clear that the challenge was not just this but also their implementation across many diverse businesses and in a culture where there would be no mandate for change.

Creating change where there is no mandate is difficult and one where the business looked to HR for leadership. The senior management support change but the organisational culture would not allow them to mandate it and leaders of each group company have the authority to make their own decisions. So it became clear that while continuing to work on the platform of best practices HR needed to focus on change management and influence the key stakeholders to engage with them if they were to succeed. We had to switch from doing the right thing ourselves to getting people to want to be involved and do the right thing themselves. This meant we were not masters of our own destiny but that if we could engage the key influencers sufficiently, we could create something much greater than the corporate team could do by itself, and change an organisation of over 300,000 people as it started its second century since its foundation. We had all seen solutions and products that have been well designed but which no one wants to use and they fall into decline and we could not allow that to happen here.

Engagement with stakeholders was a key part of the strategy, starting with a partnership between HR colleagues in Tokyo communicating with parent companies and those in the Regional Head Offices interacting with the businesses in the regions. This sounds simple in theory as we tried to meet with the key influencers in Japan who would agree to global implementation, and with those in the regions who would be champions of change in their own businesses. But in practice the process was much more complex as, for example, some had recently made changes so it was difficult for them to change direction again or the cost of change was felt to be too great.

Through our engagement strategy we wanted to create a culture of change, and it took time to build relationships, sell change and ensure participation. The corporate HR team embarked on an engagement plan; meeting with HR and business leaders across group companies, talking about their business issues and explaining how the new HR practices could make a difference and provide solutions. In doing this we realised that we shared many of the same issues – finding talent, ensuring we develop and retain our key people and so on, but without proactive engagement we could not listen, learn and find solutions. So we had to engage and build relationships in the right way, always ensuring a business focus.

There is no doubt that showing financial benefit is an important way to encourage involvement so our change journey did not just include changing HR practices but also reviewing HR service providers. Historically group companies had bought services separately which meant they paid higher prices so we worked together to create economies of scale, including buying employee benefits so that we could buy similar or better at a lower price. Providing an ROI for the time invested in change management created an incentive and interest for involvement in the areas where a financial return is not so clear or short term and helped create the culture of change we were striving to develop.

As more and more companies were involved in decision-making and buying-into company-wide solutions, it became clear that not every company could move at the same speed and for practical reasons we could not implement change at the same speed everywhere. This enabled us to pilot change in some cases and allowed those with the strongest business need or commitment to participate and demonstrate the benefits to others. This was especially helpful for some of the systems-based solutions where testing with a smaller group made sense before implementing it more widely. In the first year of our global performance management system we launched it to 5,000 staff, to 38,000 in year two and then to over 100,000 the following year.

The tireless focus on engagement means everyone in the corporate HR team has objectives around engaging with group companies; we run regular conferences, training and other events to keep all our companies informed and involved. The benefits of this go far beyond our HR change management agenda and are building a platform of strong relationships with the main influencers to deliver further change in the future.

Some achievements so far:

The programme of change started with implementing a global database as a source of consistent employee data to support management decision-making. There were soon over 250,000 employees in the database and Mercer job grading had been introduced and covered over 90 per cent of management roles. This creates an understanding of how roles differ and makes it easier to identify development roles and other opportunities. The global performance management system was piloted to measure performance in a consistent way, set clear organisational goals that cascaded down to individual level and introduced new compensation approaches. We launched a global careers site on which we have advertised thousands of roles, and we have a talent pool of tens of thousands of potential candidates who have registered their CVs. This has given Hitachi staff better visibility of job vacancies and has encouraged movement between group companies. It has also provided a coherent picture of Hitachi for external candidates and helped define our employer brand.

Participation in the new global employee survey has grown to 170,000, providing a measure of engagement by comparing with an external benchmark to identify our best practices and opportunities for improvement, and 300,000 staff use the 'Hitachi University' e-learning platform. The project to reduce employee benefits costs has made significant savings and payrolls are being consolidated with the same objective.

Some of our learning:

1   Engagement with the key stakeholders is critical for success – those who will champion, support and make change happen. The start point needs to be getting the big players on board – a small company can take as much or more time than a big player but provides a much lower return. It is really an 80:20 approach, which means not everyone can be the same level of priority for focus and resources.

2   Consider every possible way to get buy-in. For successful change management we need to consider them all – consult, discuss, listen, involve, pilot, solve problems, build relationships and so on.

3   We have to answer the question 'what's in it for me?' and being able to answer that question for businesses can open the door for buy-in. HR needs to have a strong business understanding and a financial mindset and this has implications for development and recruitment of HR staff.

4   Tenacity and resilience are important competencies. They are not perhaps always on the list when we think about what makes someone successful in HR but a tireless focus on change combined with the emotional intelligence to involve and engage others in the right way can make a real difference.

5   Create momentum and don't lose it – a partial solution which can be further developed is better than waiting for perfection and the momentum can provide the quick wins that can be communicated to show progress and create more change.

6   HR can never communicate too much – employee surveys tell us that staff always want to know more and we can sometimes assume that because we know and understand something others do too.

A continuing journey. The journey is continuing with a focus on global talent and the new approaches are becoming business as usual. With the right strategies in place to engage employees and implement effective change, this global approach to talent management is creating tangible business results: reduced recruitment costs and employee benefit costs for example. Some benefits are harder to measure but just as important, such as the attraction, retention and engagement of talent as these will underpin the continuing success of the organisation. Ultimately, it will be the financial impact on the business itself which will be the measure of success and Hitachi now has more than 50 per cent of its revenues outside Japan and its global scope is continuing to grow.

Engagement contagion

OC engagement is contagious and may spread from one individual to another, but also from one team member to another. Engagement contagion is the transfer of positive (or negative) experiences and incorporates emotional and cognitive contagions (Barsade, 2002). Cognitive contagion is the shared creation of meaning, an understanding of how to make and build sense of OC, while drawing on compatible or shared knowledge structures. Cognitive contagion is similar to emotional contagion in that an individual can adopt, synchronize or absorb the cognitive approach, beliefs and judgement patterns of others, in essence catching their perspective and way of thinking to create meaning of OC. However, cognitive contagion differs from emotional contagion in that it is not transferred via mimicry. Instead, cognitive contagion is caught through the process of sharing judgements, ideas and thoughts about OC. Cognitive contagion is passed or transmitted through the behavioural and communication cues of others. Emotional contagion like cognitive contagion can occur in teams where members of a team or individuals who work together influence the moods and judgements of those around them. Emotional contagion infuses in others an emotional response, influencing cognitions, attitudes and behaviours. Through their interactions with others at work, engaged employees can transmit their positive emotions, their physiological arousal associated with their emotions and their sense of meaning and interpretation of the purpose of OC. Rubin and colleagues (2009) found that leaders who are highly cynical about change convey their cynicism to their employees and this contributes to them being cynical and also to a decrease in their engagement. In contrast, employees who work with individuals who are engaged catch engagement through the mechanism of engagement contagion. Bakker and colleagues (2006) found that team members report higher levels of engagement when their team colleagues also report higher levels of engagement. Unless someone deliberately runs away from, avoids, argues with, fights or purposefully ignores and resists engaged employees, then the emotions of engaged employees are visible and can infect others. Even sceptical co-workers or colleagues who question the validity of the engaged employee's thoughts may become engaged themselves by diving into a heated debate or disagreement about the ideas, demonstrating their own fully focused and embraced attention on their view point.

The contagion effect of OC engagement is important for managers as they function as role models and through their behaviour can influence the engagement of their employees in a number of ways. A reverse contagion effect can also take place: just as managers may influence the OC engagement of their staff, employees may also influence that of their managers. For instance, employees' levels of OC engagement have been found to be related to managers' self-efficacy which in turn predicted line managers' performance (Luthans & Peterson, 2002). However, not everyone will catch OC engagement from others. Dynamic social impact theory (Latané & L'Herrou, 1996) suggests that when people work together, even minimally, there is a natural tendency towards: (i) consolidation – as the proportion of the people who hold a minority perspective shrinks, the diversity in the group shrinks; (ii) clustering – people become more similar to those near them than to those farther away; and (iii) continuing diversity – a few holding minority views persist within the group. Evidence from research (Latané & L'Herrou, 1996) supports these natural tendencies indicating that shared cognitions and behaviours are a natural and common phenomena when people participate in teams or work with others. There may be several reasons why OC engagement contagion is not fully passed onto others. Some reasons may be motivational, situational or dispositional while some people may purposefully choose to remain uninfected. Those individuals who do not catch OC engagement to its fullest extent may be motivated to deflect the emotional or behavioural influences because they have instrumental reasons for doing so, such as political battles or retaliatory behaviour or they may not be convinced about the need for change. If people have a reason for not wanting to engage with OC, they may be less inclined to pay attention to the engagement of others with the change or to the thoughts or comments from others about the change.

Summary

Leadership and management play important roles in creating a culture for effective OC engagement. There is, however, a need to reimage the leadership model for OC engagement. Traditional leadership styles are slowly being dismantled in favour of distributed and collaborative styles, although many organizations seem to be slow to adopt these leadership forms. Wheatley and Frieze (2011) describe this evolution of leadership as the journey from hero to host. Heroic leadership, they say, rests on the illusion that someone can be in control, yet we live in a world of complex systems whose very existence means they are inherently uncontrollable. By distributing power and decision-making about OC more widely, and particularly among those who have the most to gain, organizations can respond to the complexity and uncertainty of change by enacting collaborative leadership. This style of leadership can be deeply uncomfortable and can even produce feelings of vulnerability, particularly for leaders who are used to knowing the answers and being in control. However, the traditional transformational and transaction models to leadership need to be reframed by bringing together groups of stakeholders and allowing them to create a collective identity and shared understanding of change. Creating the momentum for this requires investment and a shift in the practice of leadership so that it is collaborative and incorporates a stakeholder perspective of OC engagement based on mutual reciprocity. The reciprocal nature of this relationship requires that employees and other stakeholders are active players in managing their own OC engagement.

Engagement with change also requires positive support from management. It is managers, given the nature of their role, who are in the best position to directly affect engagement on a daily basis at an individual and team level. This requires the reversal of traditional command and control approaches to management. It means that line managers have to create the motivation and energy a team needs for engagement and make space for stakeholders to effectively engage. It also involves translating the rationale and purpose for OC into what it means for front-line staff, identifying the implications of the change and developing the capability of the individuals and teams to deal with changes. As it is mainly, though not exclusively, through managers that employees have a relationship with the organization, managers should focus on building mutuality and social support. How line managers manage people, and the relations they build with them, impacts on levels of OC engagement. Line managers play a key role as facilitators of OC engagement in making it possible for other people to do what they must do and what they want to do and in boosting engagement levels of the people who work for them.

So while effective leadership of OC engagement is about enabling it to happen, management involves making it happen in a mutually beneficial way. Both play a vital part, along with employees and other stakeholders, in fostering OC engagement.

Implications

There are a number of practical implications which arise from the discussion in this chapter.

- Review and redefine the role of the leadership of OC engagement. Consider this role as showing the way and helping or inducing others to pursue it. How, and to what extent, do you 'show the way' in a change initiative? How do you help others to pursue it? What do you understand by engaging others to pursue the change? How do you do this? How effective is it? How can you do all this better?
- Create meaningful change. Review how connected the rationale for OC is to the activities and meaning of it for all stakeholders. The rationale and purpose of change can contribute to OC success if they are orientated towards the embodiment of concrete activities that people can use to choose their own actions and construct meaning. How can you improve this?
- Understand and practise effective management of the OC engagement process. This comprises understanding that OC engagement is a long-term and on-going process that requires continued interactions over time in order to generate obligations and a state of reciprocal interdependence; and finding out what resources and support are most desired by employees and most likely to create a sense of obligation that is returned with greater levels of OC engagement. How well do you do so? What do you need to improve? How can you do so? What do you need to do to resolve any areas of doubt?
- Identify whether and how you engage stakeholders in OC. Review whether and how you engage people in the change effort by influencing, motivating and

inspiring them to want to do what needs to be done, to devote discretionary effort to it willingly, even eagerly. To what extent do you know what motivates and inspires each of your team members, both collectively and individually, in their everyday work and in times of uncertainty and change? How do you use your position and personal power? How can you do all this better?

Chapter 8

Fostering OC engagement

Learning outcomes

After reading this chapter you will be able to:

- appreciate that OC engagement has to be fostered and maintained;
- discuss factors that generate engagement with change;
- identify the roles of stakeholders in developing OC engagement;
- apply key principles and practices for building and sustaining OC engagement.

Introduction

The idea that employees are either engaged or not, and that once engaged, the impact on performance is linear (a bit more engagement equals just that bit more performance) is of course overly simple and yet much of the practitioner literature presents this picture. OC engagement has to be fostered and maintained, which is a shared responsibility between leaders and managers, as well as employees and other stakeholders. There is, however, a lack of clarity about what organizations 'do' to generate OC engagement. In an attempt to address this issue the aim of this chapter is to identify some key principles and practices underpinning the way that OC engagement can be generated and sustained. We argue that the antecedents of OC engagement, discussed in the previous chapter, can be influenced through the following principles: inclusivity; connectivity; transparency; co-creation; equity and empathy. These principles provide ways for stakeholders to connect with change effectively.

Generic approaches

The promise of OC engagement is that it puts the stakeholder centre stage, but what then follows has to be a careful analysis of the factors that lead individuals to be engaged with change. There are, however, considerable variations in the views of authors about how OC engagement can be fostered. As Robinson and colleagues (2004: 26) rightly say, "there is no easy answer as far as engagement is concerned – no simple pulling of one or two levers to raise engagement levels". There are no shortcuts to building and maintaining OC engagement. A one size fits all approach is unlikely to be effective, as levels of OC engagement may vary according to its antecedents.

Engaging people in a change effort is challenging and demands attention. Senior executives see employee disengagement as one of the biggest threats facing their businesses but 90 per cent of them simply choose to ignore the problems caused by disengaged staff (Amble, 2010). Cynics may ask if this is due to ignorance, admitted or otherwise, of how to deal with it. Yet the literature is awash with generic checklists for improving OC engagement. Most action from consultants focuses on the use of suggestion schemes, recognition rewards and getting employees to buy into corporate values. For example, Lavigna (2013) advocates the following for improving OC engagement: provide strong and stable leadership; support employee development; articulate goals and values of the organization; emphasize the organization's vision; involve employees in decision-making; encourage risk-taking; encourage higher levels of education; accommodate unique employee needs; set clear performance expectations; and treat employees fairly. In a similar fashion, Blanchard (2012) provides a list advocating that engagement can be developed by: providing a compelling argument for change in the form of unequivocal information linking it with business performance; clarifying how individuals' efforts to make and sustain change will contribute; showing individuals how refusal to engage with change and take personal development seriously will have consequences; providing a steady dose of partnering to provide clear direction, conversation, support and accountability over a long period of time; and asking rather than telling. Such checklists are obviously good things to do but are couched at such a level of generality that they do not provide a clear basis of action for fostering OC engagement. They are also worrying since they view individuals, particularly employees in a passive role, with engagement seen as something that is driven by the organization, rather than something that is also under the control of employees and other stakeholders. Instead of OC engagement being something that is done *to* stakeholders we propose that it is done *with* them. To enable this we suggest the following principles for enhancing OC engagement.

Principles of OC engagement

The key principles we propose to help build and maintain OC engagement (see Figure 8.1) are:

- Inclusivity
- Connectivity
- Transparency
- Co-creation
- Equity
- Empathy

Inclusivity

Inclusivity enhances stakeholders' propensity to engage with OC. Research shows that being included in decisions affecting their job or work can lead to high levels of engagement among employees and that including employees in the change process, planning and implementation fosters positive employee reactions (Korsgaard et al., 2002).

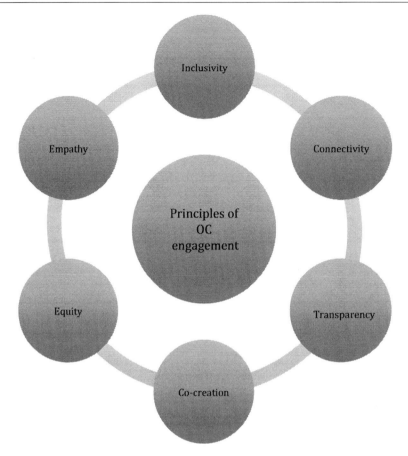

Figure 8.1 Principles of OC engagement

Inclusive work practices can generate the kinds of discretionary behaviours that lead to enhanced OC engagement. For inclusivity to be effective and for it to have a positive impact on engagement, it requires a system of management practices giving employees skills, information, motivation, latitude and power. This will enable employees to have the ability to make decisions that are important to OC and to the quality of their working lives, thus influencing their OC engagement.

Inclusivity is not just a single event but needs to be established as a principle where the focus is upon capturing the ideas of stakeholders, securing their commitment and where stakeholders are seen as central to OC. Inclusion adds a critical dimension to OC engagement as it focuses on the role that stakeholders play in the process of change. It also extends the practice of interactivity by enabling stakeholders to provide their own ideas rather than simply parrying the ideas that others present. In this way inclusivity enables stakeholders to serve as front-line content providers of change creating OC content themselves and being proactive players in the process of OC. This is in contrast to traditional OC models (such as Kotter, 1996) where leadership monopolizes the creation of OC and keeps a tight rein on its content and process or where managers resist the inclusivity of employees with OC because they believe that the process will be more efficient and quicker if fewer people are involved in it. This may well be the case, at times, especially with emergent change, but a lack of inclusivity in planned changes and decision-making processes can be perceived by employees as signs of management's lack of appreciation of the value and views of employees.

Decision-making

Inclusivity with OC can be fostered in different ways and involves a conscious and intended effort by leaders and managers to provide opportunities for individuals and/or teams to have a greater involvement in change. One practice for doing this is for individuals to be given the freedom to be involved in decisions about changes, to be able to challenge precedent, to identify problems and their root causes, and to craft solutions. In turn, it is likely that employees will reciprocate by behaving in favour of the organization (Michel & González-Morales, 2013). Research indicates a positive correlation between inclusion in decision-making and problem-solving with engagement (Sverke et al., 2008). Evidence from a Workplace Employment Relations (van Wanrooy et al., 2013) study underlines the connection between decision-making and engagement. Eighty-five per cent of the 21,000 employees surveyed, for the study, who were satisfied with their inclusion in decision-making felt proud to work for their organization. Inclusion in decision-making about changes is likely to lead to enhanced OC engagement because individuals have the opportunity to share their opinions and make an impact which has been found to be associated with decreased resistance to change (Lines, 2004). In addition, employees who are able to influence the content of a change intervention have been found to be more likely to participate in it (Nielsen et al., 2007). More specifically, inclusion in decision-making and problem-solving may increase the ability of individuals to make changes to their cognitive attitudes and beliefs towards work (van Wingerden et al., 2016).

Inclusion can be maximized when employees have to the power to carry out the decision, resulting in gaining the maximum level of OC engagement possible. This is evident in how General Electric (GE) arrived at the decision to develop and launch its Predix cloud-based industrial operation system. The initiative began when GE's CEO encouraged employees to explore how the accelerating trend towards value-added services in the industrial sector might eventually affect the company's growth. In essence, the CEO challenged his team to act as leaders of change by disrupting before being disrupted by interpreting the weak signals coming from the market. He asked them to pay special attention to how digital native companies were creating shifts in customer behaviours and to diagnose digital solutions for business challenges that had not yet taken a toll on the company's profit and loss statement. This resulted in the launch of Predix which helps companies see how their machines and infrastructure are performing so that they can improve them constantly. This example highlights the critical role of including stakeholders in responding to threats and opportunities in the external environment.

A suggested framework for considering how to implement inclusivity in decision-making is as follows. First, consideration needs to be given as to how inclusivity in OC is to be implemented, whether it will be informal or formal, whether employees will have a direct say, or be indirect as in having voting rights, being mindful that some people will have a stronger desire for being included than others, although, all should have the opportunity to be involved. Second, there has to be clarity on what issues employees can be involved in, for instance, is it just to be about job design and working conditions or strategic issues? Employees also need to be clear on what level of involvement they can expect – will they have the opportunity to express an opinion and/or to make a decision? – and they also need to know what decisions have already been made. Third, the process of decision-making needs to be clear, so employees know what to expect, for example, will decisions be made in teams, or in a confidential ballot? If their views are not taken on-board then individuals need to be given a clear rationale as to why. So feedback has to be provided to staff such as 'we have heard your views and will take them on-board' as well as which views/ideas are not valid and why that is the case.

Through participating in decisions about change, individuals can question existing work practices, craft changes, and in so doing, change the way work is done. Inclusion in decision-making and problem-solving will, therefore, increase individuals' perceived ability to influence change and, in turn, have a positive impact on OC engagement.

Practices for problem-solving and idea generation

OC engagement is often best created by involving people in identifying problems and shaping solutions. Practices to create inclusivity in problem-solving and idea generation can be informal or formal. The former can occur face-to-face, such as 'photocopier' conversations where people gather round a photocopier or similar (preferably with a cup of tea or coffee) and raise issues, concerns and ideas. As an idea comes up that may, in turn, spark other ideas, so in this informal way ideas can be generated and developed. More formal approaches are Talking Walls and Appreciative Inquiry.

TALKING WALLS

A creative practice for idea generation and problem-solving is a Talking Wall – a concept which was first described by Parsell and colleagues (1998) and is a technique of exploring issues, analyzing problems and/or developing action plans. A Talking Wall, where people stick post-it notes on a wall anonymously, can help to encourage less confident people to share their views. For example, a public sector organization used it recently to agree a new vision statement. A variety of vision statements were put on huge pieces of paper on a corridor wall and employees were invited to comment on them and consider – what they liked about them, did not like, and whether the statements were too long, too short, and if the words used were right (or not) and matched the ethos of the company. Rather than responding with words, individuals can be asked to draw something, or make something to generate ideas of how to address challenges. Themes then need to be identified, analyzed and shared. This approach can encourage people to contribute their ideas in a creative and safe way.

APPRECIATIVE INQUIRY (AI)

A framework that can help to create inclusivity in problem-solving and ideas generation at all levels across the organization is Appreciative Inquiry (AI). AI is a collaborative approach that focuses on identifying changes within organizations based on what is positive, rather than what is viewed as negative or problematic (Cooperrider et al., 2005). AI engages stakeholders through a four-cycle process which comprises Discovery,

Dream, Design and Destiny. The discovery phase involves participants sharing the strengths of the issue being reviewed and in the dream phase, they envision what should change. In design, they propose action plans to accomplish the dreams and finally, in the destiny phase, the design is implemented to achieve the desired change. So rather than telling participants what to do and how to do it, managers facilitate a process of inclusivity by asking questions to address issues and participants generate ideas based on the strengths of the organization and/or team.

Using an AI approach can promote OC engagement in a number of ways. The high levels of inclusion required in AI can lead to high-quality interactions and build relationships and trust amongst stakeholders. Moreover, since participants have a vested interest in the solutions they identify, this can enhance their commitment to proposed changes and ultimately their engagement in the transformation process.

Critique of inclusivity

Inclusivity in OC is not without its critics. It has been challenged by the work of two Australian researchers, Stace and Dunphy (2001) who argue that participative approaches are time consuming and can expose conflicting views that are difficult to reconcile. To address these concerns, Stace and Dunphy (2001) propose a contingency model which recommends using an approach which fits the context of the OC based on the following four styles of participation:

(i)   Collaborative – this involves widespread employee participation in key decisions.
(ii) Consultative – this is limited involvement in setting goals relevant to areas of responsibility.
(iii) Directive – this involves leaders and managers making decisions about change.
(iv) Coercive – this is when senior leaders impose change on the organization.

According to Stace and Dunphy (2001), collaborative and consultative approaches may not be the most effective in all situations. For example, where organizational survival depends on strategic change, they say that a directive or coercive approach is most appropriate. Admittedly in reality it is rarely practical to involve all stakeholders all the time in all the major decisions about a change initiative, especially if the change is emergent and unexpected. When decisions need to be made and implemented in a short time frame, the organization may be forced towards centralized decision-making, even when that is not the preferred philosophical option. Survival, in times of crisis, may well depend on a compliance approach. However, when the situation permits, particularly when change can be planned in more detail, there are normally decisions that stakeholders can be involved in and influence, although to ensure this is effective there needs to be trust among stakeholders.

Employees may be sceptical of being involved in decision-making about OC where there is lack of trust such as when managers are perceived as manipulating employees to gain the outcomes they desire, For example, when managers seek open participation, but circumvent this by selecting the employees that participate to ensure they get the outcome they want. Providing individuals with opportunities for inclusion is less likely to be perceived as manipulative if leaders and managers are considered to be authentic because this will generate positive perceptions of a leader's true intention for soliciting thoughts, information and concerns, and also help to build trust. This is evident in an empirical study conducted by Cottrill and colleagues (2014) which indicates a positive relationship between authentic leadership and a sense of inclusion which results in more discretionary behaviour from individuals. This is in contrast to linear, top-down approaches to pro-blem-solving which are often disconnected and time consuming, with slow feedback loops. As a result, decisions and policies often take too long to implement and are obsolete by the time they reach the ground.

A key principle for OC engagement is, therefore, to make the process of OC inclu-sive – namely, to devolve decision-making to the stakeholders most impacted by the issues. An inclusive process will encourage the creativity and enthusiasm of everyone involved. The dynamic and distributed nature of this approach, with many stakeholders making decisions, encourages engagement with change. This approach, which goes far beyond the strategies for consultation and participation that most organizations embrace, is not a one-time event or even a process. When done correctly, it reimagines leadership of change so that it becomes more distributed and collaborative.

Connectivity

OC is complex because it involves human beings who are complicated, with myriad perspectives, motivations and beliefs. While this diversity is a strength, as the world grows increasingly interconnected, the complexity grows. However, by finding ways of build-ing relationships, working together, organizing and distributing power and resources, connectivity can be developed. The experience of connectedness with others is critical to the expression of self-in-role that forms the basis of Kahn's (1990) definition of engagement. Conversely, lack of connectedness can be associated with disengagement and can result in reactions such as: "I was really shut down, not letting loose or being funny or letting them [other people] get close to me . . . I just didn't let them in" (Kahn 1990: 702).

Connectivity with other people works well when individuals operate from a base of civility – which refers to the interpersonal behaviours that demonstrate respect for others (Andersson & Pearson, 1999). A lack of civility or incivility – that is, disrespectful and rude behaviours that are milder forms of mistreatment, as compared to aggression, bullying or other negative behaviours that inflict psychological harm – is related to stress including anxiety, a decline in productivity and even worse, retaliation (Bies & Tripp, 2005). Those who are on the receiving end of incivility report greater psy-chological distress than those who are not (Cortina et al., 2001). A culture of inci-vility will inhibit the development of OC engagement because employees who are surrounded by incivility may have to spend tremendous amounts of energy coping with the stress these conflicting and negative interactions create, rather than being engaged (Shore et al., 2009).

People need to have opportunities to connect with OC since individuals will change only when they have to, or when they want to. They are usually pushed to change by circumstances outside their control. But every day people over the world rush to embrace change, because they are seduced by an opportunity to connect with something big, exciting or virtuous. To get people to engage with OC, they need to be given something worth connecting with. They need an enticing challenge that connects them and draws them to engage. As Hutton (2011) points out, the best managers and leaders are those who can create connection and eschew tricks and tactics for the steady path of being consistent and authentic. They have a knack for bringing meaning to a task and making connections for people. Whenever possible they give power away so as to transmit responsibility. Building supportive relationships in which individuals feel valued and cared for can therefore encourage a sense of connectedness.

Transparency

Transparency provides clarity about why OC needs to happen; what it means for individuals and their team and the work they do, as well as for the organization. It can also help to reduce uncertainty which is a key blocker to OC engagement.

Uncertainty

One of the difficulties with OC, particularly if it is emergent, is its complexity in that it contains a lot of unknowns, so that employees often experience a great deal of uncertainty which can affect their OC engagement. Uncertainty is the inability to assign probabilities as to the likelihood of future events (Duncan, 1979). It is a psychological state of doubt about what an event signifies or portends due to absence of information (DiFonzo & Bordia, 1998). Two specific types of uncertainty are strategic and job-related uncertainty (Bordia et al., 2006). Strategic uncertainty refers to doubt regarding organization-level issues, such as reasons for change, the future direction of the organization, its sustainability and the nature of the business environment. In contrast, job-related uncertainty refers to doubt regarding job security, promotion opportunities and changes to job roles. When employees are lacking information and are uncertain about change it is likely that they will be less willing to accommodate or accept it, will have a less positive view of change, blaming those responsible for implementing it. Despite these negative outcomes many managers fail to deal with uncertainty and impose decisions on employees.

Rather than the unrealistic goal of entirely eliminating uncertainty, attempts can be made to reduce it. Clarifying the process and procedures by which OC will be decided and decisions taken can help to reduce uncertainty. When people are faced with the prospect of OC, the possession of information about the change allows them to make sense of it. Having information about OC enables people to consider whether or not they will engage with it. In addition, information can reduce the amount of time that individuals spend in fearful anticipation of change. So attempts to be more transparent about OC can help to reduce uncertainty. Effective communications are particularly relevant for enhancing transparency.

Communication

Effective communications is important for generating transparency about change and thus encouraging engagement with it. A study of 2.5 million teams in 195 countries found that engagement improved when line managers had some form of daily communication with their staff (Zak, 2017). Similarly, research by Gallup has found that nearly eight in ten employees (77 per cent) are engaged when there is open communications (Groscurth & Shields, 2016). This is supported in a study of a corporate audit department in a large bank which was conducted by Whelan-Barry and colleagues (2003). The study found that at the group level, explicitly communicating what the change meant for the work group helped to reduce employees' anxiety about what the change meant for them and their jobs. Of course when faced with rapid emergent change it may be impossible to know what will happen next, however, whenever feasible clarity and a sense of direction need to be provided. Empirical research has consistently demonstrated that effectively managed communication during change is related to a range of positive employee outcomes including reduced anxiety (Rafferty & Restubog, 2010) and uncertainty for employees (Allen et al., 2007). Furthermore, communication can help to shape employees' reactions to change. This is illustrated in a study carried out by Jimmieson and White (2011) into a hotel undergoing a rebranding exercise which indicates that high-quality communication can help employees support and adjust to change. Through effective communication, organizations can create an environment in which employees engage with OC. In particular, managers communicating strategic and operational matters down and across the organization and employees being able to communicate upwards with their managers have been shown to facilitate the generation of employee engagement (Alfes et al., 2010).

In order to engage people in change, time and energy must be invested in communications so that fears, concerns and doubts are addressed. Barrett (2002) identifies five specific goals for communication about change. It must: (i) ensure clear and consistent messages to educate employees about what the change means to them; (ii) motivate employee support for the change; (iii) encourage discretionary effort; (iv) limit misunderstandings and rumours that may damage productivity; and (v) align employees behind the change. Such advice on how to communicate OC is helpful but is very general and tends to assume a one-way top-down communication process. Communication is too often considered as the mono-directional transfer of instructions or explanations of the change, typically from senior executives down the organizational hierarchy until it eventually reaches front-line staff. The challenge is that communication, although viewed as an important part of the change process, is often ignored and dealt with in a cursory manner. Some managers are far too fond of sending information by emails (management by email) which either go unopened and are deleted or are given a cursory glance. The overuse of emails springs from the assumption that if the case for change is presented as logically as possible then people, being rational, will buy into it and take the appropriate actions.

To address this, managers need to enhance employees' propensity to engage with OC through a wide range of organizational communication activities. For communication about change to be effective it must go up, down and across an organization's structure and be of a high quality. Effective communication requires also close attention to content and how it is translated to different audiences. Verbal communications will either engage or disengage people. For a message to make sense it must resonate with the recipients' perspectives on the change, be experienced as open and transparent and be delivered with authenticity and sincerity.

The way an organization communicates about change and the words and images it chooses to represent transformations is important. What is said about change is one thing but to whom and how it is said is just as important. Central to this is framing and rhetorical crafting. Framing is the management of meaning and connecting messages with the needs and interests of those whose engagement is needed (Fairhurst & Sarr,

1996). This can be done in various ways such as: linking the message with the benefits for stakeholders and reflecting their values and beliefs; moving from 'I' statements to 'we' statements; and expressing confidence in people's ability to engage with and achieve change. Different methods and channels of communication are also required as people have different preferences for the way they receive and process information, so the same messages need to be conveyed using different formats and styles and in a way that makes an emotional connection with people.

Stories are a powerful form of communication. Stories of those involved in the process of making OC happen or stories of people who have accomplished similar tasks make change seem real and achievable. They can also make OC come to life and help gain the engagement of those stakeholders who are still uncertain about whether or not to become involved in the change. The ultimate impact of stories will depend on not just having compelling answers to questions but also the willingness and ability of leadership to make things personal, and to engage other people openly in discussion and decision-making. This means telling different aspects of the same strategic narrative to different stakeholders. As Aetna's CEO Mark Bertolini (cited in Anthony & Schwartz, 2017) says, this means tailoring the message so it has the appropriate level of fidelity relevant to each part of the organization. A person working in a call centre might need a different set of messages than a line manager does to understand how he fits into the big picture. In Aetna's case, this has meant building a narrative of how the move away from fee-for-service reimbursement to a new business model of value-based care would change the nature of health insurance, and one day possibly render it obsolete. Instead of simply reinforcing the story about strengthening Aetna's current business, Bertolini developed a narrative about building new skills to help consumers make better health choices and building a new organization that would make money doing so. It is, however, easy to underestimate the amount of communication required. Organizations have to be tireless about it, consistent and persistent, and keep battering the core messages home week after week. Telling stories about the future is therefore an on-going activity.

Web-based technology is another potent communication channel that facilitates communication among different actors connected in a virtual but also direct way. Social media, for example, is a way of communicating with a large, highly dispersed group of stakeholders. It can facilitate dialogue and integrate employees into OC by creating a sense of community and transparency. Online forums can connect people in similar job functions or areas of expertise and enables people to ask questions and quickly obtain information, leading to increased collaboration and knowledge transfer. There is, however, evidence that achieving improved engagement through social media may not be as easy as suggested. Research (Ruta et al., 2012) warns that the use of social media will mirror the existing structure of power and politics within an organization and will only facilitate employee engagement when openness and trust are already part of the organizational make-up.

The challenge for managers is to use appropriate channels and methods of communication to convey appropriate information. While leaders will have the big picture in mind and think of the overall organizational context, employees are more focused on the relevance and impact of change on their personal circumstances, such as whether it will affect their job role, responsibilities or rewards. People need to have information about the change in order to appreciate and understand the relevance of it. It needs to be accurate, useful, adequately address employee concerns and uncertainty, and be presented in a timely and appropriate way. If stakeholders are being kept informed of OC, they are more likely to engage. Timely and accurate communications can help to reduce uncertainty and enhance employees' sense of control over the change. There are limits, however, to how far direct formal communication on its own can engage stakeholders. Instead it needs to be mixed with discursive methods.

OC conversations

Discursive methods of communication create conversations through dialogue and debate, in contrast to directive methods, such as here is a question and here is an answer. A lack of conversations can have an adverse impact on OC, as it means that the leadership of the organization are unlikely to be aware of what the rest of the organization is thinking and feeling. Leaders and managers, therefore, need to create spaces for organizational conversations that lead to and foster OC engagement through authentic discussions about the why, how, what and when of change. To create OC conversations which are authentic means suspending assumptions and entering into genuine dialogue which enables stakeholders to contribute to decisions as well as share views, concerns and ideas in an honest and open way.

Creating space for OC conversations is challenging, requires effort and may be hard if a leader or manager believes in the sanctity of positional power and that people should do as they are told. For leaders and managers with such views, engaging in conversations may seem like a waste of time and raise questions such as: Why encourage people to explore possibilities when it has already been decided what needs to happen next? What is the point in encouraging people to come up with ideas that they will only have to be dissuaded from? OC conversations may also be difficult if stakeholders are based in different countries. In order to overcome such barriers, Infosys – the Indian information technology company – has created a network to enable conversations with its employees across the globe. This initiative has captured the wisdom of the workforce through Infi tv, Infi radio and Infi bubble. The need for sharing views that Infosys finds so crucial is also key to how the US software company Cisco encourages dialogue among its employees. In order to connect its project teams from across the globe, Cisco has built an intranet network that enables them to connect and communicate. This network has been an advantage for the company since there have been a number of occasions when the executive team have been able to deal speedily with a crisis because they have had the ability to hold emergency discussions at very short notice with participants around the world (cited by Gratton, 2014). By encouraging and participating in OC conversations, leaders and managers can become more informed about stakeholders' perspectives, ideas and concerns.

It is through OC conversations, as opposed to monologue, that leaders and managers can understand what people are thinking and feeling about change and it allows them to recognize differences and agreements. To achieve this, OC conversations may need to be orchestrated which means engaging with stakeholders in a way that resembles an ordinary person-to-person conversation more than it does a series of commands from on high. Furthermore, it involves initiating practices and fostering cultural norms that instil a conversational sensibility throughout the organization. This involves understanding the essential attributes of conversations outlined by Groysberg and Slind (2012) which comprise: intimacy; interactivity; and intentionality:

- Intimacy. OC conversations enable leaders and managers to minimize the distances such as institutional, attitudinal and sometimes spatial, which typically separate them from their employees and other stakeholders. Where conversational intimacy prevails, leaders and managers can seek and earn the trust of others by cultivating the art of listening to people at all levels and by learning to speak with stakeholders directly and authentically. This intimacy distinguishes organizational conversation from other forms of organizational communication and shifts the focus from a top-down distribution of information and orders to a bottom-up exchange of ideas.
- Interactivity. Interactivity reinforces, and builds upon, intimacy. It means that leaders talk with stakeholders and not just to them. This interactivity makes the conversation open and fluid rather than closed and directive and entails shunning the simplicity of monologue and embracing the unpredictable vitality of dialogue. Too often, an organization's prevailing culture works against any attempt to transform communication into a conversation. To make this happen leaders need to foster a genuinely interactive culture that creates a welcoming space for OC conversation. This is illustrated in Cisco Systems where the CEO, John Chambers, holds various forums to keep in touch with employees; for instance every other month he leads a 'birthday chat', which is open to any Cisco employee whose birthday falls in the relevant two-month period and where the employee sets the agenda for the discussion.
- Intentionality. To be rich and rewarding, an OC conversation participant needs to have some sense of what they hope to achieve from it. In the absence of such intent, an OC conversation will either meander or come to a stop. Intent confers order and meaning on even the loosest and most digressive forms of OC conversations and should reflect a shared agenda that aligns with the strategic objectives of OC. Conversational intentionality requires leaders and managers to discuss explicitly with stakeholders the OC vision, purpose and the logic that underlies the rationale for change but also importantly to listen to their views, concerns and ideas. Intentionality will enable relevant actions from the conversation to be identified.

In sum, OC conversations can create a flow of ideas, issues and concerns in an intimate, interactive and intentional manner. Such conversations need to be allowed to emerge and flourish and should be treated as a practice to achieve OC engagement across a diverse group of stakeholders.

Listening and voice

LISTENING

OC conversations have two components: listening and voicing. To listen most effectively individuals need to enter into an OC conversation curious as to what others are thinking, and what the basis of their perceptions is. This involves putting aside personal perspectives and listening attentively to the point of view of others. In his book *On Dialogue* – a treatise on how thought is generated and sustained on a collective level – the physicist Daniel Bohm (2013: 3) writes that: "Communication can only lead to the creation of something new if people are able to freely listen to each other, without prejudice, and without trying to influence each other."

Listening without prejudice can be difficult. Bohm (2013) describes how group conversations can be like a game of Ping Pong where people are batting ideas back and forward and the object of the game is to win or to score points for themselves rather than listen to each other. What is crucial is to create a conversation where there is more of a common inclusion, in which people are not playing a game against each other, but with each other. This is supported by Gratton (2014) who describes how she has experienced inclusive conversations which unfold and are recursive rather than linear and directed. The benefit of this, Gratton (2014) says, is that it creates sensitivity within a group to the similarities and differences in views and consequently creates an environment that is non-judgemental but instead is relaxed and curious.

Listening and being attentive signals respect for people of all levels, a sense of curiosity, and even a degree of humility. This is illustrated in the 'listening sessions' initiated by Duke Energy's president and CEO, James E. Rogers. In meetings with groups of managers, Rogers invited participants to raise any issues and concerns and through these conversations he learnt information that might otherwise have escaped his attention. At one session, for example, Rogers heard from a group of supervisors about a problem related to unequal compensation and consequently was able to work with those affected by the problem to find a solution (cited by Groysberg & Slind, 2012). Listening is important since without listening there is no OC conversation and no opportunity to understand some of the personal and emotional issues that occur in response to potential changes.

VOICE

Along with listening, a vital part of OC conversations is the opportunity for stakeholders to share or 'voice' their opinions, concerns and ideas about changes. This is a multi-faceted activity which is most obviously connected to the generation of trust, fairness and procedural and informational justice (Bartunek et al., 2006). In essence, voice relates to stakeholders' ability to influence the outcome of organizational decisions about OC by having the opportunity to advance their ideas and have them considered. Hirschman (1970) was the first to introduce the concept of voice in his book, *Exit, Voice and Loyalty*, and he defined voice as any attempt at all to change an objectionable state of affairs. This definition is supported by Axelrod (2010) who notes that maximizing voice means widening the circle of inclusion to encompass those likely to be affected by the change process, including those who might be opposed or think differently. When people believe that their voice counts, a critical mass for change spontaneously emerges.

Voice enables people to be heard and to influence outcomes. The opportunity for stakeholders to have a voice in decision-making about OC is fundamental in influencing attitudes and behaviour towards the organization that employs them, and in building inclusivity with managers and other stakeholders. Voice is a building block for OC engagement as it enables individuals to express themselves. People will use their voice when they feel that their words and opinions matter and that they will be listened to and make a difference, change minds and directions and add value to OC. When this is not the case then individuals will use their voice less. If they feel that they are not being listened to then they will be silent, nod and go along with what is being proposed

(Morrison & Milliken, 2000). The lack of voice in OC can exact a high psychological price on individuals, generating feelings of anger and resentment which can contaminate every interaction, shut down creativity and undermine productivity (Perlow & Williams, 2003). Consequently, individuals will withdraw and disengage from OC. Opportunities for individuals to make their voice heard and to know that it is listened to is vital for encouraging OC conversations and generating transparency.

In sum, transparency is about providing clarity about the rationale for change as well as how it will happen and the impact it will have on individuals. It is also about letting individuals be vocal about what is most crucial for them to say and others to listen to them.

Co-creation

Co-creation is about creating an active partnership with stakeholders in the development of OC. It means constructing or negotiating OC *with,* rather than *for* stakeholders, thereby reflecting the plurality of stakeholders' interests. The co-creation of OC requires that power is more widely distributed across the organization and amongst stakeholders. This means that the organization becomes more of a collaborative community of individuals looking to co-create OC rather than a collection of people waiting to implement it. Co-creation means including people in the change process and its activities which involve collaboration, developing a sense of ownership, creating a team-based approach, and clarifying roles and responsibilities.

Collaboration

In organizations, information and decision-making are often distributed among many people, making it exceedingly difficult to map a way forward. Even identifying and creating a shared understanding of problems can be arduous when a myriad of stakeholders have differing perspectives and motivations. To address this there is a need to convene stakeholders to build common understanding and collective engagement and action. In the context of OC, the power of collaboration is the ability to bring together stakeholders.

The collective engagement for change can be actively built by establishing collaboration with multiple stakeholders in thinking about the *what* and *how* of change. Companies which do this include Morning Star and Tata. Morning Star is a California-based tomato processing company. The company has developed a number of instruments and procedures for collaboration, including the Colleague Letter of Understanding (CLOU). Every Morning Star employee has to produce a CLOU, which outlines how they will achieve their performance objectives, as well as the personal mission statement that everyone is involved in writing. A collaborative process, such as CLOU, can be used to bring employees together to discuss and to make decisions about the collective future of an organization.

Front-line staff who do a job often have a better understanding of what the problems are, and how they can best be solved. These staff tend to be rich repositories of knowledge about where potential challenges may occur, what technical and logistical issues need to be considered and how they might be addressed. This approach is used by Tata, a global enterprise headquartered in India, which has created a network – a wise crowd –

that enables employees across the globe to have their voices heard, through exchanging solutions to problems, and sharing their innovative ideas. The benefits of such collaboration are outlined by Nupur Singh, Head of the HR function in Europe at the Tata Group's Consultancy Services:

> We encourage collaboration by encouraging a leadership style that is not about micro-managing. We want people to trust each other. So we encourage leaders to define the end results, the accountability, and their responsibility. A leader defines the vision, sets the boundary but does not control the outcome phase, and creates freedom within the boundary.
>
> (cited in Gratton, 2014: 66)

Building collaboration is vital, even when people are working virtually across geographical boundaries, as it enables individuals to engage in the co-creation of ideas about OC.

Involving as many stakeholders as is feasible can help co-create change. This is illustrated by IBM who set up a 'values jam' to elicit views on organizational values, which was a website where anyone in the company could post comments, responses, suggestions and concerns. Based on the feedback received from this wise crowd, changes were made to the proposed values. Infosys also utilizes the concept of wise crowds as part of the company's annual strategy development process. Employees are asked to submit ideas on the significant trends that they see affecting their customers, from this information a list of trends is created and then a series of online forums set up in which employees can suggest how to match each trend with various customer solutions that the company might offer (cited in Groysberg & Slind, 2012). Dell does something similar with Ideastorm, a website where customers post suggestions for new features, products and services. Although ensuring broad co-creation may take longer, and may not always be feasible with emergent change, it does enable more ideas to surface from across the organization and people are also more committed when they are involved in collaborating in a plan for change.

Sense of ownership

The co-creation of OC is often taken for granted in that it is seen as a fairly straightforward and easy process to set up in which people just need to be told that they can be involved. However, it is not just a matter of stating that employees can be more involved or participate in decisions. A sense of ownership needs to be built. According to Meaney and colleagues (2010), building ownership calls for action on two fronts: (i) tightening managers' formal accountabilities; and (ii) mobilizing self-directed change in the organization. Meaney and colleagues liken the former to a military campaign and the latter to a marketing campaign. The military campaign drives delivery of the transformation through a clear governance structure with well-defined roles and objectives. This involves accountability for outcomes at four levels: (i) an executive steering committee which has overall responsibility for the initiative; (ii) a programme management office (PMO) which is charged with coordinating the programme; (iii) executive sponsors who provide leadership and guidance; and (iv) managers and project teams who are responsible for achieving individual targets and milestones. In contrast, the marketing campaign aims to enlist the active inclusion of staff at every level by tapping into the formal and informal networks across the organization.

Developing a sense of ownership as a practice, especially through 'marketing campaigns', can help develop collaboration, particularly among teams.

A team-based approach

To create co-creation there is a need for a shift from the organization as a whole to its constituent teams. To achieve this, Huy and Bresman (2017) propose a team model of strategic change based on the three stages of Discovering, Deliberating and Embedding.

i   Discovering – Teams prioritize and excel at what Huy and Bresman call 'scouting' tasks, to identify what needs to change.
ii   Deliberating – This involves teams offering their views of proposed change visions. Visions that fail to win widespread support will not be considered further, while those that are popular will inform the new strategic direction.
iii   Embedding – This requires a task coordinator role whose purpose is to translate new strategic directions into manageable, sustainable routines. This includes: coordinating with various stakeholders to address their concerns about the change; collecting evidence to reinforce the legitimacy of the new direction; and conveying timely information.

These three stages are not entirely unique to Huy and Bresman's model but are similar to components of several theories of OC. Where their model differs, according to the authors, is in transferring the stages from a context where the three are performed in linear sequence to a team-based context where they are performed simultaneously by different work units, each at its own task-appropriate pace. Such a team-based approach can be effective in the co-creation of OC, particularly where cross-team collaborations are set up.

Clarity of roles and responsibilities

Co-creation requires a genuine sharing of responsibility which needs clarity about roles and responsibilities. People are more likely to engage with change when it is clear what their responsibilities or authority is, relative to others, what decisions are theirs to make and what is expected of them. A RACI chart is a simple way to provide such clarity. RACI stands for:

- Responsible. The individuals who have responsibility for making decisions about OC and/or doing the work.
- Accountable. Individuals who are accountable for the completion of the OC, such as the project manager or project sponsor.
- Consulted. These are the people who provide information for the OC, and are often subject matter experts.
- Informed. These are stakeholders who are affected by the outcome of the OC and who need to be kept informed about progress.

A RACI matrix can be used to outline, agree and communicate roles and responsibilities. Clarifying roles and responsibilities is a key practice for helping to define ownership with the co-creation of OC.

In sum, the co-creation of OC enables stakeholders to shape change. It means OC is done 'with' rather than 'to' stakeholders and is more likely to garner engagement and increase the chance of success.

The following case of change (as illustrated in Box 8.1) in a South African public water utility highlights the importance of the co-creating change with multiple stakeholders.

Box 8.1 Engaging staff with transformation in a South African public water utility

Written by Fiona Sweeney,
Independent People and Organizational Change Consultant

The South African public water utility supplies water to approximately 1.2 million people and had approximately 250 employees at the time of the project. The utility's transformation plans had been for years stagnating due to management and labour relations issues which were characterized by conflict and disagreement. Challenges ranged from poor people management, underutilization of skilled people to ineffective planning and implementation of projects in the technical services department.

With the appointment of a new CEO, the Board launched a new agenda to rebrand the organization and to create a transformed workplace and a transformed water services sector. The transformation and reorientation of the workplace which was envisaged and which was approved by the Board of Directors was not merely an adjustment to managerial control, it involved a composite package of changes to: work organization and allocations (to address the operational challenges); grading of positions and wage and benefits adjustments; industrial relations; the way of working; and skills development throughout the organization.

There was a realization by the Board from the very beginning that the future success of the organization was contingent on the willingness of all stakeholders, within and outside the utility, to look for better ways to work together. Employee participation was vital to the success of the change initiative and HR, in conjunction with leaders in the organization, had an important role to play in getting buy-in to the changes. It was felt that improved worker participation would ensure that the utility benefited from the knowledge which workers had and that such participation might also assist in soliciting worker expertise in problem solving, elimination of waste, and cost effectiveness. It was equally important that the Unions supported the principles of the transformation and that they supported executive management in bringing about the changes.

The HR Department developed a performance enhancement system and carried out a review of the organizational structure. This led to a complete review of job profiles followed by a grading and evaluation process. The organizational redesign and performance enhancement system were designed to ensure maximum utilization of internal capacity and further advance the development of in-house skills.

A Transformation Task Team was established by the Board and consisted of key stakeholders such as the Human Resources Committee of the Board, Unions and management. The role of the team was to drive the process and address any challenges. The transformation process was based on the two pillars of change management and project management. HR took the lead on the change management aspects and, in conjunction with other key stakeholders, developed a change management plan that included communication plans, stakeholder engagement, people impact plans and specific risk management plans.

All change management processes were based on the ADKAR change management model which manages key elements of: Awareness; Desire; Knowledge; Ability; and Reinforcement. This model was adopted to guide the organizational change.

Change Management Training was given to a selection of HR and Business Leaders. And change management workshops for all employees were designed and delivered to create a common vision around the future of the utility and to equip employees to understand the rationale for the organization to undergo the change. The change management process was introduced as an inclusive process that would promote awareness and ultimately ownership. Any resistance to the change could be aired during the workshops and addressed where necessary. Leadership workshops were designed to get alignment between key leaders. They would also have the dual purpose of building change management competency. It was important that senior management drove the change process and led by example.

Communications that came out from the Board and senior managers reiterated their commitment to developing a turnaround strategy that would be implemented incrementally to address the challenges identified and their promise to their 'loyal and performing employees' to make the utility a better place to work. They asked for employee support through the process in highlighting barriers to improving communication, equity and productivity at all levels throughout the organization.

An enhanced, transparent and participatory environment was created with the support of the Chief Executive via communicative structures such as workshops, meetings and interactions. There was regular consultation and sponsor involvement at all levels across all areas in the utility. Staff were encouraged to share any concerns, views and ideas they had about the proposed changes. An impact assessment was also carried out by questionnaire to establish the readiness of the organization for change.

The Transformation Team anticipated that there would be resistance to the changes in particular from senior and middle management as they were the most impacted in the restructure. The impacted managers were to carry the change message to employees so it was vital that they were on board with the messaging around the change. The message was clear from the Board and CEO that jobs would be guaranteed but not positions. This risk was mitigated by the leadership alignment workshops that were delivered.

The unions supported the principles driving the transformation process from the beginning. This could have been a major stumbling block had they put up resistance to the change. However, the Board realized that in order to get them on board they had to engage them in the process and show them that the changes had wide ranging benefits for each and every employee at the utility irrespective of his or her level within the organization.

Although HR had a big part to play in managing the change process, a major achievement was ownership of the process by the employees. An employee engagement index of 65 per cent was achieved following a climate survey conducted amongst all employees. This was the highest it had even been in the utility.

Engagement of the unions from the outset was important. The number of disputes and grievances showed a marginal decrease in the period of implementation. However, this remains a key focus area of the Board.

With the focus on learning and development, particularly in the area of technical skills, there were lots of growth opportunities for individual employees who had been identified for fast track training to occupy skilled positions that were vacant or lacking. This helped to restore the trust in the change process demonstrating that it was delivering what it said it would.

The post implementation reinforcement process could have been better. The HR team was heavily involved in managing the process and also in the implementation of some of the major changes around people. However, there was an expectation from some senior managers that HR would continue to do this even after the project aspects had become business as usual. Managing the expectations of business managers in a post implementation world would mean that they take full accountability for embedding the changes in their area.

The key lessons learnt from the project about how to effectively engage stakeholders in transformation are:

- The importance of involving the key stakeholders in the process from the outset
- Leadership involvement and alignment
- Better understanding of the change process. Building change management competency using a structured approach that was shared across the organization
- Consistent, open and transparent process
- Change Management Training for HR – don't assume if you are good at HR you will be good at managing change
- Communicate, communicate, communicate
- Reinforce the right behaviours required for success

Equity

The generation of OC engagement requires equity. This means that stakeholders need to feel that they are fairly and justly treated, that they have or will be given the right resources for engaging with change, and that their effort will be fairly recognized and appropriately rewarded. When employees' equity is reduced or non-existent this results in loss of trust and the employment relationship between employers and employees can be damaged, often beyond repair. If organizations want more from employees, in the form of OC engagement, arguably they will have to offer employees a more substantial commitment in return, in the form of adequate resources, recognition and rewards.

Resources

Resources are key to encouraging OC engagement because they help employees cope with the change, reduce uncertainty and improve satisfaction. Moreover, taking on more responsibilities or focusing on the challenging aspects of the change facilitates employee adjustment (Amiot et al., 2006) which often requires additional or different resources. Resources can come from sources, such as line managers and co-workers who offer support or from the job itself, through control, autonomy, opportunities for development, and job or skill variety. Since employees still have to deliver their day jobs when change is happening, they are unlikely to be willing to invest extra time in the change over and above their day job if they have inadequate resources.

Resource inadequacies refer to situations where OC engagement is made harder because of problems caused by a lack of appropriate resources (Sonnentag, 2003). Resource inadequacies decrease OC engagement because they sap individuals' physical and emotional energy that could otherwise be used for productive investment in change. Sonnentag (2003) found that situational constraints involving a lack of appropriate information or materials to do the job were negatively associated with engagement in a sample of public service workers. When resources are lacking, a strategy that individuals may use to maintain functioning is to select the most important aspect of their job and ignore aspects that require a lot of investment (Baltes, 1997), such as OC. Organizations, therefore, have to identify the additional resources that can be made available to employees to cope with the strains involved with OC. Ensuring that employees have resources sufficient to do their jobs and take on any additional responsibilities as a result of changes is a key practice for developing equity.

Recognition and rewards

Rewards and recognition are other key practices for promoting equity because they represent both direct and indirect returns on the personal investment of time and energy an individual expends on OC engagement. In terms of Social Exchange Theory, this means that when employees receive rewards (and recognition) from their organization, they will feel obliged to respond with higher levels of engagement.

Rewards refer to the formal pay and benefits received as compensation associated with a job, as well as the feedback given by managers, co-workers and customers. Research suggests that employees will be more likely to engage with OC to the extent that they perceive that they receive a fair reward for their engagement (Maslach et al., 2001). A lack of fair rewards can create a sense of injustice or outrage which can lead to people being cynical about engaging with changes (Xanthopoulou et al., 2009). People will vary in their levels of OC engagement depending on their perceptions of the fairness of the rewards that they receive (Kahn, 1990). Employees need to feel that there is a clear and fair relation between the work they do on OC and the extrinsic rewards they get, such as salary, promotion and status. In accordance with Vroom's (1964) expectancy theory of motivation, people want to know that what they get for the work they put in to OC is valuable to them (called valence). If the outcome of their effort is not valuable to them, they are unlikely to be motivated to direct their efforts and energy towards engaging with change. The degree of formality of such recognition is determined by circumstances and what is appropriate. In terms of findings from empirical studies, results on the relationships between rewards and engagement are mixed. For example, Bakker et al. (2006) suggest that financial rewards are actually negatively related to perceptions of engagement, although satisfaction with fringe benefits is positively related to engagement. In contrast, Jackson and colleagues (2006) show that financial rewards are positively related to reported levels of engagement for teachers in South Africa. Similarly, a study by Gorter and colleagues (2008) concludes that rewards are positively related to engagement for dentists. This suggests that employees need to feel valued and appreciated and that they need to receive recognition for their efforts.

Recognition also involves feedback which means employees obtaining direct and clear information about the effectiveness of their performance. In a ten-year study of 20,000 managers and employees, Gostick and Eton (2007) identified the significant impact that recognition can have on engagement. Recognition when done regularly and genuinely, such as through feedback, can be a way of making individuals feel more valued. Feedback allows individuals to evaluate their growth and progress towards achieving OC goals, as well as helping them feel valued and appreciated. Research shows that feedback exhibits significant positive relationships with engagement among information technology workers (Hallberg & Schaufeli, 2006), customer service representatives (Bakker et al., 2003), teachers (Hakanen et al., 2006), dentists (Hakanen et al., 2008), military personnel (Britt, 2003), as well as employees from various nations across both private and public sectors (Salanova & Schaufeli, 2008). Feedback is a key element of recognition that provides meaningful information that can enhance engagement. Recognizing and rewarding behaviours is important because anything less will lead to perceptions of unfairness. So when employees feel fairly treated – that they are recognized and appropriately rewarded and have the right resources – then there is a sense of equity.

Empathy

Aside from the complexity and uncertainty involved in change, it also creates different reactions from different people. To understand and respond to how individuals react to change, a key principle for engendering OC engagement is empathy. Empathy is the capacity to understand or feel what another person is experiencing from within the other person's frame of reference; that is, the capacity to place oneself in another's position. Decety and Yoder (2016) define empathy as a multifaceted construct used to account for the capacity to share and understand the thoughts and feelings of others. These authors differentiate between emotional and cognitive empathy. Emotional empathy is the capacity to share or become affectively aroused by others' emotional states at least in valence and intensity, and cognitive empathy is the ability to consciously put oneself into the mind of another person to understand what he or she is thinking or feeling. It involves feeling the way someone else feels, and understanding how someone else feels. In other words, empathy comprises of being able to put yourself in someone else's position both intellectually and emotionally.

Leaders and managers have a key role to play in supporting the emotional side of OC. However, many may find managing the emotional side of change daunting and mistakenly believe that emotions have no place at work and should be relegated to the personal or social realms of life. Studies, however, attest to the opposite. For example, in a meta-analysis of hundreds of cross-sectional, longitudinal and experimental studies, Lyubomirsky and colleagues (2005) examined the relationship between happiness and success at work and found that happiness and success are not only correlated, but that happiness leads to success. Research suggests that leaders play an important role in managing emotions such as happiness (Pescosolido, 2002) since when an event that necessitates conducting an OC occurs, organizational members may look to a leader or line manager to help them make sense of that event. A leader may interpret change for individuals by demonstrating an emotional response, such as hope and passion for conducting a change, which can affect individuals' emotional states both individually and collectively, particularly if individuals personally identify with and trust the leader (Gill & Caza, 2015). Research shows that if emotions are properly managed rather than shut out at work, they can drive trust, loyalty and commitment, productivity, innovation, good decision-making and effective performance (Holbeche & Springett, 2004). Consequently, leaders and managers need to be able to recognize and understand the emotional landscape which means tuning in to what people are not just thinking but also feeling. To increase this awareness means raising their emotional intelligence.

Emotional intelligence is defined as a set of interrelated skills concerning the ability to perceive accurately, appraise and express emotion, the ability to access and/or generate feelings when they facilitate thought, and the ability to regulate emotions to promote emotional and intellectual growth (Mayer & Salovey, 1997). Research supports a positive relationship between leaders with high emotional intelligence and employee engagement (Ravichandran et al., 2011). Raising the emotional intelligence of employees themselves may be another way of increasing engagement. Studies have shown that emotionally intelligent employees are more prone to positively appraise potentially stressful events such as OC (Gerits et al., 2004). Emotional intelligence can support managers in empathizing with and addressing reactions to change.

Reactions to OC

Employees will have their own opinions about OC and experience a range of emotional responses to it, which in turn will be manifested in how they engage with change. As Vakola and Nikolaou (2005: 162) say, "change can be received with excitement and happiness or anger and fear, while employees' responses to it may range from positive intentions to support the change to negative intentions to oppose it." Individuals' assessment of change thus concerns the evaluation of how positive or negative they perceive the change to be. Although, it is not always as simple as this, as is evident in the increase of the complexity of researchers' conceptualizations of reactions to change over the years. Studies which focus on behavioural reactions to change can be divided into three main categories. The first includes studies that conceptualize behavioural reactions as explicit behaviours, taking the form either of the active involvement in OC or withdrawal behaviours, such as intentions to quit due to the change (for example, Neves, 2009). The second category focuses on behavioural intentions to resist, sabotage (Stensaker et al., 2002) or support the change (Herold et al., 2007; Hornung & Rousseau, 2007; Stanley et al., 2005). The third set of studies considers coping as a behavioural outcome that represents explicit behavioural reactions to change (Amiot et al., 2006) taking the form of either individuals' stress-related coping strategies or individuals' reported functioning given the conditions of change (Cunningham, 2006).

Whereas past research has tended to treat reactions to change as monolithic, it is now the norm to treat reactions to change as multidimensional constructs. Individuals' explicit reactions to OC are either affective (how they feel), cognitive (what they think) or behavioural (what they intend to do). Starting with the affective reactions, a number of researchers focus on either positive or negative reactions to change (for example, Oreg, 2003). More specifically, researchers consider positive reactions to change, such as change related satisfaction (Jones et al., 2005), positive emotions and affective aspects of change commitment (Walker et al., 2007). Seo and colleagues (2012) explore the role of employees' affective experiences (positive feelings) in shaping their engagement and behavioural responses to OC at its start and then 12 months later. They found that unsurprisingly, employees' engagement, resistant and creative behavioural responses to change are related to their affective experiences and that employees' affective experiences at the start of OC predict both engagement and behavioural responses to change 12 months later. An individual's evaluation of the potential consequences of change, particularly for their job, is a critical appraisal that influences their reactions to change (Bordia et al., 2006). Such assessment is subjective in nature and determines behaviour (Armenakis et al., 2007). Research has pointed out that negative evaluations of OC are likely to influence an individual's awareness of its negative, disliked aspects (Herscovitch & Meyer, 2002). In contrast, employees who assess changes in a positive manner are more motivated to collaborate by displaying extra-role behaviours that benefit their organization. In line with this argument, Kunz and Linder (2015) found that the relationship between need for achievement and intention to engage in innovative behaviour was positive for individuals with a positive attitude towards the change and negative for individuals less open to new ideas. Factors underlying openness towards change include a willingness to engage with change and a positive view of change (Wanberg & Banas, 2000). In contrast, employees who are cynical about OC are likely to have doubts about the success of any particular initiative and are unlikely to engage with it (Bernerth et al., 2007). Individuals will, therefore, differ in the way they react to change and consequently the level of an individual's OC engagement will vary from change to change.

UNDERSTANDING AND ADDRESSING REACTIONS TO OC

The importance of understanding how individuals within organizations react to changes helps determine the extent to which they will engage with OC. Anyone attempting to engage stakeholders with change in an organization knows to expect some opposition as change is not a rational process; it is natural for humans to struggle with it. Opposition to change manifests itself in many ways, from foot-dragging and inertia to petty sabotage and outright rebellions. The main sources of opposition to OC are highlighted by Buchanan and Huczynski (2017) as: self-interest – wanting to protect the status quo; a lack of understanding about the need or rationale for change; different assessments of the costs and benefits of change; and low tolerance for ambiguity and uncertainty. Understanding why individuals may object to change is vital as opposition to OC is not necessarily damaging, indeed it is not just desirable but necessary, in order to prevent the implementation of weak ideas and ineffective proposals. A difference of opinion can often be constructive as it exposes the positive and negative aspects of a proposed change. Rather than assuming those who raise objections to change are resistors, Doty (2017) proposes that they are treated as 'guardians' who see what needs to be protected and are mindful that trust can be destroyed by a shortcut or a blind spot. When managers approach guardians as responsible, thinking adults rather than seeing them as purely 'resistors' they demonstrate genuine respect for the views of others. As Maurer (2010: 23) says "sometimes we need to hear the resistance in order to know that our plans are doomed to failure." This is also advocated by Ford and Ford (2009: 100) who say that "even difficult people can provide valuable input when you treat their communication with respect and are willing to reconsider some aspect of the change you're initiating." In support of this, Jick and Peiperl (2010) suggest that leaders should rethink the concept of 'resistance', and see it as a natural part of the change process and as a potential source of energy and feedback. In other words, the power of resistance can be used to build support for change and treating so-called resistors with respect can build trust and improve the chances of identifying solutions that will be effective. While advocating a similar approach, Maurer (2010) also warns that there are situations where focusing on dissent can be counterproductive, for instance, where challenges to proposed changes are not well informed or where OC is necessary for organizational survival.

Although managers cannot always make people feel comfortable with change, they can minimize discomfort by identifying the root causes of concerns and opposition to change and where possible work with stakeholders to eradicate or lessen them since failure to pay attention to managing personal concerns can result in lost momentum or the erosion of OC engagement. If the personal concerns of individuals are ignored and their engagement is lost, the negative impact of individuals withdrawing their support, either openly or covertly, can be highly damaging to OC.

Summary

In this chapter we have focused on creating conditions in which stakeholders are likely to engage with OC. Fostering OC engagement should not be something else an employee, manager or leader has to do, instead, it should be how OC gets done and engagement concepts need to be incorporated in the organizational culture. This is illustrated by the case in Box 8.2 written by Lindsey Agness. As the case highlights, enhancing OC engagement is something to do *with* someone, not *to* someone. It is important to involve staff at all levels so they understand why change needs to occur, the urgency and importance of making the change work, how they can contribute, and that their contribution is valued.

We propose that OC engagement can be influenced to varying degrees through the principles of inclusivity; connectivity; transparency; co-creation; equity and empathy. These principles provide ways for stakeholders to connect with change effectively. Such principles help to build the antecedents of OC engagement such as trust and fairness which are closely related to the employees' perceptions that their opinions are sought, they are listened to and their views treated with respect. The challenge is for organizations to operationalize these principles in everyday practice, which means changing the way that OC engagement is viewed in organizations. There might be, of course, other principles that are important for different organizations and stakeholders, so a 'one size fits all' approach to OC engagement is ineffective since levels of engagement and its drivers will vary according to the size of the organization, stakeholder groups, the individual and the nature of OC.

Generating OC engagement is a gradual but by no means straightforward process. Organizations can but offer opportunities for employees to experience engagement activities positively, but they cannot force them to engage. It is about developing a more creative, flexible approach suited to the demands of the complexity of OC. The challenge is, of course, for organizations to operationalize these principles in everyday practice as illustrated in the following case (Box 8.2).

Box 8.2 Adopting a top-down and bottom-up approach to culture change

Written by Lindsey Agness,
Managing Director, The Change Corporation

The case organisation is a public-sector local authority with a new CEO who wanted to understand the reasons why the level of morale and well-being was at rock bottom in their largest directorate – the Planning Service. He also wanted recommendations about what could be done to turn around the culture. The CEO wanted an accelerated approach where the root causes could be identified quickly and action taken at all levels within the service. It was also important to design a methodology that could be easily packaged and subsequently rolled out to other departments to embed the new culture across the whole organisation.

My consultancy team used an approach which builds on the work of Oshry (2007) and the concept of tops (senior managers), middles (middle managers) and bottoms (front-line staff), as a way of engaging the whole system. Our approach (as illustrated in Figure 8.2) engages with the tops and coaches them to lead the change, cascades down to the middles and mobilises the bottoms to create ownership.

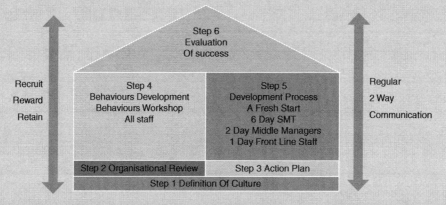

Figure 8.2 Approach to creating sustainable culture change

This involves the following steps:

Step I – Define what good looks like in terms of the desired culture

The new CEO was concerned that the dominant leadership culture within the service had moved too far towards a focus on task and away from a focus on people and teams. His vision was to build a more balanced culture where people were highly valued, nurtured and motivated. He wanted to begin the process in the service area since he was receiving feedback from staff within this service that their well-being was at an all-time low. He asked us to investigate and gather evidence about what was happening on the ground and to make recommendations for change.

Step 2 – Reviews where the organisation is now

We agreed with the client that a bespoke survey would be designed and sent out to all members of the Planning Service. The aim of the survey was to identify areas of strength within the Planning Service and areas for development. The purpose was to test out the hypothesis that the leadership style had moved too far in the direction of task and away from people and team, leaving staff feeling demotivated and disengaged. The design was based on the McKinsey Seven-S model – a framework for investigating how well an organisation is functioning across seven key areas (Strategy, Structure, Systems, Style, Staff, Skills, Shared Values). It was important that we engaged with all levels of staff in order to understand their feelings about how they were being managed and to hear the reasons for their apparent discontent. To achieve this, our review was conducted in three stages:

i   (i) an initial survey was developed and sent out to staff to provide a baseline of data;
ii (ii) the results of the survey were further explored via a series of focus groups with front-line staff, team leaders and one-to-one meetings with senior staff. All staff had the opportunity to contribute to the process;
iii (iii) a final report was written that outlined the key issues based on the evidence from the review and also included recommendations.

There were some early stakeholder challenges as our client was a different head of service and not the relevant head of service. This was a deliberate choice by the organisation so that there was no conflict of interest within the process. This meant that we had to work hard to build rapport with the relevant head of service and to get their buy-in to our approach prior to the launch of the survey and wider project.

The total number of staff invited to participate in this stage was 120. The 91 responses to the survey represented a 76 per cent response rate. The 94 people engaged through the face-to-face process represented 78 per cent of the total staff group. Whilst the results of the quantitative data were mixed, something unusual happened with the results of the qualitative data. We received over 20,000 words that equates to approximately 50 pages of typed text. Clearly staff were keen to participate. We believe that they saw it as an opportunity to anonymously put their views across without fear of any reprisals, they welcomed the chance to be heard and the survey provided a channel to raise anxieties that had been building up over a long period. The results of the survey reinforced the concerns about the task-based environment with a lack of empathy for the pressures of work. It was also evident from the survey data that there was a widespread lack of well-being among employees.

Step 3 – Develop an Action Plan

Our recommendations and actions that came out of the survey were based on the principle goal to move all the service managers towards a more people focused style of management. We were engaged to work with the team to turn the culture around.

A crisis in the service area, partly precipitated by a delay between the publication of the report and the start of our work due to other distractions in the organisation, including a major restructure and a holiday period, meant that when we did start, we were working in an emergent and rapid way over a period of ten weeks. We began working in parallel with both top-down and bottom-up layers of the service. We also had to work hard to get the service senior managers on board as they had been heavily criticised by the report, and some were initially shocked by, and defensive of, the findings from the survey.

Step 4 – Behaviour workshops

We ran a number of behaviour workshops with front-line and team leader level staff. These workshops were designed in conjunction with a small team from within the service and two members of our own design team. They were designed to be interactive and engaging. Staff were asked to identify the new behaviours that they felt would deliver the desired culture as well as the behaviours they no longer wanted to experience. From this, our team identified four key themes and the behaviours that represented and did not represent each theme. These included the following: Communicating Effectively; Being Inclusive; Valuing each Other; Taking Responsibility for Delivering a Great Service; and Embracing Creativity and Change.

We received feedback from staff that the workshops had been very cathartic for them and that they were helping to build a common purpose and vision for the future.

Step 5 – Provide development and support to drive the culture change

At the same time as we were delivering the behaviour workshops, we also began to work with the service's senior leadership team. There was some critical rapport building that needed to be done initially to get them all on board. We worked hard to help them understand that we were all working towards the same outcome and that we had the means by which to support them make the behavioural shifts they urgently needed to make. In less than a week after we began the work, each member of the senior team had their own personal coach. We also had developed a high-level design for a development programme to transfer a toolkit to them that would develop them into more proficient people managers. The programme consisted of six one-day modules delivered over a six-week period.

Our overall approach for the programme is illustrated in Figure 8.3.

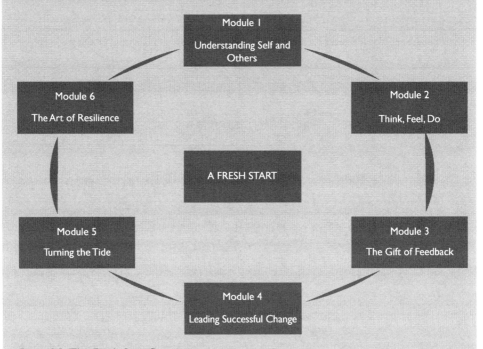

Figure 8.3 The Fresh Start Programme

We know that this process from our evaluation had a major impact on the leadership team. Some of the key learning points identified by participants included:

- Developing a shared language
- Having the time and space to think and reflect
- Learning about each other's personal behavioural styles
- Building a stronger rapport and understanding in the team
- Improving communication and engagement with the front-line staff
- Creating focus on people rather than task
- Using frequent feedback
- Helping to manage the restructure
- Being more confident and positive about the future.

Culture change requires constant reinforcement to be sustained and we strongly recommended that the new behaviours were reinforced through HR policies and procedures. The case organisation will conduct a review of HR to include a strategic policy review, development of people plans and a training and development programme.

Step 6 – Measure and evaluate success

We built in space at the end of the programme to evaluate success and engage with all levels of the organisation via focus groups and one-to-one meetings. We will also be repeating the survey in the Autumn. Early signs show a very positive start with a visible shift in the behaviour of the senior team. An example of this is when the head of service gave a heart-felt apology to the whole service for allowing the culture and behaviour of managers to go unchecked for so long. This act was symbolic for many staff and represented the start of the new culture.

Our attempts to engage staff in this initiative have led to a shift towards an optimistic workforce who feel that their work environment has become a much more positive place to be in. However, at the time of writing this case, it is still early days and not the time to lose focus. It will be important to mirror these changes across other departments to build a people focused organisational wide culture.

There are several key lessons from this project:

- Keep the time lag between the publication of the initial report of the survey results and the start of the work as short as possible. Because of the high levels of engagement through the survey process, expectations of staff were that something was about to change immediately. When nothing happened for almost two months the frustration levels of staff contributed towards the situation that meant we were urgently called back on site.
- Keep key stakeholders on board throughout all stages of the project. We spent time rebuilding relationships with critical stakeholders at the point that we needed to get on with the implementation phase. This could have been avoided if we had managed their expectations and kept closer to them during the survey process. While we did have one-to-one interviews with each member of the service area management team to get their feedback on the survey results before the report was published, we could have had more regular communication with them in the form of weekly email updates or attending their regular management team meeting.
- We had feedback from our later evaluation that staff were concerned about the sustainability of the changes especially as the organisation has a poor history of delivering change in a sustainable way. Other initiatives have 'fizzled out' over time.

> • We know that we have engaged extensively with both the 'tops' and 'the bottoms'. However, our engagement with the 'middles' has been more ad hoc. They are critical stakeholders as they can both help to cascade the changes to their teams and to support the management team in the delivery of the new culture.

Implications for practice

There are a number of practical implications which arise from the discussion in this chapter.

- Co-create change. The co-creation of OC can be developed by setting up working groups with different representatives from different grades across the organization; for instance, a change group with a specific role, such as pulling together communications. These need to be genuine attempts, not just a tick box, to make sure different views of the organization are represented. How might you improve on how you do this?
- Be clear on negotiables and non-negotiables. There is a need to be very clear with stakeholders about what is within their power to shape with OC, what is not up for negotiation, and why. This will help with managing expectations and help people understand and accept the decisions which need to be made without their input. Review how you engage stakeholders and what you can do differently.
- Use various communication channels. Employees should be given the space and support they need to be able to speak up and share their views, ideas and concerns. Review how you engage people through various forms of communication, such as via staff meetings, and drop-in sessions – not just emails – give people the space to ask questions and get answers.
- Demonstrate that you listen to stakeholders' views. Take time to listen and to feedback to stakeholders about what they said and your response to it. For example, 'You said . . . We did . . .'. If it is not possible to take action based on views and ideas then give reasons. Consider how you might improve on this.
- Identify relevant behaviours. Managers need to identify behaviour that indicates a lack of engagement or opposition to the change, discuss these behaviours with the individual/s concerned and address the issues which may be concerning individuals, such as job security, financial impact, work relationships, levels of responsibility and learning and development needs. How might you identify root causes of opposition to change?
- Review how you respond to personal concerns and reactions of people to the change. Employees at different levels of an organization have different experiences of the reality of the organization. Managers should not just assume that employees will view the need for change in the same way they do. Because of the knowledge front-line staff hold and their experience, they may have very different perspectives and ideas about what needs to change. They need the opportunity to share these in OC conversations. Consider ways you can stimulate conversations about change.

Chapter 9

Conclusions and reflections on OC engagement

This final chapter will synthesize the conclusions made in the book and outline the practical implications for creating effective OC engagement.

The meaning of OC engagement

To explore the concept of OC engagement we have created a unifying definition that combines the relevant concepts across definitions; capturing the key components that make OC engagement unique from other constructs; integrating key perspectives; separating the antecedent and consequence constructs from the definition itself; and considering engagement at different levels. Taking these into account for the purposes of this book we refer to OC engagement at different levels in an organization. At an individual and team level it is a transient attitude, where an individual or team is *focused* on and aligned with the goals of OC, and channels their *emotional* and *cognitive* self to transform change into *purposeful accomplishment*. While at an organizational level, OC engagement is a process by which an organization increases the involvement of its employees and other stakeholders with OC. OC engagement is, therefore, an *active role* not something that is happening *to* people but instead something they are engaging *with*. Stakeholders need to be given the ability to own the change, that is, to take personal responsibility for those aspects of the change which they can control or influence.

The practice of OC engagement

Generating OC engagement is not a one-way, purely top-down exercise, nor a cookie-cutter approach that ignores individuals' personal needs. Instead it is, as outlined in this book, an art that needs to reflect individuals' and organizational needs with OC. As such, OC engagement is a dynamic and fragile phenomenon which involves placing people at the heart of change, whenever feasible and practical to do so.

OC engagement needs to be fostered in order to build its resilience. The fragility of OC engagement is a function of how vulnerable individuals feel and are when they risk being involved in OC. People do not get engaged simply because they get enough breaks, like runners who train simply with intervals of running and resting. OC engagement is a far more delicate phenomenon, hard to create and even harder to sustain. In order to build its resilience OC engagement needs to be not only fostered but also maintained. This means that organizations must avoid complacency and understand and recognize that OC engagement has to be anchored in the organizational culture. To achieve this involves understanding the two potential approaches to OC engagement. First, transactional OC engagement, where OC engagement is an event related to the annual employee survey, followed up with a few actions to show some commitment. Second, transformational OC engagement, where OC engagement is a way of life and part of the organizational culture. Organizations need to evolve from looking at OC engagement from a transactional perspective towards an organization where engagement is a way of life since OC engagement is a process, not an event.

As a process, OC engagement is a shared endeavour and requires an active partnership between stakeholders based on the principles of inclusivity; connectivity; transparency; co-creation; equity and empathy. These principles provide ways for stakeholders to connect with change effectively and must be fostered and sustained, as they will distinguish organizations that create effective OC engagement from those that do not. These principles matter because stakeholders need to be included in OC rather than having it forced on them.

If employers want to retain and motivate people, keeping them connected with the organization, they need to foster a culture of OC engagement. This means that leaders need to be proactive, accessible and approachable and willing to listen and act on what they hear and managers must provide support and resources and keep a finger on the pulse of how people are feeling and help to ensure stakeholders engage effectively with OC.

An important success factor, which sometimes is overlooked, is ensuring genuine and real commitment from leaders in the organization. The commitment from leaders to improving OC engagement is a fundamental catalyst of change within an organization, for two reasons. First, it contributes to gaining management buy-in and second, it ensures that employees, and other stakeholders, know that engagement with change is a business imperative and not simply another initiative. So due to the challenge and complexity that OC engagement presents, neither leaders, managers nor other stakeholders can be complacent about it, instead they need to continue to seek ways of evolving their approach and raising the bar for OC engagement.

Organizations need to be equipped not just for gradual incremental change but to thrive in continuous change and react to emergent change in a timely manner. To effectively change an organization requires an ethical, values-based, learning culture where stakeholders are actively involved in change rather than it being thrust upon them. Developing the ability to change requires contributions from all concerned: employees, and other stakeholders, need to be willing to be engaged and take responsibility for advancing their organization's effectiveness; leaders need to be willing to collaborate and develop the kind of distributed and collaborative direction setting that makes sense in times of accelerating change; managers need to embrace change as the norm and adopt agile working methods that fit the context and improve practices to ensure that stakeholders are able to engage with OC. To enable all this requires active OC conversations, support and resources to ensure that people are willing and able to embrace change as the norm, rather than as a threat. A shared learning approach is vital – both in intent and in practice – to enable the organization and its stakeholders to proactively sense and seize opportunities and address threats to the benefit of all concerned.

Practitioners have provided valuable insights into OC engagement which we can use, along with the key discussions in the book to draw several conclusions about implementing OC engagement:

- No 'one size fits all'. Organizations operate in different business contexts and need different approaches to foster engagement within their workforce. Implementing the same initiatives or approaches in different organizations might not produce the same effect in other organizations, as the organizational culture and the working environments are likely to differ. Practitioners should therefore be inspired by the OC engagement principles presented in this book, but at the same time, ensure that the initiatives they implement are tailored to fit the goals and objectives of their organizations. What works well in one organization might not work at all in another organization.

- Adopt a stakeholder approach to OC engagement. Developing OC engagement cannot be done by leaders in isolation. OC engagement initiatives are much more successful if other organizational groups such as line managers are involved and if the OC engagement has the full support of both management and leadership and focuses on involving stakeholders from the beginning.

- Embed OC engagement in the organizational culture. OC engagement is much more powerful when it becomes part of the way that the organization lives and operates. When it becomes an integrated part of the culture of OC and a mainstream way of working and behaving in an organization, OC engagement is more likely to be sustained.

- Align OC engagement with other change priorities. OC engagement is not an ideal state that people attain. The most effective approach to engagement is not 'stop and start', but instead it is an on-going process that works alongside OC activities. An organization cannot conduct a change initiative, complete the process and move on to other things. OC engagement should not be something else that an employee, manager or leader has to do; instead it should be how change gets done. Building engagement is therefore an on-going process. It is a way of doing change in the organization that requires on-going monitoring, adaptation and action.

To illustrate the challenges of engaging stakeholders with change, Box 9.1, written by Mark Crabtree, provides us with novel insights:

Box 9.1 The Story of Perkin

Written by Mark Crabtree,
Assistant Director of Human Resources, Durham University

As a trainer, coach and facilitator, over the years I have supported many managers and staff through change initiatives, from small tweaks and amendments to large transformational change projects. Since we have adopted the American Military term VUCA (Volatile, Uncertain, Complex and Ambiguous) and applied it to business environments I seem to be spending more of my time coaching managers on how to lead their staff through change.

I am an advocate for using storytelling and metaphors in the work that I do as I believe it creates a narrative that all participants with varied experiences, expectations and values can identify with. I also like playing around with graphics and pictures. So let me tell you "The Story of Perkin", which I use to explore change and transition. Perkin lives on an island, which in

Perkin's mind is lush, green and comfortable; in fact Perkin has lived on the island for many years and leads a contented life. What needs to happen to encourage (or maybe coerce) Perkin to move? This part of the story is familiar to those who are trying to instigate change which means moving from one state that for some people is very familiar, comfortable and well lived in, to another which is untried and untested. How often are managers trying to encourage people to embark on organizational change, when they are currently comfortable and contented? When I ask participants to discuss how they can energize Perkin and encourage Perkin to move, the most popular initial strategy is to create an incentive. "Make the other island an attractive alternative" (see Figure 9.1).

Figure 9.1 Engaging people to change

The idea of the incentive on the other island being a 'pub' was my idea, perhaps it shows how my mind works. However, after telling this story a number of times the 'pub' choice has taken on more significance. I chose the 'pub' because I like craft beer and visiting country pubs and I thought, probably unwisely, that this was a 'tongue in cheek' safe(ish) picture to use. However, I started to be challenged on my choice of picture. "I don't drink", "I don't visit pubs" or "why a pub?" are comments that I often receive. "What would you choose?" is my retort and I get a variety of replies from art galleries to gyms. What then follows is often a deep conversation about how we incentivize staff to engage with change. Do we sell a convincing positive vision of the future to the people affected by change? Whilst most managers say that they do accept the importance of selling and communicating the 'future state' some may tend to do this using language and future scenarios that resonate with their aspirations and needs and not necessarily with the aspirations and needs of those staff who will be impacted by the change. How much do we know about our people so that we can contextualize the vision of the future in such a way that it appeals to them? Do we know their career drivers and work-based values? We may need to understand our people a little more so we can hone our message. I am not advocating being manipulative but being aware of the fact that our people are key stakeholders in the future version of the organization. Perhaps we should think about how we can translate the key messages many times over so that everyone can see the benefits of the future state. How can we ensure that everyone appreciates that they have a stake in the future?

The next chapter of my story focuses on whether, once we have communicated a compelling vision of the future (be it a pub, art gallery, gym or something else that appeals), Perkin will or will not start to engage in the move to the other island. Do we appreciate or understand how attached Perkin is to the current land? Even though the new place may look appealing is the vision solid enough to appear a real and a strong possibility? When we discuss this part of the story, it always strikes me how long some people's memories are relating to organizational changes that did not come to fruition. It leads to suggestions of change being described as "just rhetoric", "more false promises", or "we have seen it all before". In the large organizations I have worked with, people seem to remember the changes that have faltered or failed rather than the ones that have succeeded. The promise of a better future sometimes does not hold as much water as senior managers think it does. Perhaps some like it just the way it currently is and no matter how enticing the future may be it still doesn't compete with the current level of comfort. The discussion then tends to move on to telling "home truths" or creating "burning platforms". There is an acceptance that as well as describing the (positive) future, there is a need to be open and honest about the implications of not changing.

In the story, for Perkin, things may get a little hot and unpleasant. I am not advocating a scorched earth policy here; however we need to communicate clearly the impact of maintaining the status quo. There is a need to explain why engaging in the change and buying into the future vision is better than keeping things as they are. Keeping things as they are may be unsustainable in the future, lead to a drop in customer satisfaction or may impact in a negative way on how people perceive their job or organization. However the story here needs to be balanced, it should not be all doom and gloom with a weak vision of the future which is likely to create unnecessary anxiety. If the future vision is too ethereal it will be seen as a mirage.

Will Perkin now move; or will Perkin just want to stay and see what happens? Most of those that I talk to can recite instances of when, no matter how compelling the argument for change is, or how well communicated the vision and the implications of not changing are, there are always those who want to stay put and not engage with the change. Spending time exploring the reasons behind this standpoint is always worthwhile and the reasons can be plentiful. In "The Story of Perkin", there is the distance between the two islands to contend with. Can Perkin swim? How many sharks or other Perkin eating creatures may lurk below the surface of the sea? The challenges involved in making the move may far out-way the pull of the future vision or the impending difficulties that staying may bring. Perkin may decide that it is better to stay and to see how things pan out rather than taking, what Perkin perceives to be, a life-threatening risk. I am always interested in listening to the examples that people share which illustrate that no matter how comprehensive the communication is about the need to change, there is sometimes little information on how the change can be started; little exploration of how people perceive the challenges along the way; and what can help with the journey.

Every time I tell the story of Perkin, the audience suggests building a bridge between the two islands. "Build a bridge for Perkin to cross" as if this bridge is the answer to Perkin's transport issues between the two islands. During the conversations with the audience, people can recall their own bridges, the plans that have been put in place to help facilitate change. I continue to be amazed about how detailed these plans are. It seems as though the audience are very aware of the need to build the metaphorical bridge. Is it that easy?

In July 2013, my wife, Chris, and I went on holiday to County Antrim, a beautiful part of Northern Ireland. At Ballintoy you can visit Carrick-a-Rede, which is run by the National Trust. The Trust's membership handbook says:

> Connected to the cliffs by a rope bridge across the Atlantic Ocean, this rocky island is the ultimate clifftop experience. Jutting out from the Causeway Coastal Route, the 30 metre deep and 20 metre wide chasm separating Carrick-a-Rede from the mainland is traversed by an amazing rope bridge that was traditionally erected by salmon fishermen.

To Chris, who does not like heights, the words cliff, rope bridge (even an amazing one) and chasm were very daunting. The fact that many a Trip Adviser review stated that it is safe (these days), didn't really help. Now Chris did cross the bridge, although very slowly; however, when we were there I saw many people who decided not to cross despite the reassurance from the National Trust staff that it was safe. Perhaps this is how Perkin may feel when asked to cross the bridge in the story. How robust is the change plan? Has it been tested? What are the risks?

Does Perkin see the bridge as safe, will it hold Perkin's weight, what is the bridge made of, how is it attached to the cliff? These are some of the questions that Perkin may be contemplating before one foot is placed on the bridge. This chapter of the story of Perkin creates some interesting debates. Whilst the audience does suggest building a bridge, some people, when I mention Carrick-a-Rede, say that they would not venture across.

When we are planning change, what is our metaphorical bridge? Do those impacted by the change see and appreciate the integrity of the plans? Do they see the plans as being securely hitched to something solid, like the bridge in the story which needs to be securely hitched to the cliffs? Or do they see the plan as being potentially weak and one that will not bear much weight?

You may notice that there is another Perkin on the other side (see Figure 9.1). There seems to be a growing trend in organizations of identifying champions. Perhaps having change champions may help encourage people to embrace change and to see it as something that they should embrace. However, in the story of Perkin, how much do we know of this new character? Are they a friend of Perkin? Can they be trusted? Does Perkin see this person as having the same values and beliefs? Is this new character "a chip off the old Perkin block"? Whilst I am not criticizing the practice of identifying champions to help facilitate change, careful thought needs to be taken over who these champions are. They should be of the people and for the people. They should be held in high esteem, be trustworthy and display high levels of integrity. If I were scared of heights (I'm not), I would not be encouraged to cross Carrick-a-Rede rope bridge by someone wearing a "Freddy Kruger – Nightmare on Elm Street mask". So, the plan (the bridge) needs to be perceived as safe and the change champion trustworthy.

One time when I was telling the story of Perkin, a member of the audience suggested a helicopter. "Why not just hire a helicopter and fly Perkin across?" I have to admit I had not thought of this so, rather than be rude and just push this suggestion to one side, I decided to explore this in some depth. "What could the helicopter be?" I asked. Coaching, one to one support, personalized treatment was amongst the suggestions given. I decided to add the helicopter to the story. In some organizations, when resources allow, it may be worthwhile investing in personal, individually bespoke interventions. I would advocate a fleet of helicopters if resources would allow it and it could be shown that there is a good return on this investment. However, in times when resources are tight, it may be a luxury transport that most organizations cannot afford. I did welcome the suggestion though.

As the helicopter flies off into the distance (see Figure 9.2) we have to be careful that Perkin doesn't think the helicopter is there to help with the journey across to the other island. Often high cost resources are mooted in change scenarios; resources that do not materialize. Imagine how Perkin would feel if the helicopter flew low then off over the horizon. False hope can be devastating, so the resources that are employed to support people on the change journey need to be realistic and ones that can actually be employed.

Figure 9.2 The safety-net of engagement

Organizations may have chosen their "change champion" well; they may be encouraging; and in "The Story of Perkin", Perkin might start to make the journey across. But Perkin will need to feel safe along the way. This led me to think about helping people feel safe even if they feel uncertain. For this reason there is a "lifebuoy" half-way across the bridge. Perhaps the lifebuoy isn't the perfect metaphor and maybe there should be a chair or a refuge to allow Perkin to have a rest.

It is important that organizations consider the plans they are putting in place around change; how they can make people feel safe. Also, in Perkin's case, it may be helpful to have distance markers at key points along the bridge so Perkin knows that progress is being made. It is often the case that the plan for change is a long one and there needs to be stages along the way where people can see that progress has been made.

The vision of the future and the implications of not changing may be well communicated, the bridge may be firmly in place, Perkin's trusted friend may be beckoning Perkin across with a smiling face and encouraging gestures, there may be a refuge or a lifebuoy partway along the bridge; however, to Perkin the sharks and the "Perkin eating" creatures may still be circling. After all, in some change scenarios, there are those who remain reluctant. What then?

When I ask what else could we need for Perkin, the unanimous response is always a safety-net (as illustrated in Figure 9.2). This is the final part of the story and the final metaphor, although I accept there could be plenty more. So I ask my audience what the safety-net could be and the answers range from skills training, self-help groups and retraining to outplacement counselling and voluntary severance schemes.

The happy ending to my story is one where Perkin crosses the bridge and engages with the new environment. However, in some versions of the story Perkin may decide to stay and when things get tough jump off the island. Or, Perkin may fall off the bridge because it does sway a little too much. Or in a darker version of the story Perkin may be pushed. In reality, Perkin is like you and I with fears and aspirations, with skills that may be obsolete and that need replacing or refreshing, with caring responsibilities, with a future. Perhaps we should think more carefully about the safety-net for those who do not make it across first time or at all. What can we put in place that supports people to engage with the process of change, that allows them to feel safe, even though the journey may be treacherous and uncertain. How can we help people feel some degree of safety in this VUCA world?

For now that is the end of the story of Perkin. We have not explored how, once Perkin moves to the other island, Perkin's life develops. Does Perkin embrace life on the new island? That is perhaps the cue for another story, one that looks at embedding change.

Future research

This book has examined OC engagement. Unlike many traditional theories of management and behaviour, OC engagement and its ideas are still relatively fluid; they have yet to be fully defined and understood, and are far from widely recognized and used in the field of OC. Of course there is the danger of overgeneralizing from the broad perspective covered in this book and the various sources of data. The desire for breadth has meant that depth has been sacrificed in certain areas, such as not considering in depth OC engagement by specific sector, firm size, age or gender grouping. Since no book is complete, in its own right, there is always scope for further research. For OC engagement to thrive and survive in the longer term, it will need to be backed by a stronger evidence base addressing its drivers and consequences. Evidence of an association between OC engagement and specific antecedents and specified outcomes should be reflected in longitudinal studies. The perspectives of different groups of stakeholders in different sectors across the globe with OC engagement also requires further investigation. There is also scope to examine in more depth the nature of leadership and management required for a more engaged organization and importantly also the views of employees, which tend to be neglected in the organizational change literature.

The aim in this book has been to highlight a number of important issues and complexities of OC engagement and take forward the debate not only about the gaps in theory and knowledge but also in practice. For as Hutton (2010: 395) says: "We are starting to understand the link between fairness, prosperity and the good life. Now we just have to deliver it. After all, we deserve better."

References

Abrahamson, E. (2004). *Change without Pain*. Cambridge, MA: Harvard Business Press.

Agarwal, U. A. and Bhargava, S. (2013). Effects of psychological contract breach on organizational outcomes: Moderating role of tenure and educational levels. *Vikalpa*, 38(1), 13–26.

Aitken, C. and Keller, S. (2007). 'The CEO's role in leading transformation', *McKinsey Quarterly*, February. Available at www.mckinsey.com

Aitken, C. and Keller, S. (2009). 'The irrational side of change management', *McKinsey Quarterly*, April. Available at www.mckinsey.com

Aitken, C. and Scott, S. (2007). 'The CEO's role in leading transformation', *McKinsey*. Available at www.mckinsey.com

Ajzen, I. and Fishbein, M. (1980). *Understanding attitudes and predicting social behavior*. London: Prentice Hall.

Alavi, S. B. and Gill, C. (2017). Leading change authentically: How authentic leaders influence follower responses to complex change. *Journal of Leadership and Organizational Studies*, 24(2), 157–171.

Albrecht, S. (2013). *Handbook of employee engagement: Perspectives, issues, research and practice*. Cheltenham: Elgar.

Alderfer, C. P. (1972). *Existence, relatedness, and growth: Human needs in organizational settings*. NY: Free Press.

Alfes, K., Truss, C., Soane, E.C., Rees, C., and Gatenby, M. (2010). *Creating an engaged workforce*. Wimbledon: CIPD.

Ali, A., Ahmad-Ur-Rehman, M., Haq, I. U., Jam, F. A., Ghafoor, M. B., and Azeem, M. U. (2010). Perceived organizational support and psychological empowerment. *European Journal of Social Sciences*, 17(2), 186–192.

Allen, J., Jimmieson, N. L., Bordia, P., and Irmer, B. E. (2007). Uncertainty during organizational change: Managing perceptions through communication. *Journal of Change Management*, 7(2), 187–210.

Amble, B. (2010). CEOs misunderstand employee engagement. *Management-Issues*, 7 December.

Amiot, C. E., Terry, D. J., Jimmieson, N. L., and Callan, V. J. (2006). A longitudinal investigation of coping processes during a merger: Implications for job satisfaction and organizational identification. *Journal of Management*, 32(4), 552–574.

Amis, J., Slack, T., and Hinings, C. R. (2004). The pace, sequence, and linearity of radical change. *Academy of Management Journal*, 47(1), 15–39.

Andersson, L. M. and Pearson, C. M. (1999). Tit for tat? The spiraling effect of incivility in the workplace. *Academy of Management Review*, 24(3), 452–471.

Anthony, S. and Schwartz, E. I. (2017) What the best transformational leaders do, *Harvard Business Review*, Digital Articles, 2–9.

Appelbaum, S. H., Habashy, S., Malo, J. L., and Shafiq, H. (2012). Back to the future: Revisiting Kotter's 1996 change model. *Journal of Management Development*, 31(8), 764–782.

Archer, D. and Cameron, A. (2009). *Collaborative leadership: How to succeed in an interconnected world.* London: Routledge.

Armenakis, A., Bernerth, J., Pitts, J., and Walker, H. (2007). Organizational change recipients' beliefs scale: Development of an assessment instrument. *Journal of Applied Behavioural Science*, 43 (4), 481–505.

Armenakis, A. A. and Harris, S. G. (2002). Crafting a change message to create transformational readiness. *Journal of Organizational Change Management*, 15(2), 169–183.

Armenakis, A., Harris, S., and Mossholder, K. (1993). Creating readiness for organizational change. *Human Relations*, 46(6), 681–703.

Armor, D. A. and Taylor, S. E. (1998). Situated optimism: Specific outcome expectancies and self-regulation. In *Advances in experimental social psychology*. San Diego, CA: Academic Press, (30), 309–379.

Arthur, W. B. (2009). *The nature of technology: What it is and how it evolves.* NY: Simon and Schuster.

Aryee, S., Walumbwa, F. O., Zhou, Q., and Hartnell, C. A. (2012). Transformational leadership, innovative behavior, and task performance: Test of mediation and moderation processes. *Human Performance*, 25(1), 1–25.

Ashforth, B. E. and Kreiner, G. E. 2013. Profane or profound? Finding meaning in dirty work. In B. J. Dik, Z. S. Byrne, and M.F. Steger (eds) *Purpose and meaning in the workplace.* Washington: American Psychological Association, 127–150.

Atluri, V., Dietz, M., and Henke, N. (2017). Competing in a world of sectors without borders. *McKinsey Quarterly*, July.

Augier, M. and Teece, D. J. (2005). Reflections on (Schumpeterian) leadership: A report on a seminar on leadership and management education. *California Management Review*, 47(2), 114–136.

Auster, E. R. and Ruebottom, T. (2013). Navigating the politics and emotions of change. *MIT Sloan Management Review*, 54(4), 31–36

Avey, J. B., Reichard, R. J., Luthans, F., and Mhatre, K. H. (2011). Meta-analysis of the impact of positive psychological capital on employee attitudes, behaviors, and performance. *Human Resource Development Quarterly*, 22(2), 127–152.

Avolio, B. J. (2011). *Full range leadership development.* Thousand Oaks, CA: Sage.

Axelrod, R. H. (2010). *Terms of engagement: Changing the way we change organizations.* San Francisco, CA: Berrett-Koehler.

Badaracco, J. (2002). *Leading quietly: An unorthodox guide to doing the right thing.* Cambridge, MA: Harvard Business Press.

Baker, W., Cross, R., and Wooten, M. (2003). Positive organizational network analysis and energizing relationships. *Positive Organizational Scholarship: Foundations of a New Discipline*, 328–342.

Bakker, A. B. and Bal, M. P. (2010). Weekly work engagement and performance: A study among starting teachers. *Journal of Occupational and Organizational Psychology*, 83(1), 189–206.

Bakker, A. B. and Demerouti, E. (2007). The job demands-resources model: State of the art. *Journal of Managerial Psychology*, 22(3), 309–328.

Bakker, A., Demerouti, E., & Schaufeli, W. (2003). Dual processes at work in a call centre: An application of the job demands–resources model. *European Journal of Work and Organizational Psychology*, 12(4), 393–417.

Bakker, A. B., Emmerik, H. V., and Euwema, M. C. (2006). Crossover of burnout and engagement in work teams. *Work and Occupations*, 33(4), 464–489.

Bakker, A. B., Hakanen, J. J., Demerouti, E., and Xanthopoulou, D. (2007). Job resources boost work engagement, particularly when job demands are high. *Journal of Educational Psychology*, 99 (2), 274.

Balain, S. and Sparrow, P. (2009). *Engaged to perform: A new perspective on employee engagement: Academic report.* Centre for Performance-led HR, Lancaster University Management School.

Baldry, C., Bain, P., Taylor, P., Hyman, J., Scholarios, D., Marks, A., Watson, A., Gilbert, K., Gall, G., and Bunzel, D. (2007). *The meaning of work in the new economy*. Basingstoke: Palgrave.

Balogun, J. and Hailey, V. H. (2004). *Exploring strategic change* (2nd ed). London: Prentice Hall.

Baltes, P. B. (1997). On the incomplete architecture of human ontogeny: Selection, optimization, and compensation as foundation of developmental theory. *American Psychologist*, 52(4), 366–380.

Bamford, D. R. and Forrester, P. L. (2003). Managing planned and emergent change within an operations management environment. *International Journal of Operations and Production Management*, 23(5), 546–564.

Bandura, A. (ed.) (1995). *Self-efficacy in changing societies*. Cambridge: Cambridge University Press.

Bardwick, J. M. (2007). *One foot out the door: How to combat the psychological recession that's alienating employees and hunting American business*. NY: AMACOM.

Barrett, D. J. (2002). Change communication: Using strategic employee communication to facilitate major change. *Corporate Communications: An International Journal*, 7(4): 219–231.

Barrick, M. R., Mount, M. K., and Judge, T. A. (2001). Personality and performance at the beginning of the new millennium: What do we know and where do we go next? *International Journal of Selection and assessment*, 9(1–2), 9–30.

Barsade, S. G. (2002). The ripple effect: Emotional contagion and its influence on group behavior. *Administrative Science Quarterly*, 47(4), 644–675.

Barsade, S. and O'Neill, O. A. (2016). Manage your emotional culture. *Harvard Business Review*, 94 (1), 58–66.

Bartel, C. A. (2001). Social comparisons in boundary-spanning work: Effects of community outreach on members' organizational identity and identification. *Administrative Science Quarterly*, 46 (3), 379–413.

Bartol, K. M. and Martin, D. C. (1994). *Management*. NY: McGraw-Hill.

Bartunek, J. M., Rousseau, D. M., Rudolph, J. W., and DePalma, J. A. (2006). On the receiving end sensemaking, emotion, and assessments of an organizational change initiated by others. *Journal of Applied Behavioral Science*, 42(2), 182–206.

Bass, B. M. (1997). Does the transactional–transformational leadership paradigm transcend organizational and national boundaries? *American Psychologist*, 52(2), 130–139.

Bass, B. M. and Avolio, B. J. (1994) Introduction. In B. M. Bass and B. J. Avolio (eds) *Improving organizational effectiveness through transformational leadership*. Thousand Oaks, CA: Sage.

Bass, B. M. and Steidlmeier, P. (1999). Ethics, character, and authentic transformational leadership behavior. *Leadership Quarterly*, 10(2), 181–217.

Bates, S. (2004). Getting engaged, *HR Magazine*, 49(2), 44–51.

Baumeister, R. F. (1991). *Meanings of life*. NY: Guilford Press.

Beard, M. (2017). *Women and power: A manifesto*. London: Profile Books.

Beardwell, J., and Claydon, T. (eds) (2007). *Human resource management: A contemporary approach*. London: Pearson.

Becker, H. S. (1960). Notes on the concept of commitment. *American Journal of Sociology*, 66(1), 32–40.

Beer, M. (1990). *Leading change*. Cambridge, MA: Harvard Business School.

Beer, M. and Nohria, N. (2000). Cracking the code of change. *Harvard Business Review*, May–June, 133–141.

Bernerth, J. B., Armenakis, A. A., Feild, H. S., and Walker, H. J. (2007). Justice, cynicism, and commitment: A study of important organizational change variables. *Journal of Applied Behavioral Science*, 43(3), 303–326.

Bies, R. J. and Tripp, T. M. (2005). Badmouthing the company: Bitter employee or concerned citizen? In R. Kidwell and C. Martin (eds) *Managing organizational deviance*. Thousand Oaks, CA: Sage, 97–108.

Bissola, R. and Imperatori, B. (2014). The unexpected side of relational e-HRM: Developing trust in the HR department. *Employee Relations*, 36(4), 376–397.

Blanchard, H. (2012). How do you get leaders to change? *Chief Learning Officer*, October, 26–29.

Blau, P. M. (1964). *Exchange and power in social life*. NY: Wiley.

Bledow, R., Schmitt, A., Frese, M., and Kühnel, J. (2011). The affective shift model of work engagement. *Journal of Applied Psychology*, 96(6), 1246.

Blizzard, R. (2003). Employee engagement: Where do hospitals begin? *Gallup Poll Tuesday Briefing*, 11(2), 91.

Boal, K. B. and Schultz, P. L. (2007). Storytelling, time, and evolution: The role of strategic leadership in complex adaptive systems. *Leadership Quarterly*, 18(4), 411–428.

Boaz, N. and Fox, E. A. (2014). Change leader, change thyself. *McKinsey Quarterly*, March.

Bohm, D. (2013). *On dialogue*. London: Routledge.

Bolino, M., Long, D., and Turnley, W. (2016). Impression management in organizations: Critical questions, answers, and areas for future research. *Annual Review of Organizational Psychology and Organizational Behavior*, 3, 377–406.

Bono, J. E. and Judge, T. A. (2003). Self-concordance at work: Toward understanding the motivational effects of transformational leaders. *Academy of Management Journal*, 46(5), 554–571.

Bordia, P., Jones, E., Gallois, C., Callan, V. J., and DiFonzo, N. (2006). Management are aliens! Rumors and stress during organizational change. *Group and Organization Management*, 31(5), 601–621.

Bordia, P., Restubog, D., Jimmieson, N. L., and Irmer, B. E. (2011). Haunted by the past – effects of poor change management history on employee attitudes and turnover . *Group and Organization Management*, 36(2) 191–222.

Bovey, W. and Hede, A. (2001). Resistance to organizational change: the role of cognitive and affective processes. *Leadership and Organization Development Journal*, 22(8), 372–382.

Bowditch, J. L., Buono, A. F., and Stewart, M. M. (2001). *A primer on organizational behavior*. NY: Wiley.

Brammer, S., Rayton, B., and Millington, A. I. (2006). Do CSR policies affect employees' commitment to their organisations? *People Management*, 12(3), 14.

Bremmer, I. (2014). The new rules of globalization. *Harvard Business Review*, 92(1), 103–107.

Britt, T. W. (2003). Aspects of identity predict engagement in work under adverse conditions. *Self and Identity*, 2(1), 31–45.

Brown, P., Lauder, H., and Ashton, D. (2010). *The global auction: The broken promises of education, jobs, and incomes*. Oxford: Oxford University Press.

Brown, S. and Eisenhardt, K. (1997). The art of continuous change: linking complexity theory and time-paced evolution in relentlessly shifting organizations. *Administrative Science Quarterly*, 42, 1–34.

Bruch, H. and Menges, J. I. (2010). The acceleration trap. *Harvard Business Review*, 88(4), 80–86.

Buchanan, D. A. (2016). I couldn't disagree more: Eight things about organizational change that we know for sure but which are probably wrong. In Burnes, B. and Randall, J. (eds) *Perspectives on change: What academics, consultants and managers really think about change*. London: Routledge, 6–21.

Buchanan, D. A. and Badham, R. J. (2008). *Power, politics and organizational change* (2nd ed). London: Sage.

Buchanan, D. A. and Huczynski, A. A. (2017). *Organizational behaviour* (9th ed). Essex: Pearson.

Buchanan, D. and Storey, J. (1997). Role-taking and role-switching in organizational change: the four pluralities. *Innovation, Organizational Change and Technology*, 127–145.

Burke, W.W. (2002). *Organization change: Theory and practice*. Thousand Oaks, CA: Sage.

Burnes, B. (1996). No such thing as … a "one best way" to manage organizational change. *Management Decision*, 34(10), 11–18.

Burnes, B. (2006). *Managing change: A strategic approach to organisational dynamics* (6th ed). Harlow: Prentice Hall.

Burnes, B. (2009). Reflections: ethics and organizational change–time for a return to Lewinian values. *Journal of Change Management*, 9(4), 359–381.

Burnes, B. and Randall, J. (eds) (2016). *Perspectives on change: What academics, consultants and managers really think about change*. London: Routledge.

Burns, J. M. (1978). *Leadership*. NY: Harper and Row.

By, R. T. (2005). Organisational change management: A critical review. *Journal of Change Management*, 5(4), 369–380.

By, R. T. and Burnes, B. (eds). (2013). *Organizational change, leadership and ethics: Leading organizations towards sustainability*. London: Routledge.

By, R. T., Hughes, M., and Ford, J. (2016). Change leadership: Oxymoron and myths. *Journal of Change Management*, 16(1), 8–17.

Byeon, J. H. (2005). A systems approach to entropy change in political systems. *Systems Research and Behavioral Science*, 22(3), 223–231.

Caldwell, R. (2003). Change leaders and change managers: Different or complementary? *Leadership and Organization Development Journal*, 24(5), 285–293.

Campbell, C. H., Ford, P., Rumsey, M. G., and Pulakos, E. D. (1990). Development of multiple job performance measures in a representative sample of jobs, *Personnel Psychology*, 43, 277–300.

Carr, A. H. (1940). *America's last chance*. NY: Thomas Crowell.

Cartwright, S. and Cooper, C. L. (eds). (2008). *The Oxford handbook of personnel psychology*. Oxford: Oxford Handbooks.

Carver, C. S., Scheier, M. F., Miller, C., and Fulford, D. (2009). *Oxford handbook of positive psychology*. Oxford: Oxford University Press.

Caza, A. (2012). Typology of eight domains of discretion in organisations. *Journal of Management Studies*, 49(1) 144–177.

CBI and IPA (2011). *Transformation through employee engagement: Meeting the public services challenge*. London: Confederation of British Industry.

Cellan-Jones, R. (2014). Stephen Hawking warns artificial intelligence could end mankind. *BBC News*, 2.

Chalofsky, N. and Krishna, V. (2009). Meaningfulness, commitment, and engagement: The intersection of a deeper level of intrinsic motivation. *Advances in Developing Human Resources*, 11 (2), 189–203.

Chanlat, J. F. (1997). Conflict and politics. In A. Sorge & M. Warner (eds) *Handbook of Organizational Behaviour*. London: International Thomson, 472–480.

Chen, J. and Wang, L. (2007). Locus of control and the three components of commitment to change. *Personality and Individual Differences*, 42(3), 503–512.

Cherim, S. (2002). Influencing organizational identification during major change: A communication based perspective. *Human Relations*, 55, 1117–1137.

Christensen, C. M., Raynor, M. E., and McDonald, R. (2015). What is disruptive innovation? *Harvard Business Review*, 93(12), 44–53.

Christian, M. S., Garza, A. S., and Slaughter, J. E. (2011). Work engagement: A quantitative review and test of its relations with task and contextual performance. *Personnel Psychology*, 64(1), 89–136.

CIPD (2009). *Employee engagement, factsheet*. London: CIPD.

CIPD (2011). *Sustainable organisation performance: What really makes the difference?*London: CIPD.

Clinton, H. (2017). *What happened*. NY: Simon and Schuster.

Clinton, M. and Woollard, S. (2012). *Facing continuing uncertainty: The state of HR*. London: King's College.

Cole, M. S., Walter, F., Bedeian, A. G., and O'Boyle, E. H. (2012). Job burnout and employee engagement: A meta-analytic examination of construct proliferation. *Journal of Management*, 38 (5), 1550–1581.

Collins, D. (1998). *Organizational change: Sociological perspectives*. London: Routledge.

Colquitt, J. A., Conlon, D. E., Wesson, M. J., Porter, C. O., and Ng, K. Y. (2001). Justice at the millennium: A meta-analytic review of 25 years of organizational justice research. *Journal of Applied Psychology*, 86(3), 425–445.

Conference Board (2006). *Employee engagement: A review of current research and its implications*. NY: The Conference Board.

Conway, E. and Monks, K. (2008). HR practices and commitment to change: An employee-level analysis. *Human Resource Management Journal*, 18(1), 72–89.

Cooperrider, D. L., Whitney, D., and Stavros, J. M. (2005) *Appreciative inquiry handbook: The first in a series of AI workbooks for leaders of change*. San Francisco, CA: Berrett-Koehler.

Cortina, L. M., Magley, V. J., Williams, J. H., and Langhout, R. D. (2001). Incivility in the workplace: Incidence and impact. *Journal of Occupational Health Psychology*, 6(1), 64–80.

Cottrill, K., Denise Lopez, P., and Hoffman, C. (2014). How authentic leadership and inclusion benefit organizations. *Equality, Diversity and Inclusion: An International Journal*, 33(3), 275–292.

Cropanzano, R. and Mitchell, M. S. (2005). Social exchange theory: An interdisciplinary review. *Journal of Management*, 31(6), 874–900.

Csikszentmihalyi, M. (2000). *Beyond boredom and anxiety*. San Francisco, CA: Jossey-Bass.

Csikszentmihalyi, M., Abuhamdeh, S., and Nakamura, J. (2005). Flow. In A. J. Elliot and C. S. Dweck (eds) *Handbook of competence and motivation*. NY: Guilford Publications, 598–608.

Csikszentmihalyi, M. and Rathunde, K. (1993). The measurement of flow in everyday life: Toward a theory of emergent motivation. In J. E. Jacobs (ed.) *Developmental perspectives on motivation*. Lincoln: University of Nebraska Press, 57–97.

Cummings, T. G. and Worley, C. G. (2014). *Organization development and change*. London: Cengage learning.

Cunningham, C. E., Woodward, C. A., Shannon, H. S., Macintosh, J., Lendrum, B., Rosenbloom, D., and Brown, J. (2002). Readiness for organizational change: A longitudinal study of workplace, psychological, and behavioural correlates. *Journal of Occupational and Organizational Psychology*, 75, 377–392.

Cunningham, G. B. (2006). The relationships among commitment to change, coping with change, and turnover intentions. *European Journal of Work and Organizational Psychology*, 15(1), 29–45.

Dawson, P. (1994). *Organizational change: A processual approach*. London: Chapman.

Dawson, P. (2003). *Reshaping change: A processual perspective*. Oxon: Routledge.

Dawson, P. (2005). Changing manufacturing practices: An appraisal of the processual approach. *Human Factors and Ergonomics in Manufacturing and Service Industries*, 15(4), 385–402.

Dawson, P. and Andriopoulos, C. (2014). *Managing change, creativity and innovation*. London: Sage.

De Braine, R. D. and Roodt, G. (2011). The Job Demands-Resources model as predictor of work identity and work engagement: A comparative analysis. *SA Journal of Industrial Psychology*, 37(2), 52–62.

De Haan, E. and Kasozi, A. (2014). *The leadership shadow: How to recognize and avoid derailment, hubris and overdrive*. London: Kogan Page.

Decety, J. and Yoder, K. J. (2016). Empathy and motivation for justice: Cognitive empathy and concern, but not emotional empathy, predict sensitivity to injustice for others. *Social Neuroscience*, 11(1), 1–14.

Deloitte (2013). Organization acceleration. Available at www2.deloitte.com/content/dam/Deloitte/global/Documents/HumanCapital/dttl-hc-organizationacceleration-8092013.pdf

Demerouti, E. and Cropanzano, R. (2010). From thought to action: Employee work engagement and job performance. *Work Engagement: A Handbook of Essential Theory and Research*, 65, 147–163.

Demerouti, E., Xanthopoulou, D., Petrou, P., and Karagkounis, C. (2017). Does job crafting assist dealing with organizational changes due to austerity measures? Two studies among Greek employees. *European Journal of Work and Organizational Psychology*, 26(4), 574–589.

Development Concepts and Doctrine Centre (DCDC) (2010). *Global strategic trends*. London: Ministry of Defence.

DiFonzo, N. and Bordia, P. (1998). A tale of two corporations: Managing uncertainty during organizational change. *Human Resource Management*, 37(3–4), 295–303.

Dirks, K. T. and Ferrin, D. L. (2001). The role of trust in organizational settings. *Organization Science*, 12(4), 450–467.

Doty, E. (2017). Us versus them: Reframing resistance to change, *Strategy + Business*, January 30, January 30, Summer, Issue 87.

Duncan, R. (1979). Organizational learning: Implications for organizational design. *Research in Organizational Behavior*, 1, 75–123.

Dunphy, D. and Stace, D. (1993). The strategic management of corporate change. *Human Relations*, 46(8), 905–918.

Dutton, J. E. (2003). *Energize your workplace: How to create and sustain high-quality relationships at work.* NY: Jossey-Bass.

Dutton, J. E. and Heaphy, E. (2003). The power of high quality connections. In K. S. Cameron, J. E. Dutton, and R. E. Quinn (eds) *Positive organizational scholarship: foundations of a new discipline.* San Francisco, CA: Berrett-Koehler, 263–278.

Edmondson, A. C., Haas, M., Macomber, J. D., and Zuzul, T. (2015). The role of multiplier firms and megaprojects in leading change for sustainability. In R. Henderson, R. Gulati, and M. Tushman (eds) *Leading sustainable change: An organizational perspective.* Oxford: Oxford University Press, 273–297.

Edwards, A. R. (2005). *The sustainability revolution: Portrait of a paradigm shift.* Canada: New Society.

Egan, G. (1994) *Working the shadow side: A guide to positive behind-the-scenes management.* London: Jossey-Bass.

Erickson, T. J. (2010). *What's next, Gen X?: Keeping up, moving ahead, and getting the career you want.* Cambridge, MA: Harvard Business Press.

Fairhurst, G. and Sarr, R. (1996). *The art of framing.* San Francisco, CA: Jossey-Bass.

Fairhurst, G. T. and Uhl-Bien, M. (2012). Organizational discourse analysis: Examining leadership as a relational process. *Leadership Quarterly*, 23(6), 1043–1062.

Fairlie, P. (2011). Meaningful work, employee engagement, and other key employee outcomes: Implications for human resource development. *Advances in Developing Human Resources*, 13(4), 508–525.

Farndale, E., Pai, A., Sparrow, P., and Scullion, H. (2014). Balancing individual and organizational goals in global talent management: A mutual-benefits perspective. *Journal of World Business*, 49(2), 204–214.

Ferris, G. R. and Kacmar, K. M. (1992). Perceptions of organizational politics. *Journal of management*, 18(1), 93–116.

Ferris, G. R. and King, T. R. (1991). Politics in human resources decisions: A walk on the dark side. *Organizational Dynamics*, 20(2), 59–71.

Flamholtz, E. and Randle, R. (2011). *Corporate culture: The ultimate strategic asset.* Stanford: Stanford Business Books.

Fleck, S. and Inceoglu, I. (2010). A comprehensive framework for understanding and predicting engagement. In S. Albrecht (ed.) *Handbook of employee engagement: Perspectives, issues, research and practice.* Cheltenham: Edward Elgar, 31–42.

Fong, T. C. T. and Ng, S. M. (2012). Measuring engagement at work: Validation of the Chinese version of the Utrecht Work Engagement Scale. *International Journal of Behavioral Medicine*, 19(3), 391–397.

Ford, J. D. and Ford, L. W. (2009). Decoding resistance to change. *Harvard Business Review*, 87(4), 99–103.

Ford, J. D. and Ford, L. W. (2012). The leadership of organizational change: A view from recent empirical evidence. In W. Pasmore, R. Woodman, and A. Shani (eds). *Research in organization change and development.* Bingley: Emerald, 1–36.

Ford, C. and Sullivan, D. M. (2004). A time for everything: How the timing of novel contributions influences project team outcomes. *Journal of Organizational Behavior*, 25(2), 279–292.

Francis, H. and Reddington, M. (2012). Employer branding and organisational effectiveness. *People and organisational development: A new agenda for organisational effectiveness*, London: CIPD.

Fredrickson, B. L. (2001). The role of positive emotions in positive psychology: The broaden-and-build theory of positive emotions. *American Psychologist*, 56(3), 218–226.

Freeman, R. E., Wicks, A. C., and Parmar, B. (2004). Stakeholder theory and the corporate objective revisited. *Organization Science*, 15(3), 364–369.

Frese, M. (2008). The word is out: We need an active performance concept for modern workplaces. *Industrial and Organizational Psychology*, 1(1), 67–69.

Friedman, T. L. (2016). *Thank you for being late*. London: Allen Lane.

Friedman, T. L. (2017). From hands to heads to hearts. *The New York Times*. Available at www.nytimes.com/2017/01/04/opinion/from-hands-to-heads-to-hearts.html

Fuchs, S. and Edwards, M. R. (2012). Predicting pro-change behaviour: The role of perceived organisational justice and organisational identification. *Human Resource Management Journal*, 22(1), 39–59.

Fugate, M., Prussia, G. E., and Kinicki, A. J. (2012). Managing employee withdrawal during organizational change: The role of threat appraisal. *Journal of Management*, 38(3), 890–914.

Fugate, M., Kinicki, A. J., and Scheck, C. L. (2002). Coping with an organizational merger over four stages. *Personnel Psychology*, 55(4), 905–928.

Galvin, C. (2011). Starless horizons. *The Sunday Times Magazine*, 6 November, 59.

Gandini, A. (2016). Coworking: The freelance mode of organisation? *The Reputation Economy*. London: Palgrave, 97–105.

Gardner, W. L., Cogliser, C. C., Davis, K. M., and Dickens, M. P. (2011). Authentic leadership: A review of the literature and research agenda. *Leadership Quarterly*, 22(6), 1120–1145.

George, J. M. (2010). More engagement is not necessarily better: The benefits of fluctuating levels of engagement. In S. L. Albrecht (ed.) *New horizons in management. Handbook of employee engagement: Perspectives, issues, research and practice*. Northampton: Elgar, 253–263.

George, J. M. and Zhou, J. (2007). Dual tuning in a supportive context: Joint contributions of positive mood, negative mood, and supervisory behaviors to employee creativity. *Academy of Management Journal*, 50(3), 605–622.

Gersick, C. (1991). Revolutionary change theories: A multilevel exploration of the punctuated equilibrium paradigm. *Academy of Management Review*, 16, 10–36.

Gerits, L., Derksen, J. J., and Verbruggen, A. B. (2004). Emotional intelligence and adaptive success of nurses caring for people with mental retardation and severe behavior problems. *Mental Retardation*, 42(2), 106–121.

Gibson, J. W. and Tesone, D. V. (2001). Management fads: Emergence, evolution, and implications for managers. *Academy of Management Executive*, 15(4), 122–133.

Gill, C. and Caza, A. (2015). An investigation of authentic leadership's individual and group influences on follower responses. *Journal of Management*, 44(2), 530–554.

Gillet, N., Huart, I., Colombat, P., and Fouquereau, E. (2013). Perceived organizational support, motivation, and engagement among police officers. *Professional Psychology: Research and Practice*, 44(1), 46.

Goffee, R. and Jones, G. (2009). Authentic leadership. *Leadership Excellence*, 26(7), 3–4.

Goffman, E. (1961). *Asylums. Essays on the social situation of mental patients and other inmates*. NY: Doubleday Anchor.

Gorter, R. C., Te Brake, H. J., Hoogstraten, J., and Eijkman, M. A. (2008). Positive engagement and job resources in dental practice. *Community Dentistry and Oral Epidemiology*, 36(1), 47–54.

Gostick, A. and Eton, C. (2007). *The carrot principle: How the best managers use recognition to engage their people, retain talent, and accelerate performance*. NY: Simon and Schuster.

Gould, S. J. (1978). *Ever since Darwin: Reflections in natural history*. London: Burnett.

Graen, G. B. and Uhl-Bien, M. (1995). Relationship-based approach to leadership: Development of leader–member exchange (LMX) theory of leadership over 25 years: Applying a multi-level multi-domain perspective. *Leadership Quarterly*, 6, 219–247.

Graetz, F. (2000). Strategic change leadership. *Management Decision*, 38(8), 550–562.

Grant, A. M. and Ashford, S. J. (2008). The dynamics of proactivity at work. *Research in Organizational Behavior*, 28, 3–34.

Grant, A. M., Campbell, E. M., Chen, G., Cottone, K., Lapedis, D., and Lee, K. (2007). Impact and the art of motivation maintenance: The effects of contact with beneficiaries on persistence behavior. *Organizational Behavior and Human Decision Processes*, 103, 53–67.

Gratton, L. (2014). *The key*. London: McGraw-Hill.

Greenberg, E., Hirt, M., and Smit, S. (2017). The global forces inspiring a new narrative of progress. *McKinsey Quarterly*, 2, 35–52.

Gronn, P. (2000). Distributed properties: a new architecture for leadership. *Educational Management Administration and Leadership*, 28, 317–338.

Groscurth, C. and Shields, S. (2016). Managing in tough financial times: Does engagement help? *Gallup News*, June 7.

Groysberg, B. and Slind, M. (2012). Leadership is a conversation. *Harvard Business Review*, 90(6), 76–84.

Guest, D. (2014). Employee engagement: A sceptical analysis. *Journal of Organizational Effectiveness: People and Performance*, 1(2), 141–156.

Guimaraes, T. and Armstrong, C. (1998). Empirically testing the impact of change management effectiveness on company performance. *European Journal of Innovation Management*, 1(2), 74–84.

Gyurjyan, G., Parsons, I., and Thaker, S. (2014). *A health check for Pharma: Overcoming change fatigue in the pharmaceutical industry*. London: McKinsey.

Hakanen, J. J., Schaufeli, W. B., and Ahola, K. (2008). The Job Demands-Resources model: A three-year cross-lagged study of burnout, depression, commitment, and work engagement. *Work and Stress*, 22(3), 224–241.

Hakanen, J. J., Bakker, A. B., and Schaufeli, W. B. (2006). Burnout and work engagement among teachers. *Journal of School Psychology*, 43(6), 495–513.

Halbesleben, J. R. B. (2010). A meta-analysis of work engagement: Relationships with burnout, demands, resources, and consequences. In A. B. Bakker and M. P. Leiter (eds) *Work engagement: A handbook of essential theory and research*. Hove: Psychology Press.

Halbesleben, J. R., Harvey, J., and Bolino, M. C. (2009). Too engaged? A conservation of resources view of the relationship between work engagement and work interference with family. *Journal of Applied Psychology*, 94(6), 1452.

Hallberg, U. E. and Schaufeli, W. B. (2006). "Same same" but different? Can work engagement be discriminated from job involvement and organizational commitment? *European Psychologist*, 11(2), 119–127.

Hameed, I., Roques, O., and Arain, G. A. (2013). Nonlinear moderating effect of tenure on organizational identification (OID) and the subsequent role of OID in fostering readiness for change. *Group and Organization Management*, 1–27.

Hamel, G. (2012). *What matters now: How to win in a world of relentless change, ferocious competition, and unstoppable innovation*. London: Wiley.

Hamel, G. and Breen, B. (2007). *The future of management*. Boston: Harvard Business School Press.

Hamel, G. and Zanini, M. (2014). Build a change platform, not a change program. *McKinsey Insights*, 18 November.

Hardy, C. and Clegg, S. R. (1996). Some dare call it power. In S. Clegg, C. Hardy, & W. R. Nord (eds) *Handbook of organization studies*. London: Sage, 622–641.

Harter, J. K., Schmidt, F. L., and Hayes, T. L. (2002). Business-unit-level relationship between employee satisfaction, employee engagement, and business outcomes: A meta-analysis. *Journal of Applied Psychology*, 87, 268–279.

Harter, J. K., Schmidt, F. L., Killham, E. A., and Agrawal, S. (2009). *Gallup Q12® meta-analysis: The relationship between engagement at work and organizational outcomes.* London: Gallup.

Hatch, M. J. (2018). *Organization theory: Modern, symbolic, and postmodern perspectives.* (4th ed) Oxford: Oxford University Press.

Haudan, J. (2008). *The art of engagement: Bridging the gap between people and possibilities.* NY: McGraw-Hill.

Hayward, S. (2010). Engaging employees though whole leadership. *Strategic HR Review*, 9(3), 11–17.

Heaphy, E. D. and Dutton, J. E. (2008). Positive social interactions and the human body at work: Linking organizations and physiology. *Academy of Management Review*, 33(1), 137–162.

Herold, D. M., Fedor, D. B., and Caldwell, S. D. (2007). Beyond change management: A multi-level investigation of contextual and personal influences on employees' commitment to change. *Journal of Applied Psychology*, 92(4), 942–951.

Herold, D. M., Fedor, D. B., Caldwell, S., and Liu, Y. (2008). The effects of transformational and change leadership on employees' commitment to a change: A multilevel study. *Journal of Applied Psychology*, 93(2), 346–357.

Herscovitch, L. and Meyer, J.P. (2002). Commitment to organizational change: Extension of a three-component model. *Journal of Applied Psychology*, 87, 474–487.

Hirschman, A. O. (1970). *Exit, voice, and loyalty: Responses to decline in firms, organizations, and states.* Cambridge, MA: Harvard University Press.

Hirt, M. and Willmott, P. (2014). Strategic principles for competing in the digital age. *McKinsey Quarterly*, 5, 1.

Hobfoll, S. E. (1989). Conservation of resources: A new attempt at conceptualizing stress. *American Psychologist*, 44(3), 513–524.

Hodges, J. (2011). The role of the CEO and leadership branding: Credibility not celebrity. In R. Burke, G. Martin, and C. Cooper (eds) *Corporate reputation: Managing opportunities and threats.* London: Gower.

Hodges, J. (2016). *Managing and leading people through organizational change: The theory and practice of sustaining change through people.* London: Kogan Page.

Hodges, J. and Gill, R. (2014). *Sustaining change in organizations.* London: Sage.

Hodges, J. and Howieson, B. (2017). The challenges of leadership in the third sector. *European Management Journal*, 35(1), 69–77.

Hofstede, G. (1979). *Cultures and organisations: Software of the mind intercultural cooperation and its importance for survival.* London: McGraw-Hill.

Holbeche, L. (2017). *HR leadership.* London: Routledge.

Holbeche, L. and Matthews, G. (2012). *Engaged: Unleashing your organization's potential through employee engagement.* London: Wiley.

Holbeche, L. and Springett, N. (2004). *In search of meaning in the workplace.* Horsham: Roffey Park.

Holt, D. T., Armenakis, A. A., Field, H. S., and Harris, S. G. (2007). Readiness for organizational change: The systematic development of a scale. *Journal of Applied Behavioural Science*, 43, 232–255.

Hooper, A., and Potter, J. (2000). *Intelligent leadership.* London: Random House.

Hope-Hailey, V., Searle, R., and Dietz, G. (2012). *Where has all the trust gone.* London: CIPD.

Hornung, S. and Rousseau, D. M. (2007). Active on the job—Proactive in change how autonomy at work contributes to employee support for organizational change. *Journal of Applied Behavioral Science*, 43(4), 401–426.

Hulin, C. L. and Judge, T. A. (2003). Job attitudes. In W. Borman and D. Ilgen (eds) *Handbook of psychology: Industrial and organizational psychology.* NY: Wiley, 255–276.

Hüttermann, H. and Boerner, S. (2011). Fostering innovation in functionally diverse teams: The two faces of transformational leadership. *European Journal of Work and Organizational Psychology*, 20(6), 833–854.

Hutton, W. (2010). *Them and us: Changing Britain – why we need a fair society*. London: Hachette.

Hutton, W. (2011). Staff lead the focus on recovery. *The Sunday Times*, 6 March.

Huy, Q. N. (2001). In praise of middle managers. *Harvard Business Review*, 79(8), 72–79.

Huy, Q. N. and Bresman, H. M. (2017). Orchestrating organizational change in fast moving environments: A team-based model. *Academy of Management Proceedings*, 2017(1), 12026.

Ibarra, H. and Hansen, M. T. (2011). Are you a collaborative leader? *Harvard Business Review*, 89 (7/8), 68–74.

Imperatori, B. (2017). *Engagement and disengagement at work: Drivers and organizational practices to sustain employee passion and performance*. Switzerland: Springer.

Inoue, A., Kawakami, N., Ishizaki, M., Shimazu, A., Tsuchiya, M., Tabata, M., and Kuroda, M. (2010). Organizational justice, psychological distress, and work engagement in Japanese workers. *International Archives of Occupational and Environmental Health*, 83(1), 29–38.

Institute of Leadership and Management (2011). *Great expectations: Managing Generation Y*. Ashridge: Ashridge Business School.

Jackson, L. T., Rothmann, S., and Van de Vijver, F. J. (2006). A model of work-related well-being for educators in South Africa. *Stress and Health*, 22(4), 263–274.

Ji, Y. Y. and Oh, W. Y. (2014). An integrative model of diffusion and adaptation of executive pay dispersion. *Journal of Managerial Issues*, 70–85.

Jick, T. and Peiperl, M. (2010). *Managing change: Cases and concepts: Text and cases*. London: McGraw-Hill.

Jimmieson, N. L. and White, K. M. (2011). Predicting employee intentions to support organizational change: An examination of identification processes during a re-brand. *Journal of Social Psychology*, 50(2), 331–341.

Jones, R. A., Jimmieson, N. L., and Griffiths, A. (2005). The impact of organizational culture and reshaping capabilities on change implementation success: The mediating role of readiness for change. *Journal of Management Studies*, 42(2), 361–385.

Judge, T. A., Thoresen, C. J., Bono, J. E., and Patton, G. K. (2001). The job satisfaction–job performance relationship: A qualitative and quantitative review. *Psychological Bulletin*, 127(3), 376–407.

Kahn, W. A. (1990). Psychological conditions of personal engagement and disengagement at work. *Academy of Management Journal*, 33, 692–724.

Kahn, W. A. (1992). To be fully there: Psychological presence at work. *Human Relations*, 45(4), 321–349.

Kanter, R. M. (1997). *Rosabeth Moss Kanter on the frontiers of management*. Cambridge, MA: Harvard Business Press.

Kanter, R. M., Stein, B. A., and Jick, T. D. (1992). *The challenge of organizational change*. NY: The Free Press.

Kanungo, R. N. (1982). Measurement of job and work involvement. *Journal of Applied Psychology*, 67(3), 341–349.

Karatepe, O. M. (2013). High-performance work practices and hotel employee performance: The mediation of work engagement. *International Journal of Hospitality Management*, 32, 132–140.

Kast, F. E. and Rosenzweig, J. E. (1973). *Contingency views of organization and management*. NY: Science Research Associates.

Kataria, A., Garg, P., and Rastogi, R. (2013). Employee engagement and organizational effectiveness: The role of organizational citizenship behavior. *International Journal of Business Insights & Transformation*, 6, 102–113.

Kelliher, C., Clarke, C., Hailey, V. H., and Farndale, E. (2012). Going global, feeling small: An examination of managers' reactions to global restructuring in a multinational organisation. *International Journal of Human Resource Management*, 23(11), 2163–2179.

Keenoy, T. (2014). Engagement: A murmuration of objects? In K. Truss, *et al.* (eds) *Employee engagement in theory and practice*. Routledge: London, 197–220.

Kenexa Research Institute (2008). *Engaging the employee: A Kenexa Research Institute World Trends Report.* NY: Kenexa Research Institute.

Kenexa Research Institute (2010). *WorkTrends(TM) Annual Report.* NY: Kenexa Research Institute.

Kenexa Research Institute (2012). *Beyond engagement: The definitive guide to employee surveys and organizational performance.* NY: IBM.

Kernaghan, K. (2011). Getting engaged: Public-service merit and motivation revisited. *Canadian Public Administration*, 54(1), 1–21.

Khurana, R. (2002). The curse of the superstar CEO. *Harvard Business Review*, 80(9), 60–66.

Kiefer, T. (2005). Feeling bad: Antecedents and consequences of negative emotions in ongoing change. *Journal of Organizational Behavior*, 26(8), 875–897.

Kim, H. J., Shin, K. H., and Swanger, N. (2009). Burnout and engagement: A comparative analysis using the Big Five personality dimensions. *International Journal of Hospitality Management*, 28(1), 96–104.

Konovsky, M. A. (2000). Understanding procedural justice and its impact on business organizations. *Journal of Management*, 26(3), 489–511.

Konovsky, M. A. and Organ, D. W. (1996). Dispositional and contextual determinants of organizational citizenship behavior. *Journal of Organizational Behavior*, 253–266.

Korsgaard, M. A., Sapienza, H. J., and Schweiger, D. M. (2002). Beaten before begun: The role of procedural justice in planning change. *Journal of Management*, 28(4), 497–516.

Korunka, C., Kubicek, B., Schaufeli, W. B., and Hoonakker, P. (2009). Work engagement and burnout: Testing the robustness of the Job Demands-Resources model. *Journal of Positive Psychology*, 4(3), 243–255.

Kotter, J. P. (1996). *Leading change.* Boston, MA: Harvard Business School Press.

Kotter, J. P. (2012). Accelerate! *Harvard Business Review*, 90(11), (November), 45–58.

Kumar, K. and Thibodeaux, M. S. (1990). Organizational politics and planned organization change: A pragmatic approach. *Group and Organization Management*, 15(4), 357–365.

Kunz, J. and Linder, S. (2015). With a view to make things better: Individual characteristics and intentions to engage in management innovation. *Journal of Management and Governance*, 19(3), 525–556.

Langley, A. and Tsoukas, H. (2010). Introducing perspectives on process organization studies. *Process, Sensemaking, and Organizing*, 1(9), 1–27.

Latané, B. and L'Herrou, T. (1996). Spatial clustering in the conformity game: Dynamic social impact in electronic groups. *Journal of Personality and Social Psychology*, 70(6), 1218–1230.

Lavigna, R. J. (2013). *Engaging government employees: Motivate and inspire your people to achieve superior performance.* NY: AMACOM.

Lawrence, P. (2014). *Leading change: How successful leaders approach change management.* London: Kogan Page.

LePine, J. A., Podsakoff, N. P., and LePine, M. A. (2005). A meta-analytic test of the challenge stressor–hindrance stressor framework: An explanation for inconsistent relationships among stressors and performance. *Academy of Management Journal*, 48(5), 764–775.

Lester, P. B., Hannah, S. T., Harms, P. D., Vogelgesang, G. R., and Avolio, B. J. (2011). Mentoring impact on leader efficacy development: A field experiment. *Academy of Management Learning and Education*, 10(3), 409–429.

Levitt, T. (1960). Marketing myopia. *Harvard Business Review*, 38 (July–August 1960), 24–47.

Lewin, K. (1951). *Field theory in social sciences.* NY: Harper and Row.

Lines, R. (2004). Influence of participation in strategic change: Resistance, organizational commitment and change goal achievement. *Journal of Management Studies*, 40(3), 193–215.

Liu, Y. and Perrewe, P. L. (2005). Another look at the role of emotion in the organizational change: A process model. *Human Resource Management Review*, 15(4), 263–280.

Liu, Y., Caldwell, S. D., Fedor, D. B., and Herold, D. M. (2012). When does management's support for a change translate to perceptions of fair treatment? The moderating roles of change attributions and conscientiousness. *Journal of Applied Behavioral Science*, 48(4), 441–462.

Locke, E. A. (1976). The nature and causes of job satisfaction. In M. D. Dunnette (ed.) *Handbook of industrial and organizational psychology*, Vol. 1, 1297–1343.

Lockwood, N. R. (2007). Leveraging employee engagement for competitive advantage. *Society for Human Resource Management Research Quarterly*, 1, 1–12.

Lodahl, T. M. and Kejner, M. (1965). The definition and measurement of job involvement. *Journal of Applied Psychology*, 49, 24–33.

Luecke, R. (2003). *Managing change and transition*. Boston, MA: Harvard Business School Press.

Luisis-Lynd, L. and Myers, P. (2010). *How, why and when are organizations engaging with engagement?* Paper presented at the CIPD Conference, Keel University, UK.

Luthans, F. (2002). The need for and meaning of positive organizational behavior. *Journal of Organizational Behavior*, 23(6), 695–706.

Luthans, F. and Avolio, B. J. (2003). Authentic leadership: A positive developmental approach. In K. S. Cameron, J. E. Dutton, and R. E. Quinn (eds) *Positive organizational scholarship*. San Francisco, CA: Barrett-Koehler, 241–261.

Luthans, F. and Peterson, S. J. (2002). Employee engagement and manager self-efficacy. *Journal of Management Development*, 21(5), 376–387.

Luthans, F., Avolio, B. J., Avey, J. B., and Norman, S. M. (2007). Positive psychological capital: Measurement and relationship with performance and satisfaction. *Personnel Psychology*, 60(3), 541–572.

Luthans, F., Youssef, C. M., and Avolio, B. J. (2015). *Psychological capital and beyond*. Oxford: Oxford University Press.

Lyubomirsky, S., King, L., and Diener, E. (2005). The benefits of frequent positive affect: Does happiness lead to success? *Psychological Bulletin*, 131(6), 803–855.

Macey, W. H. and Schneider, B. (2008). The meaning of employee engagement. *Industrial and Organizational Psychology*, 1(1), 3–30.

Macey, W. H., Schneider, B., Barbera, K. M., and Young, S. A. (eds). (2009). *Employee engagement: Tools for analysis, practice, and competitive advantage*. New York: Blackwell.

MacLeod, D. and Clarke, N. (2009). *Engaging for success: Enhancing performance through employee engagement: A report to government*. London: Department for Business, Innovation and Skills.

Madhok, A. (2006). Revisiting multinational firms' tolerance for joint ventures: A trust-based approach. *Journal of International Business Studies*, 37(1), 30–43.

Mainemelis, C. (2001). When the muse takes it all: A model for the experience of timelessness in organizations. *Academy of Management Review*, 26(4), 548–565.

Manyika, J. (2017). *Technology, jobs and the future of work: A briefing note*. Washington: McKinsey.

Manyika, J., Lund, S., Robinson, K., Valentino, J., and Dobbs, R. (2015). *A labor market that works: Connecting talent with opportunity in the digital age*. Washington: McKinsey.

Manyika, J., Lund, S., Bughin, J., Woetzel, J. R., Stamenov, K., and Dhingra, D. (2016). *Digital globalization: The new era of global flows*. Washington: McKinsey.

Markoff, J. (2015). *Machines of loving grace: The quest for common ground between humans and robots*. London: HarperCollins.

Marshak, R. (1993). Lewin meets Confucius: A re-review of the OD model of change. *Journal of Applied Behavioural Science*, 24(4), 393–415.

Maslach, C. (2003). Job burnout: New directions in research and intervention. *Current Directions in Psychological Science*, 12(5), 189–192.

Maslach, C. and Jackson, S. E. (1981). The measurement of experienced burnout. *Journal of Organizational Behavior*, 2(2), 99–113.

Maslach, C. and Leiter, M. P. (1997). *The truth about burnout*. San Francisco, CA: Jossey-Bass.

Maslach, C., Schaufeli, W. B., and Leiter, M. P. (2001). Job burnout. *Annual Review of Psychology*, 52, 397–422.

Maslow, A. (1968). Some educational implications of the humanistic psychologies. *Harvard Educational Review*, 38(4), 685–696.

Masson, R. C., Royal, M. A., Agnew, T. G., and Fine, S. (2008). Leveraging employee engagement: The practical implications. *Industrial and Organizational Psychology*, 1, 56–59.

Mast, M. S., Hall, J. A., and Schmidt, P. C. (2010). Wanting to be boss and wanting to be subordinate: Effects on performance motivation. *Journal of Applied Social Psychology*, 40(2), 458–472.

Masten, A. S. (2001). Ordinary magic: Resilience processes in development. *American Psychologist*, 56(3), 227–238.

Mauno, S., Kinnunen, U., Mäkikangas, A., and Feldt, T. (2010). Job demands and resources as antecedents of work engagement: A qualitative review and directions for future research. In S. Albrecht (ed.) *Handbook of employee engagement: Perspectives, issues, research and practice.* Cheltenham: Elgar, 111–128.

Maurer, R. (2010). *Beyond the wall of resistance: Why 70% of all changes still fail… and what you can do about it.* Austin: Bard.

May, D. R., Gilson, R. L., and Harter, L. M. (2004). The psychological conditions of meaningfulness, safety and availability and the engagement of the human spirit at work. *Journal of Occupational and Organizational Psychology*, 77(1), 11–37.

Mayer, J. D. and Salovey, P. (1997). What is emotional intelligence? In P. Salovey and D. Sluyter (eds) *Emotional development and emotional intelligence: Educational implications.* NY: Basic Books, 3–31.

McCourt, W. (1997). Discussion note: Using metaphors to understand and to change organizations: A critique of Gareth Morgan's approach. *Organization Studies*, 18(3), 511–522.

Meaney, M., Pung, C., and Wilson, S. (2010). *Voices on transformation: Insights from business leaders on creating lasting change.* Washington: McKinsey.

Menon, S. T. (2001). Employee empowerment: An integrative psychological approach. *Applied Psychology: An International Review*, 50(1), 153–180.

Meyer, J. and Allen, N. (1991). A three-component conceptualization of organizational commitment. *Human Resource Management Review*, (1), 61–89.

Meyer, J. P. and Herscovitch, L. (2001). Commitment in the workplace: Toward a general model. *Human Resource Management Review*, 11(3), 299–326.

Meyerson, D. (2001). *Tempered radicals.* Boston, MA: Harvard Business School.

Michel, A. and González-Morales, M. G. (2013). Reactions to organizational change: An integrated model of health predictors, intervening variables, and outcomes. In S. Oreg (ed.) *The psychology of organizational change: Viewing change from the employee's perspective.* Cambridge: Cambridge University Press, 65–91.

Michela, J. L. & Vena, J. (2012). A dependence–regulation account of psychological distancing in response to major organizational change. *Journal of Change Management*, 12(1), 77–94.

Mishra, A. K. and Spreitzer, G. M. (1998). Explaining how survivors respond to downsizing: The roles of trust, empowerment, justice, and work redesign. *The Academy of Management Review*, 23 (3), 567–588.

Mone, E. M. and London, M. (2010). *Employee engagement through effective performance management: A practical guide for managers.* London: Routledge.

Moorhouse Consulting (2012). *Too much change?* London: Moorhouse.

Moorhouse Consulting (2014). *Barometer on change.* London: Moorhouse.

Moran, J. W. and Brightman, B. K. (2001) Leading organizational change. *Career Development International*, 6(2), 111–118.

Morgan, G. (2006). *Images of organization* (Updated ed). London: Sage.

Morgan, N. (2001). Do you have change fatigue? *Harvard Business School Working Knowledge Home.*

Moritz, S. C. (2017). *Examination of badges to increase nursing student engagement: A quasi-experimental study* (Doctoral dissertation, Capella University).

Morrison, E. W. and Milliken, F. J. (2000). Organizational silence: A barrier to change and development in a pluralistic world. *Academy of Management Review*, 706–725.

Mostert, K. and Rothmann, S. (2006). Work-related well-being in the South African Police Service. *Journal of Criminal Justice*, 34(5), 479–491.

Mostert, K. and Rathbone, A. D. (2007). Work characteristics, work-home interaction and engagement of employees in the mining industry. *Management Dynamics: Journal of the Southern African Institute for Management Scientists*, 16(2), 36–52.

Mudrack, P. E. (2004). Job involvement, obsessive-compulsive personality traits, and workaholic behavioral tendencies. *Journal of Organizational Change Management*, 17(5), 490–508.

Murphy, K. R. (1994). Toward a broader conception of jobs and job performance: Impact of changes in the military environment on the structure, assessment, and prediction of job performance. *Personnel Selection and Classification*, 85–102.

Nadella, S. (2017). *Hit refresh*. London: Collins.

Nadler, D. and Tushman, M. (1995). Types of organizational change: from incremental improvements to discontinuous transformation. In D. Nadler, R. Shaw, and A. Walton (eds) *Discontinuous change: Leading organizational transformation*. San Francisco, CA: Jossey-Bass, 15–34.

Nahavandi, A. (2000). *The art and science of leadership*. NJ: Prentice Hall.

Näswall, K., Sverke, M., and Hellgren, J. (2005). The moderating role of personality characteristics on the relationship between job insecurity and strain. *Work and Stress*, 19(1), 37–49.

Nelson, L. (2003). A case study in organizational change: Implications for theory. *The Learning Organization*, 10(1), 18–30.

Nembhard, I. M. and Edmondson, A. C. (2006). Making it safe: The effects of leader inclusiveness and professional status on psychological safety and improvement efforts in health care teams. *Journal of Organizational Behavior*, 27(7), 941–966.

Neves, P. (2009). Readiness for change: Contributions for employee's level of individual change and turnover intentions. *Journal of Change Management*, 9(2), 215–231.

Newman, D. A. and Harrison, D. A. (2008). Been there, bottled that: Are state and behavioral work engagement new and useful construct "wines"? *Industrial and Organizational Psychology*, 1 (1), 31–35.

Niedhammer, I., Chastang, J. F., David, S., Barouhiel, L., and Barrandon, G. (2006). Psychosocial work environment and mental health: Job-strain and effort-reward imbalance models in a context of major organizational changes. *International Journal of Occupational and Environmental Health*, 12(2), 111–119.

Nielsen, K., Randall, R., and Albertsen, K. (2007). Participants' appraisals of process issues and the effects of stress management interventions. *Journal of Organizational Behavior*, 28(6), 793–810.

Nielsen, K., Taris, T. W., and Cox, T. (2010). The future of organizational interventions: Addressing the challenges of today's organizations. *Work and Stress*, 24(3), 219–233.

Northouse, P. G. (2012). *Leadership: Theory and practice*. London: Sage.

NyeJr, J. S. (2014). Transformational and transactional presidents. *Leadership*, 10(1), 118–124.

Ogilvy and Mather (2016). *The velocity 12 report: The reshaping of global growth*. Available at www.ogilvy.com

Oreg, S. (2003). Resistance to change: Developing an individual differences measure. *Journal of Applied Psychology*, 88(4), 680.

O'Regan, N. and Ghobadian, A. (2012). John Lewis Partnership lessons in logical incrementalism and organic growth. *Journal of Strategy and Management*, 5(1), 103–112.

Orlikowski, W. and Hofman, J. (1997). An improvisational model for change management: The case of groupware technologies. *Sloan Management Review*, 38(2), 11–21.

Oshry, B. (2007). *Seeing systems: Unlocking the mysteries of organizational life* (2nd ed). San Francisco, CA: Berrett-Koehler Publishers.

Oswick, C., Keenoy, T., and Grant, D. (2002). Note: Metaphor and analogical reasoning in organization theory: Beyond orthodoxy. *Academy of Management Review*, 27(2), 294–303.

O'Toole, J. and Bennis, W. (2009). A culture of candor. *Harvard Business Review*, 87(6), 54–61.

Overell, S. (2008). *Inwardness: The rise of meaningful work*. London: Work Foundation.

Overell, S., Mills, T., Roberts, S., Lekhi, R., and Blaug, R. (2010). *The employment relationship and the quality of work*. London: Work Foundation.

Park, C. L. (2010). Making sense of the meaning literature: An integrative review of meaning making and its effects on adjustment to stressful life events. *Psychological Bulletin*, 136(2), 257.

Parkes, L. P. and Langford, P. H. (2008). Work–life balance or work–life alignment? A test of the importance of work-life balance for employee engagement and intention to stay in organisations. *Journal of Management and Organization*, 14(3), 267–284.

Parsell, G., Gibbs, T., & Bligh, J. (1998). Three visual techniques to enhance interprofessional learning. *Postgraduate Medical Journal*, 74, 387–390.

Paton, R. and McCalman, J. (2008). *Change management: A guide to effective implementation* (3rd ed). London: Sage.

Pearce, C. L. and Sims, H. P. J. (2002). Vertical vs shared leadership as predictors of the effectiveness of change management teams: An examination of aversive, directive, transactional, transformational, and empowering leader behaviors. *Group Dynamics: Theory, Research, and Practice*, 6(2), 172–197.

Perlow, L. and Williams, S. (2003). Is silence killing your company? *Harvard Business Review*, May, 52–58.

Pescosolido, A. T. (2002). Emergent leaders as managers of group emotion. *Leadership Quarterly*, 13 (5), 583–599.

Peterson, U., Demerouti, E., Bergström, G., Samuelsson, M., Åsberg, M., and Nygren, Å. (2008). Burnout and physical and mental health among Swedish healthcare workers. *Journal of Advanced Nursing*, 62(1), 84–95.

Petrou, P., Demerouti, E., Peeters, M. C., Schaufeli, W. B., and Hetland, J. (2012). Crafting a job on a daily basis: Contextual correlates and the link to work engagement. *Journal of Organizational Behavior*, 33(8), 1120–1141.

Pettigrew, A. M. (1977). Strategy formulation as a political process. *International Studies of Management and Organization*, 7(2), 78–87.

Pettigrew, A. M. and Whipp, R. (1993). *Managing change for competitive success*. Cambridge: Blackwell.

Pettigrew, A., Woodman, R., and Cameron, K. (2001). Studying organizational change and development: Challenges for future research. *Academy of Management Journal*, 44, 697–713.

Pfeffer, J. (1992). Understanding power in organizations. *California Management Review*, 34(2), 29–50.

Prochaska, J. O., DiClemente, C. C., Velicer, W. F., and Rossi, J. S. (1993). Standardized, individualized, interactive, and personalized self-help programs for smoking cessation. *Health Psychology*, 12, 399–405.

Pugh, D. (1993). Understanding and managing organizational change. In C. Mabey and B. Mayon-White (eds) *Managing change*. London: Chapman.

Purcell, J. (2014). Disengaging from engagement. *Human Resource Management*, 24, 241–254.

Purcell, J. (2013). Employee voice and engagement. In C. Truss, K. Alfes, R. Delbridge, and A. Shantz (eds) *Employee engagement in theory and practice*. London: Routledge.

Rabinowitz, S. and Hall, D. T. (1977). Organizational research on job involvement. *Psychological Bulletin*, 84(2), 265–288.

Rafferty, A. E. and Restubog, S. L. D. (2010). The impact of change process and context on change reactions and turnover during a merger. *Journal of Management*, 36(5), 1309–1338.

Rafferty, A. E., Jimmieson, N. L., and Armenakis, A. A. (2013). Change readiness: A multilevel review. *Journal of Management*, 39(1), 110–135.

Ravichandran, K., Arasu, R., and Kumar, S. A. (2011). The impact of emotional intelligence on employee work engagement behavior: An empirical study. *International Journal of Business and Management*, 6(11), 157.

Rayton, B., Dodge, T., and D'Analeze, S. (2012). *The evidence: Employee engagement task force "Nailing the evidence" workgroup.* London: Engage for Success.

Reed, M. (1990). From paradigms to images: The paradigm warrior turns post-modernist guru. *Personnel Review*, 19(3), 35–40

Rees, C., Alfes, K., and Gatenby, M. (2013). Employee voice and engagement: Connections and consequences. *International Journal of Human Resource Management*, 24(14), 2780–2798.

Resurreccion, P. F. (2012). Performance management and compensation as drivers of organization competitiveness: The Philippine perspective. *International Journal of Business and Social Science*, 3 (21), 20–30.

Rhoades, L. and Eisenberger, R. (2002). Perceived organizational support: A review of the literature. *Journal of Applied Psychology*, 87(4), 698–714.

Rhoades, L., Eisenberger, R., and Armeli, S. (2001). Affective commitment to the organization: The contribution of perceived organizational support. *Journal of Applied Psychology*, 86(5), 825–836.

Rich, B. L., Lepine, J. A., and Crawford, E. R. (2010). Job engagement: Antecedents and effects on job performance. *Academy of Management Journal*, 53(3), 617–635.

Rieley, J. and Clarkson, I. (2001). The impact of change on performance. *Journal of Change Management*, 2(2), 160–172.

Robbins, S. P. (2005). *Organizational behaviour.* Harlow: FT/Prentice Hall.

Robinson, D., Perryman, S., and Hayday, S. (2004). *The drivers of employee engagement.* Brighton: IES.

Robinson, I. (2006). *Human resource management in organisations.* London: CIPD.

Rogers, E. M. (1961). *Diffusion of innovations.* NY: The Free Press.

Rosenthal, S. A. and Pittinsky, T. L. (2006). Narcissistic leadership. *Leadership Quarterly*, 17(6), 617–633.

Rosso, B. D., Dekas, K. H., and Wrzesniewski, A. (2010). On the meaning of work: A theoretical integration and review. *Research in Organizational Behavior*, 30, 91–127.

Rothbard, N. P. (2001). Enriching or depleting? The dynamics of engagement in work and family roles. *Administrative Science Quarterly*, 46(4), 655–684.

Rotter, J. B. (1966). Generalized expectancies for internal versus external control of reinforcement. *Psychological Monographs: General and Applied*, 80(1), 1.

Rubin, H. (2009). *Collaborative leadership: Developing effective partnerships for communities and schools.* Thousand Oaks, CA: Corwin Press.

Rubin, R. B., Rubin, A. M., and Haridakis, P. M. (2009). *Communication research: Strategies and sources.* London: Cengage Learning.

Ruta, C. D., Imperatori, B., and Cavenaghi, J. (2012). The effects of ICT on sports fan management. *Social e-Enterprise: Value creation through ICT.* Hershey, PA: IGI Global, 243–262.

Ryan, R. M. and Deci, E. L. (2000). Self-determination theory and the facilitation of intrinsic motivation, social development, and well-being. *American Psychologist*, 55(1), 68.

Saks, A. M. (2006). Antecedents and consequences of employee engagement. *Journal of Managerial Psychology*, 21(6), 600–619.

Saks, A. M. (2008). The meaning and bleeding of employee engagement: How muddy is the water? *Industrial and Organizational Psychology*, 1, 40–43.

Salancik, G. R. and Pfeffer, J. (1978). Who gets power—and how they hold on to it: A strategic-contingency model of power. *Organizational Dynamics*, 5(3), 3–21.

Salanova, M., Agut, S., and Peiró, J. M. (2005). Linking organizational resources and work engagement to employee performance and customer loyalty: The mediation of service climate. *Journal of Applied Psychology*, 90(6), 1217–1227.

Salanova, M. and Schaufeli, W. B. (2008). A cross-national study of work engagement as a mediator between job resources and proactive behaviour. *International Journal of Human Resource Management*, 19(1), 116–131.

Salanova, M., Schaufeli, W. B., Xanthopoulou, D., and Bakker, A. B. (2010). The gain spiral of resources and work engagement: Sustaining a positive worklife. In A. B. Bakker and M. P. Leiter (eds) *Work engagement: A handbook of essential theory and research*. NY: Psychology Press, 118–131.

Saunders, M. N. and Thornhill, A. (2003). Organisational justice, trust and the management of change: An exploration. *Personnel Review*, 32(3), 360–375.

Schaufeli, W. B. and Bakker, A. B. (2004). Job demands, job resources, and their relationship with burnout and engagement: A multi-sample study. *Journal of Organizational Behavior*, 25(3), 293–315.

Schaufeli, W. and Enzmann, D. (1998). *The burnout companion to study and practice: A critical analysis*. Washington: Taylor and Francis.

Schaufeli, W. B., Bakker, A. B., and Salanova, M. (2006a). The measurement of work engagement with a short questionnaire: A cross-national study. *Educational and Psychological Measurement*, 66 (4), 701–716.

Schaufeli, W. B., Salanova, M., Gonzalez-Roma, V., and Bakker, A. B. (2002). The measurement of engagement and burnout: A two-sample confirmatory factor analytic approach. *Journal of Happiness Studies*, 3, 71–92

Schaufeli, W. B., Taris, T. W., and Bakker, A. B. (2006b). Dr. Jekyll or Mr. Hyde: On the differences between work engagement and workaholism. *Research Companion to Working Time and Work Addiction*. Cheltenham: Elgar, 193–217.

Schaufeli, W. B., Taris, T. W., and Van RhenenW. (2008). Workaholism, burnout, and work engagement: three of a kind or three kinds of employee well-being? *Applied Psychology*, 57(2), 173–203.

Schein, E. H. (1997). *Organizational culture and leadership* (3rd ed). San Francisco, CA: Jossey-Bass.

Schneider, B. (1990). *Organizational climate and culture*. San Francisco, CA: Jossey-Bass.

Schoorman, F. D., Mayer, R. C., and Davis, J. H. (2007). An integrative model of organizational trust: Past, present, and future. *Academy of Management Review*, 32(2), 344–354.

Schrage, M. (2012). Are you driving too much change, too fast? *HBR Blog Network*, 14 November.

Scroggins, W. A. (2008). Antecedents and outcomes of experienced meaningful work: A person-job fit perspective. *Journal of Business Inquiry*, 7(1), 68–78.

Seidlitz, L. and Diener, E. (1993). Memory for positive versus negative life events: Theories for the differences between happy and unhappy persons. *Journal of Personality and Social Psychology*, 64(4), 654.

Seligman, M. (2002). Positive psychology, positive prevention, and positive therapy. In C. Snyder and S. Lopez (eds). *Handbook of positive psychology*. Oxford: Oxford University Press, 3–12.

Seligman, M. E. & Csikszentmihalyi, M. (2000). Special issue on happiness, excellence, and optimal human functioning. *American Psychologist*, 55(1), 5–183.

Senior, B. (2002). *Organisational change* (2nd ed). London: Prentice Hall.

Seo, M.-G., Taylor, M. S., Hill, N. S., Zhang, X., Tesluk, P. E., and Lorinkova, N. M. (2012). The role of affect and leadership during organizational change. *Personnel Psychology*, 65, 121–165.

Shamir, B. (1991). Meaning, self and motivation in organizations. *Organization Studies*, 12(3), 405–424.

Shaw, P. (2002). *Changing conversations in organizations: A complexity approach to change*. London: Routledge.

Sheth, J. N. (2007). *The self-destructive habits of good companies*. London: Pearson.

Sherif, K. (2006). An adaptive strategy for managing knowledge in organizations. *Journal of Knowledge Management*, 10(4), 72–80.

Shimazu, A., Schaufeli, W. B., Kosugi, S., Suzuki, A., Nashiwa, H., Kato, A., and Goto, R. (2008). Work engagement in Japan: Validation of the Japanese version of the Utrecht Work Engagement Scale. *Applied Psychology*, 57(3), 510–523.

Shore, L. M., Coyle-Shapiro, J. A.-M., Chen, X.-P., & Tetrick, L. P. (2009). Social exchange in work settings: Content, process, and mixed models. *Management and Organization Review*, 5, 289–302.

Sidhu, R. (2015). Communication and engagement. In R. Smith*et al.* (eds) *The effective change manager's handbook*. London: Kogan Page.

Siegrist, J. (1996). Adverse health effects of high-effort/low-reward conditions. *Journal of Occupational Health Psychology*, 1(1), 27.

Siegrist, J., Starke, D., Chandola, T., Godin, I., Marmot, M., Niedhammer, I., and Peter, R. (2004). The measurement of effort–reward imbalance at work: European comparisons. *Social Science and Medicine*, 58(8), 1483–1499.

Siltaloppi, M., Kinnunen, U., and Feldt, T. (2009). Recovery experiences as moderators between psychosocial work characteristics and occupational well-being. *Work and Stress*, 23(4), 330–348.

Simon, B. and Kirchgaessner, S. (2010). Toyota lost way in rapid expansion, *Financial Times*, February 24. Available at www.ft.com/content/b955b84e-2089-11df-bf2d-00144feab49a

Smollan, R. K. and Sayers, J. G. (2009). Organizational culture, change and emotions: A qualitative study. *Journal of Change Management*, 9(4), 435–457.

Soane, E. (2014). Leadership and employee engagement. *Employee engagement in theory and practice*. London: Routledge, 149–162.

Sonnentag, S. (2003). Recovery, work engagement, and proactive behaviour: A new look at the interface between nonwork and work. *Journal of Applied Psychology*, 88, 518–528.

Sonnentag, S., Binnewies, C., and Mojza, E. J. (2010). Staying well and engaged when demands are high: The role of psychological detachment. *Journal of Applied Psychology*, 95(5), 965.

Sousa-Lima, M., Michel, J. W., and Caetano, A. (2013). Clarifying the importance of trust in organizations as a component of effective work relationships. *Journal of Applied Social Psychology*, 43, 418–427.

Sparrow, P. R. and Balain, S. (2010). Engaging HR strategists: Do the logics match the realities. In S. Albrecht (ed.) *The handbook of employee engagement: Perspectives, issues, research and practice*. Cheltenham: Elgar, 263–296.

Spector, P. E. (1997). *Job satisfaction: Application, assessment, causes, and consequences*. London: Sage.

Spillane, J. P. (2006). *Distributed leadership*. San Francisco, CA: Jossey-Bass.

Stace, D. and Dunphy, D. C. (2001). *Beyond the boundaries: Leading and re-creating the successful enterprise*. London: McGraw-Hill.

Stanley, D. J., Meyer, J. P., and Topolnytsky, L. (2005). Employee cynicism and resistance to organizational change. *Journal of Business and Psychology*, 19(4), 429–459.

Stensaker, I., Meyer, C. B., Falkenberg, J., and Haueng, A. C. (2002). Excessive change: Coping mechanisms and consequences. *Organizational Dynamics*, 31(3), 296–312.

Stoughton, A. and Ludema, J. (2012). The driving forces of sustainability. *Journal of Organizational Change Management*, 25(4), 501–517.

Styhre, A. (2002). Non-linear change in organizations: Organization change management informed by complexity theory. *Leadership and Organization Development Journal*, 23(6), 343–351.

Sulea, C., Virga, D., Maricutoiu, L. P., Schaufeli, W., Zaborila Dumitru, C., and Sava, F. A. (2012). Work engagement as mediator between job characteristics and positive and negative extra-role behaviors. *Career Development International*, 17(3), 188–207.

Sundarajan, A. (2015). The Gig Economy is coming: What will it mean for work? *Guardian Newspaper*, 25 July.

Sverke, M., Hellgren, J., Näswall, K., Göransson, S., and Öhrming, J. (2008). Employee participation in organizational change: Investigating the effects of proactive vs. reactive implementation of downsizing in Swedish hospitals. *Journal of Human Resource Management*, 22(2), 111–129.

Sweetman, D. and Luthans, F. (2010). The power of positive psychology: Psychological capital and work engagement. *Work engagement: A handbook of essential theory and research*. New York: Psychology Press, 54–68.

Taipale, S., Selander, K., Anttila, T., and Nätti, J. (2011). Work engagement in eight European countries: The role of job demands, autonomy, and social support. *International Journal of Sociology and Social Policy*, 31(7/8), 486–504.

Tajfel, H. and Turner, J. C. (1986). The social identity theory of intergroup behavior. In S. Worchel and W. G. Austin (eds) *Psychology of intergroup relations*. Chicago: Nelson-Hall, 7–24.

Tamkin, P., Pearson, G., Hirsh, W., and Constable, S. (2010). *Exceeding expectation: The principles of outstanding leadership*. London: The Work Foundation.

Taris, T. W., Horn, J. E. V., Schaufeli, W. B., and Schreurs, P. J. (2004). Inequity, burnout and psychological withdrawal among teachers: A dynamic exchange model. *Anxiety, Stress & Coping*, 17(1), 103–122.

Taris, T. W., Schaufeli, W. B., and Shimazu, A. (2010). *The push and pull of work: The differences between workaholism and work engagement*. Hove: Psychology Press.

Taylor, P. and Hirst, J. (2001). Facilitating effective change and continuous improvement: The Mortgage Express way. *Journal of Change Management*, 2(1), 67–71.

Terkel, S. (1974). *Working*. NY: Pantheon.

Thomas, R. and Hardy, C. (2011). Reframing resistance to organizational change. *Scandinavian Journal of Management*, 27(3), 322–331.

Thornhill, J. (2018). Why automation may be more evolution than revolution. *Financial Times*, 24 January, 4.

Tims, M. and Bakker, A. B. (2010). Job crafting: Towards a new model of individual job redesign. *Journal of Industrial Psychology*, 36(2), 1–9.

Tims, M., Bakker, A. B., and Derks, D. (2013). The impact of job crafting on job demands, job resources, and well-being. *Journal of Occupational Health Psychology*, 18(2), 230–240.

Tims, M., Bakker, A. B., and Xanthopoulou, D. (2011). Do transformational leaders enhance their followers' daily work engagement? *Leadership Quarterly*, 22(1), 121–131.

Tinker, T. (1986). Metaphor or reification: Are radical humanists really libertarian anarchists? *Journal of Management Studies*, 23(4), 363–384.

Torkelson, E. and Muhonen, T. (2003). Coping strategies and health symptoms among women and men in a downsizing organisation. *Psychological Reports*, 92(3), 899–907.

Towers Watson (2013). *Want super engaged members? Learn how your members think, feel and act*. Australia: Towers Watson.

Towers Perrin. (2006). *The ISR employee engagement report*. NY: Towers Perrin.

Towers Perrin. (2003). Working today: Understanding what drives employee engagement. *The 2003 Towers Perrin Talent Report*. NY: Towers Perrin.

Treviño, L. K. and Brown, M. E. (2005). The role of leaders in influencing unethical behavior in the workplace. *Managing Organizational Deviance*, 69–87.

Truss, K., Soane, E., Edwards, C. Y. L., Wisdom, K., Croll, A., and Burnett, J. (2006). *Working life: Employee attitudes and engagement 2006*. London: CIPD.

Tsoukas, H. (1993). Analogical reasoning and knowledge generation in organization theory. *Organization Studies*, 14(3), 323–346.

Tushman, M. and Romanelli, E. (1985). Organizational evolution: a metamorphosis model of convergence and reorientation. In B. Staw and I. Cummings (eds) *Research in organization behaviour* (7), Greenwich: JAI Press, 171–222.

Tyler, T. R. and Blader, S. L. (2003). The group engagement model: Procedural justice, social identity, and cooperative behavior. *Personality and Social Psychology Review*, 7(4), 349–361.

United Nations (2014). *World urbanisation prospects*. New York: United Nations.

Vakola, M. and Nikolaou, I. (2005). Attitudes towards organizational change: What is the role of employees' stress and commitment? *Employee Relations*, 27(2), 160–174.

van Beek, I., Taris, T. W., and Schaufeli, W. B. (2011). Workaholic and work engaged employees: Dead ringers or worlds apart? *Journal of Occupational Health Psychology*, 16(4), 468.

Van de Ven, A. H. (1992). Suggestions for studying strategy process: A research note. *Strategic Management Journal*, 13(5), 169–188.

Van de Ven, A. H. and Polley, D. (1992). Learning while innovating. *Organization Science*, 3(1), 92–116.

Van den Broeck, A., Ferris, D. L., Chang, C.-H., and Rosen, C. C. (2016). A review of self-determination theory's basic psychological needs at work. *Journal of Management*, 42, 1195–1229.

van Wanrooy, B., Bewley, H., Bryson, A., Forth, J., Freeth, S., Stokes, L., and Wood, S. (2013). *Employment relations in the shadow of recession*. London: Palgrave.

van Wingerden, J. V., Bakker, A. B., and Derks, D. (2016). A test of a job demands-resources intervention. *Journal of Managerial Psychology*, 31(3), 686–701.

Vancouver, J. B., Thompson, C. M., Tischner, E. C., and Putka, D. J. (2002). Two studies examining the negative effect of self-efficacy on performance. *Journal of Applied Psychology*, 87(3), 506–516.

Vince, R. and Broussine, M. (1996). Paradox, defense and attachment: Accessing and working with emotions and relations underlying organizational change. *Organization Studies*, 17(1), 1–21.

Vincent-Höper, S., Muser, C., and Janneck, M. (2012). Transformational leadership, work engagement, and occupational success. *Career Development International*, 17(7), 663–682.

Vorhauser-Smith, S. (2012). Going glocal: How smart brands adapt to foreign markets. Available at www.forbes.com

Vroom, V. H. (1964). *Work and motivation*. NY: Wiley.

Walker, H. J., Armenakis, A., and Bernerth, J. B. (2007). Factors influencing organizational change efforts: An integrative investigation of change content, context, processes and individual differences. *Journal of Organizational Change Management*, 20(6), 761–773.

Walumbwa, F. O., Avolio, B. J., Gardner, W. L., Wernsing, T. S., and Peterson, S. J. (2008). Authentic leadership: Development and validation of a theory-based measure. *Journal of Management*, 34(1), 89–126.

Wanberg, C. R., and Banas, J. T. (2000). Predictors and outcomes of openness to changes in a reorganizing workplace. *Journal of Applied Psychology*, 85(1): 132–142.

Wang, D. S. and Hsieh, C. C. (2013). The effect of authentic leadership on employee trust and employee engagement. *Social Behavior and Personality: An International Journal*, 41(4), 613–624.

Wang, X. L., Shi, Z. B., Ng, S. M., Wang, B., and Chan, C. L. (2011). Sustaining engagement through work in postdisaster relief and reconstruction. *Qualitative Health Research*, 21(4), 465–476.

Ward, M. (1994). *Why your corporate culture change isn't working*. Aldershot: Gower.

Wefald, A. J. and Downey, R. G. (2009). Job engagement in organizations: Fad, fashion, or folderol? *Journal of Organizational Behavior*, 30(1), 141–145.

Weick, K. (2000). Emergent change as a universal in organizations. In M. Beer and N. Nohria (eds) *Breaking the code of change*. Boston: Harvard Business Review Press.

Weiss, H. M. and Cropanzano, R. (1996). Affective events theory: A theoretical discussion of the structure, causes and consequences of affective experiences at work. In B. Staw & L. Cummings (eds) *Research in organizational behavior: An annual series of analytical essays and critical reviews*. Greenwich, CT: JAI Press (19), 1–74.

Welbourne, T. (2011). Engaged in what? So what? A role-based perspective for the future of employee engagement. In A. Wilkinson and K. Townsend (eds) *The future of employment relations: New Paradigms*. Basingstoke: Palgrave.

Wellins, R. S., Bernthal, P., and Phelps, M. (2005). *Employee engagement: The key to realising competitive advantage*. Development Dimensions International, 1–30.

Wheatley, M. and Frieze, D. (2011). *Walk out walk on: A learning journey into communities daring to live the future now*. San Francisco, CA: Berrett-Koehler.

Whelan-Barry, K., Gordon, J. R., and Hining, C. R. (2003). Strengthening organizational change processes: Recommendations and implications from a multilevel analysis. *Journal of Applied Behavioral Science*, (39), 186–207.

Whetten, D. A. (2009). Modeling theoretic propositions. In A. S. Huff (ed.) *Designing Research for Publication*. London: Sage, 217–250.

Wilson, M. (2004). *Constructing measures: An item response modeling approach*. London: Routledge.

Winkler, S., König, C. J., & Kleinmann, M. (2012). New insights into an old debate: Investigating the temporal sequence of commitment and performance at the business unit level. *Journal of Occupational and Organizational Psychology*, 85(3), 503–522.

Winslow, J. H., Nielsen, K., and Borg, V. (2009). Generating support from supervisors to their subordinates in organizations under external pressure: A multilevel, multisource study of support and reciprocation in Danish elder care. *Journal of Advanced Nursing*, 65(12), 2649–2657.

Witters, D. and Agrawal, S. (2015). Well-being enhances benefits of employee engagement. *Gallup Business Journal*, 27 October.

Witzel, M. (2015). *Management consultancy*. London: Routledge.

Wrzesniewski, A. and Dutton, J. E. (2001). Crafting a job: Revisioning employees as active crafters of their work. *Academy of Management Review*, 26, 179–201.

Xanthopoulou, D., Bakker, A. B., Demerouti, E., and Schaufeli, W. B. (2009). Reciprocal relationships between job resources, personal resources, and work engagement. *Journal of Vocational Behavior*, 74(3), 235–244.

XenikouA. and FurnhamA. (2013). *Group dynamics and organizational culture: Effective work groups and organizations*. Hampshire: Palgrave.

Yahaya, A., Yahaya, N., Maalip, H., Ramli, J., and Md Kamal, M. (2012). The relationship between the occupational stress, organizational commitment, and job satisfaction with organizational citizenship behavior. *Archives Des Sciences*, 65(3), 55–73.

Youssef-Morgan, C. and Bockorny, K. (2013). Engagement in the context of positive psychology. In C. Truss, K. Alfes, R. Delbridge, A. Shantz, and E. C. Soane (eds) *Employee engagement in theory and practice*. London: Routledge

Yukl, G. (2006). *Leadership in organization* (6th ed). London: Pearson.

Zak, P. J. (2017). The neuroscience of trust: Management behaviors that foster employee engagement. *Harvard Business Review*, (January/February), 84–90.

Index

Note: Page numbers in italic type refer to figures.
Page numbers followed by 'n' refer to notes.

Abrahamson, E. 53–54
absenteeism 107
absorption 34–35
academia 33–37; engagement perspectives 33–37; physical, emotional and cognitive aspects 33–34, 39–41
Academy of Management Journal (Kahn) 59
acceleration trap 54
accomplishment, purposeful 39–40, 181
accountability 27, 166, 170
action phase 50
adaptability 27–28, 135; failure 1–2
ADKAR change management model 167
Aetna 159
Affective Events Theory (AET) 104
Affective Shift Theory 37–38
affectivity, positive/negative 101, 173–174
Agness, L. 175–180
Airbnb 17
Aitken, C., and Keller, S. 132
Ajzen, I., and Fishbein, M. 39
Alderfer, C. 40
Alfes, K., *et al.* 34, 81, 110
Ali, A., *et al.* 119
Alibaba 17, 52
Altimeter Group 13
altruism 30
Amazon 29, 52
American Psychological Association (APA) 60
Amis, J., *et al.* 54
antecedents 88–106; contextual 88–94; individual 100–106; and outcomes *89*, 106–113; processual 94–100
anxiety 158
Aon 30
Appelbaum, S., *et al.* 45
Apple 17

Archer, D., and Cameron, A. 122
Armenakis, A., and Harris, S. 93
Arthur, W. 10
artificial intelligence (AI) 10, 12, 18–21, 133
Ashford, S., and Grant, A. 142
Ashforth, B., and Kreiner, G. 62–63
assumptions 44–46, 109
AT&T 107
attachment 30
attention 34
attitude 35, 109; transient 38–40
Aurora Transact 108
Auster, E., and Ruebottom, T. 123
Australia 16, 20, 81
authenticity 132–133, 157, 160
automation 11–12, 19–21
Autonomous Job Marketplace (DAJ) 12
autonomy 61–62, 82–85, 105–106, 120, 142
Avolio, B., and Bass, B. 119
awareness 133
Axelrod, R. 162

Badaracco, J. 122
Bakker, A.: *et al.* 103, 146, 169; and Schaufeli, W. 68, 96, 111
Balain, S., and Sparrow, P. 33
Balogun, J., and Hailey, V. 48
bandwagon effect 136
Bardwick, J. 139
Barrett, D. 158
Barsade, S., and O'Neill, O. 105
Bass, B.: and Avolio, B. 119; and Steidlmeier, P. 121
Bates, S. 77
Beard, M. 126
Becker, H. 66–67
Beer, M. 45; and Nohria, N. 55

behaviour 5, 34–38, 78, 128; discretionary 152; extra-role, effort and advocacy 64, 112; health 50; organizational citizenship (OCB) 67–70, 76; political 130–131; positive 112, 129; positive organizational (POB) 102; reactions to OC 173–175; revisions 44; Say, Stay and Strive 30; shifts 155, 178–180; workplace 63; workshops 175–176
beliefs 130
belongingness 96
Bennis, W., and O'Toole, J. 141
Bertolini, M. 159
best practice approaches 144
bias 136
black elephant 16
black swan 16
Blanchard, H. 151
Blasé, W. 107
Blau, P. 141
Blockbuster 1
Blockchain 10, 52, 108
Blocklancer 12
Bloomberg 84
Boaz, N., and Fox, E. 132
Boerner, S., and Hüttermann, H. 121
Bohm, D. 161–162
Borders Books 2
Bordia, P., et al. 92
boredom 104
Bowditch, J., et al. 101
Breen, B., and Hamel, G. 139
Bremmer, I. 14
Bresman, H., and Huy, Q. 165
Brightman, B., and Moran, J. 28
Broussine, M., and Vince, R. 45
Brown, S., and Eisenhardt, K. 53
Bruch, H., and Menges, J. 54
Buchanan, D. 45; and Huczynski, A. 100, 172
Burke, W. 52
Burnes, B. 42–45, 49–51
burnout 5, 36–37, 54, 77, 80
buy-in 144–145, 166, 175, 180

Cadbury's chocolate factories 141
Caldwell, R. 131
Cameron, A., and Archer, D. 122
Campbell, C., et al. 68
Carr, A. 11
causality 76
certainty 42, 109
Chambers, J. 161
change 28, 63, 145, 182; content 28; crisis-driven 53; cyclical theories and phases 49–50; discontinuous 50–51; emergent 46–47; environment creation 117–149; kaleidoscope 48; management training

(ADKAR model) 167; meaning and achievement relationship 134–135; nature and organization history 92–93; overload 78–79; planned 44–46, 50; process 49, 56–57; punctuated equilibrium 53; readiness and beliefs 93–94; strategic 28–29; structural 140; theories, critics and implications 42–58; top-down and bottom-up approach 175–180, 176; transformational 51–54
Change without Pain (Abrahamson) 54
chaos 42
Chartered Institute of Professional Development (CIPD) 32–33
chatbots 12, 18
Chen, J., and Wang, L. 102
Cherim, S. 90
China 17, 52, 120
Christian, M., et al. 29, 76
Cisco Systems 160–161
civility 156
clarity 135–136, 151, 157, 163; roles and responsibilities RACI chart 165–166
Clarke, N., and MacLeod, D. 76
Climate Action Conference (2016) 16
Clinton Cards 2
Clinton, H. 1, 28
Clinton, M., and Woollard, S. 77
Cloud 20
CNBC (cable/news channel) 84
co-creation 5, 163–168, 173, 180; collaboration 163–165; roles and responsibilities clarity 165–166; sense of ownership 164–165; stages 167; team-based approach 167
Cole, M., et al. 36
collaboration 20, 27, 108–109, 163–165; and leadership 122–123; workspaces 12, 20
Collaborative Leadership: Effective Partnerships for Communities and Schools (Rubin) 122
Collaborative Leadership: How to Succeed in an Interconnected World (Archer and Cameron) 122
Colleague Letter of Understanding (CLOU) 163
Collins, D. 42
Colquitt, J., et al. 95
commitment 4, 22, 29–30, 66–67, 104, 180
communication 20, 81, 94–96, 141, 146, 157–163, 167, 183; effective 157–158; framing and goals 158–159; listening 161–162; OC conversations 160–161; verbal and stories 158–159, 162–163; web-based technology 159
community 27, 38, 159
competence 61

competition 17, 77
complacency 2
Confederation of British Industry (CBI) 118
Conference Board 32
confidence 91, 129
conflict 16, 25, 36, 42–46, 49, 84, 133–135, 140, 166; of interest 123–124, 175; views 155–156
connectivity 5, 156–157, 173, 180
Conservation of Resources (COR) theory 61–62, 70
consistency 42
consultancy 30–32, 107, 111, 126, 151; engagement perspectives 30–32; fad or fashion 75–77; fees 77
contemplation phase 50
contextual antecedents 88–94
continuity 42, 89
control 101–102, 105–106, 147–148
conversations 160–161, 178–180, 184; attributes 162–163
coping mechanisms 79, 93, 102
coral bleaching 16
Cortana 12
Cottrill, K., et al. 156
Crabtree, M. 181–186; and The Story of Perkin 182, 189–194, 185
creativity 20, 28, 103
across cultures 80–86; countries 81–85; Mauritius case study 82–85; sectors 80; theoretical perspectives 5
cryptocurrencies 108
culture, organizational 89–90, 93
Cummings, T., and Worley, C. 49
cyber security 12–13, 17
cynicism 36, 54, 146

Darwin, C. 19–21; digital 19; evolution theory 53; survival of the fittest 21
data smelting 11; and analytics 143
Davies, A. 97–100
Dawson, P. 46, 49, 125
decentralization 28
Decety, J., and Yoder, K. 170
decision-making 153–154, 162
dedication 35
Deloitte 53
Demerouti, E., et al. 142–143
demographics 15–16, 36, 43
depression 130
determinism 48
Development Concepts and Doctrine Centre (DCDC) 15
digital business models 13
digital disruption 11–14
digital skills 20

digital workplace report 13, 23n7
digitization 18–20
dimensiondata.com 13
discipline 27
discretionary effort 31–32, 79, 87, 111–112, 140–141, 149, 160
discrimination 63
dispositions 101–102
diversity of thinking 108–109
Downey, R., and Wefald, A. 75
Duke Energy 162
Dunphy, D., and Stace, D. 155
Dutton, J. 96

e-cards 2
e-learning 145
ecosystems 17
Edmondson, A., and Nembhard, I. 96
education 19; and digital skills 20
effectiveness 102–104, 112, 123, 142–143; management 138–139; mechanisms 103
efficacy see effectiveness
efficiency 12, 12–13, 17, 23n3, 43, 60, 84
effort 2, 22, 30–35, 39–40, 43, 60–67, 77, 86–88, 93, 99, 104, 118–124, 132–137, 149–153, 160, 168–169; discretionary 31–32, 79, 87, 111–112, 140–141, 149, 158; levels 129
Effort-Reward Imbalance (ERI) Theory 65
Egan, G. 130
Eisenhardt, K., and Brown, S. 53
EMC 132
emergence 19, 27, 38; change 46–47
emotional skills 20
emotions 34, 39–40, 80, 104–105, 170–173, 179; and intelligence 171; key positive 110–111; negative 65, 78–80, 111, 171–172; positive 171
empathy 5, 170–173, 180; behavioural reactions to OC 171–173; cognitive 170
employees 30–31, 132; disengagement 77–78, 86–87, 151; job crafting 142–143; role 141–143; types 30–37, 64, 68
engagement 2–5, 22, 145, 184; antecedents, outcomes and implications 87–113; conscious and unconscious approach 137–138; contagion (cognitive/emotional) 146–147; definitions and limitations 4, 33, 38–40, 76, 87–88, 156; dilemmas and drivers 5, 75–86; and disengagement 36–37; existence requirements 32; facets 34; fad or fashion 75–77, 85; in-the-wild 32; insights 180–181; levels 40–41, 106; meaning 29–41, 62–63, 134–135, 179; paradox 77–79; perspectives on 30–36; practice 185–187; principles 150–178; respectful 96; roots

59–60; theoretical perspectives and implications 59–71; think, feel and act 31; trait, state and behavioural 35–37; as transient experience 37–38

Engaging for Success (MacLeod and Clarke) 76

environment 29, 48, 60–63, 83–84; employee roles 141–143; and engagement contagion 146–147; implications 148–149; leadership 118–123, 134–137; manager and leader roles 117, 131–133, 137–141; OC culture creation 117–149; power and politics 124–131; stakeholder relationships 123–124

Epicenter 12

equity 5, 168–170, 173, 180; recognition and rewards 169–170; resources 168–169

Erickson, T. 21

error monitoring 120

ethics 5, 28, 79–80, 85–86, 180

Eton, C., and Gostick, A. 169

eudaimonic approach 110

European Union (EU) 15

exhaustion 36–37, 78–80

Exit, Voice and Loyalty (Hirschmann) 162

expectations 79

Facebook 17–18, 21, 27

fairness 94–97, 168–170

fatigue 54, 78–80

feedback 61–62, 164, 169–170, 174–178; mechanisms 27

Ferris, G.: and Kacmar, K. 130; and King, T. 130

Financial Times 11

Fishbein, M., and Ajzen, I. 39

Flamholtz, E., and Randle, R. 52

Fleck, S., and Inceoglu, I. 112

flexibility 28, 109

flow 35, 42, 69–70

focus 38–40, 55–56, 145–146

Ford, J., and Ford, L. 172

fostering 150–181; case study 166–168; generic approaches 150–151; OC engagement principles 150–178; top-down and bottom-up approach 173–178, *174*

Fox, E., and Boaz, N. 132

framing 158–159

France 81; police 81–82

freedom 27

Freelancer.com 20

Freelancers Union (US) 20

Frese, M. 66

Fresh Start Programme 176–177, *176*

Friedman, T. 2, 21

Frieze, D., and Wheatley, M. 147

Fruitpickingjobs.com 20

gain spirals 62

Gallup 3, 30–31, 81, 111, 159

Gandini, A. 20

General Electric (GE) 54, 153

Generation Y 15, 21

Gersick, C. 52–53

Gerstner, L. 54

Gibson, J., and Tesone, D. 75

gig economy 14, 20

Gill, R., and Hodges, J. 137

Gillet, N., *et al.* 81–82

globalization 14–16, 43

Goffee, R., and Jones, G. 139

Goffman, E. 34

golden handcuff rule 67

Google 19, 27

Gorter, R., *et al.* 169

Gostick, A., and Eton, C. 169

Gould, S. 53

gradualism 51–53

Graetz, F. 43

Grant, A.: and Ashford, S. 142; *et al.* 110

Gratton, L. 123, 162

Great Barrier Reef system (Australia) 16

Groysberg, B., and Slind, M. 160–161

Guest, D. 76–77

guidelines 28, 49

guru groups 76

Gutenberg, J.G. 1

hackathons 133

Hailey, V., and Balogun, J. 48

Hakanen, J., *et al.* 108

Halbesleben, J., *et al.* 101

Hallberg, U., and Schaufeli, W. 34

Hameed, I., *et al.* 90

Hamel, G. 27; and Breen, B. 139; and Zanini, M. 43

happiness 170–171

Harris, S., and Armenakis, A. 93

Harrison, D., and Newman, D. 35

Harter, J., *et al.* 106

Harvard Business Review 14

Hatch, M. 45

Haudan, J. 133

Hawking, Prof. S. 19

hedonic approach 110

HERO (hope/efficacy/resilience/optimism) 102–104, 123, 147

Herscovitch, L., and Meyer, J. 66

Hewlett-Packard 54

Hirschmann, A. 162

Hirt, M., and Willmott, P. 10–11

Hitachi Europe 143; change management case study 143–146; University 145

HMV 1–2

Hodges, J., and Gill, R. 137
Hofman, J., and Orlikowski, W. 47
Holbeche, L. 22; and Matthews, G. 139
Hooper, A., and Potter, J. 135
hope 102–104, 123
House Oversight Committee (US) 54
Huczynski, A., and Buchanan, D. 100, 172
human relations movement 60
Human Resource Management (HRM)
    22–24, 29, 32, 81, 98, 126, 143–146,
    164–168, 177; Committee 166; perfor-
    mance enhancement system 166–168
Hüttermann, H., and Boerner, S. 121
Hutton, W. 156, 187
Huy, Q. 121; and Bresman, H. 165

IBM 164
Ideastorm 164
Images of Organizations (Morgan) 25
incentive 182–183
Inceoglu, I., and Fleck, S. 112
inclusivity 5, 151–156, 162, 173, 180; Appre-
    ciative Inquiry process 158–159; critique
    159–160; and decision-making 153–154;
    participation styles 155; problem-solving and
    idea generation practices 154–155; Talking
    Walls 154
India 14, 19, 163–164
individual antecedents 100–106
individuals 132; and sense-making 136
industrial revolution, fourth 11
Industry Use Cases 109
inefficacy, sense of 36
inertia 2
Infosys 132, 160, 164
initiative 30
initiatives (programmes) 2; workplace 81
innovations 9, 43, 52, 107–110, 112; case study
    108–110
Inoue, A., *et al.* 95
instability 54, 99
Institute of Employment Studies (IES) 32
Institute of Leadership and Management
    (ILM) 21
Institute of Practitioners in Advertising
    (IPA) 118
intellectual property rights (IPR) 109
intelligence 175; artificial (AI) 10, 12,
    18–21, 133
intentionality 162–163
intentions to leave 111–112
interactivity 154, 162–163
internalization 90
Internet Saathi 19
Internet of Things (IoT) 12, 143
interpretations 79

intimacy 160–161
involvement 4, 30–31, 35, 68–70

Jackson, L., *et al.* 169
JC Penney 54
Ji, Y., and Oh, W. 54
Jick, T., and Peiperl, M. 172
Jimmieson, N., and White, K. 158
job crafting 142–143
Job Demands-Resources (JD-R) theory 60–64,
    70, 88, 142
John Lewis Partnership 51
Johnson, R. 54
Jones, G., and Goffee, R. 139
Judge, T., *et al.* 137
justice 94–97, 168–170; distributive 94;
    informational 94; interactional 94–95;
    interpersonal 94; procedural 94–95

Kacmar, K., and Ferris, G. 130
Kahn, W. 33–40, 59, 62–65, 81, 156
Kanter, R. 125; *et al.* 45, 52
Kast, F., and Rosenzweig, J. 26
Keenoy, T. 75–76
Keller, S., and Aitken, C. 132
Kelliher, C., *et al.* 81
Kenexa Research Institute 30, 118
Kennedy, John F. 134
key concepts 24–41; engagement 29–41; per-
    spectives on organizations 25–28
Khurana, R. 120
Kiefer, T. 105
Kim, Dr J. Y. 16
King, M. L. 16
King, T., and Ferris, G. 130
Konovsky, M., and Organ, D. 67
Kotter, J. 45, 52
Kraft 141
Kreiner, G., and Ashforth, B. 62–63
Kumar, K., and Thibodeaux, M. 130
Kunx, J., and Linder, S. 172

labour supply 19–20
Lafley, A. G. 135
Lardi & Partner Consulting GmbH 11
Lardi, K. 11
Lavigna, R. 151
Lawrence, P. 140
leader, role 117, 131–133, 137–141
leadership 5, 13, 43, 169; authenticity 132–133;
    collaborative 122–123, 147; and culture
    creation 133–135; definition 118;
    dependence 83; distributed 121–122;
    enablers 134–137; engaged 133;
    environment 118–123, 134–137; importance
    118–119; management role 137–141;

narrative and sense-making 135–136; perspectives on 119–123; power and politics 124–131; proactive 137; roles 117, 131–133, 137–141; signals 131–132; team presence 99–100; theoretical perspectives 119–123; transactional 120–121; transformational 119–122; visionary 121

Lean (planning and improvement methodology) 56

Lebovitz, A. 69

Legal Research Network (LRN) 20

Leiter, M., and Maslach, C. 36

Levitt, T. 17

Lewin, K. 44–45; critics 44; driving principle (theory) 44; main preoccupation 44–45; managerialist accounts 45

Linder, S., and Kunx, J. 172

Linear Arc Solutions 82

linear frameworks 10, 44–46, 50, 56–57, 119, 150, 156, 162, 165; curvi- 50; models and steps 45; non- 27, 46, 49, 56

LinkedIn learning 13

Linux 20

listening 128, 163–164

Lockwood, N. 104

logical incrementalism 51

Ludema, J., and Stoughton, A. 131

Luecke, R. 45

Luisis-Lynd, L., and Myers, P. 32

Luthans, F., and Sweetman, D. 104

Lyubomirsky, S., et al. 170

Ma (Japanese concept) 109

McCalman, J., and Paton, R. 45, 55

McCourt, W. 25

McDonald, R. 54

Macey, W.: et al. 60, 77, 107; and Schneider, B. 35, 38–39, 66

machine-learning systems 11, 18

Machines of Loving Grace (Markoff) 11

McKinsey & Co 12, 132; Seven-S model 178–179

MacLeod, D., and Clarke, N. 76

Magnitogorsk Iron and Steel Works (Russia) 11

maintenance phase 50

management 5, 38, 43; effective and levels 138–139; engagement perspectives 32–33, 139–140; global performance system 144–146; Hitachi case study 143–146; ineffective 139; line 139–140; practices 75–76, 152; relationship building and support provision 20, 140–141; stakeholder principles 123–129; talent 143; trust building and maintenance 141

manager, role 117, 131–133, 137–141

Managing and Leading People Through Organizational Change (Hodges) 56

Manyika, J., et al. 18–20

Markoff, J. 11

Marshak, R. 44

Maslach, C.: et al. 34; and Leiter, M. 36

Maslow, A. 40, 134

Massive Open Online Courses (MOOC) 13

Masson, R., et al. 77

Mast, M., et al. 125

Masten, A. 103

Matthews, G., and Holbeche, L. 139

Mauno, S., et al. 88

Maurer, R. 172

Mauritius 82; stockbroking company case study 82–85

May, D., et al. 22

Meaney, M., et al. 164

Menges, J., and Bruch, H. 54

meritocracy 27

metaphor 184; and The Story of Perkin 182, 185–190, 185

Meyer, J., and Herscovitch, L. 66

Meyerson, D. 122

Microsoft 133

migration 16

Minimum Viable Product 109

mobile performance management (MPM) 12

Moorhouse Consulting 78; Barometer on Change 133

Moran, J., and Brightman, B. 28

Morgan, G. 25–26

Morgan, N. 121

Morning Star 165

motivation 22, 29, 39, 54, 60–61, 119, 138, 182; power 125; self-concept-job fit 134; theory 37, 40, 134, 169

multichannel networks (MCNs) 17

multinational corporations (MNCs) 81–82, 85

Murphy, K. 68

Muslim Futurists 14

mutuality 79, 96, 119, 141–142, 147–148

Myers, P., and Luisis-Lynd, L. 32

Nadella, S. 133

Nahavandi, A. 131

Nailing the Evidence (Rayton et al.) 76

Narayan Murthy, N. R. 132

narrative 135–136; stories as communication practice 159; strategic 135–136

National Aeronautics and Space Administration (NASA) 134

National Health Service (NHS) 47

Needs Satisfying Theory 62–64; meaning, safety, availability 62–64

Nelson, L. 53

Nembhard, I., and Edmondson, A. 96
Netflix 54
networks 48, 96; digital 108
New York Times 21
Newman, D., and Harrison, D. 35
Niedhammer, I., *et al.* 65
Nike 29
Nikolaou, I., and Vakola, M. 171
Nohria, N., and Beer, M. 55
North American Free Trade Agreement
    (NAFTA) 15
Nye, J. 121

Ogilvy and Mather 14
Oh, W., and Ji, Y. 54
On Dialogue (Bohm) 161–162
O'Neill, O., and Barsade, S. 105
online shopping 52
openness 27, 91
optimism 88, 102–104
Organ, D., and Konovsky, M. 67
organizational change (OC) 28–29; complexity
    theories 46–47, 56–57; contingency theories
    47–49; cyclical 49–50; definitions 24–25,
    28–29; discontinuous 50–51; focus 55–56;
    gradualism 51–53; implications 57–58; the
    phenomenon 43; planned 44–46; processual
    theories 49, 56–57; punctuated equilibrium
    53; rate of occurrence 53–58; scale and pat-
    tern 50–53, 57, 92–93; transformational
    51–53
organizational citizenship behaviour (OCB)
    67–70, 76
organizational culture 89–90, 93; bonds 89–90;
    identification 90
organizations 25–28; as closed/open systems
    26–28; metaphors and critics 25–26; per-
    spectives on 25–28
Orlikowski, W., and Hofman, J. 47
Oshry, B. 174
O'Toole, J., and Bennis, W. 141
outcomes 106–113; and antecedents 88–106,
    89
Overell, S. 79; *et al.* 18
ownership 168–169

Parsell, G., *et al.* 158
participation 138, 144–145; styles 157
Paton, R., and McCalman, J. 45, 55
Peiperl, M., and Jick, T. 172
perceived organizational support (POS) 81–82
perceptions 79, 100–106
performance 30, 35, 60, 68–70, 76, 103–107,
    111–112, 134, 143; enhancement system
    166–168; moments of task 37; targets 56
personality 101–105

perspectives 25–41, 109; on engagement
    30–36; on leadership 119–123; OC
    theories and categories 42–58; on
    organizations
    25–28, *see also* theoretical perspectives
Pettigrew, A. 130; *et al.* 49
Pfeffer, J. 130
Philippines 82
Pierce, S. 143–146
Pittinsky, T., and Rosenthal, S. 125
Planning Service 173–174
pluralism 26
politics 46, 130–131; and power 124–131
pollution 16
population 17; ageing 15
populist evolution 15–16
positive organizational behaviour (POB) 102
Potter, J., and Hooper, A. 135
power 124–131, 147; motivation 125; and
    silent veto 129–130; stakeholders 124–131
pre-contemplation phase 50
predictability 27
preparation phase 50
principles 124, 150–178, *152*, 181; case study
    166–168; co-creation 163–166; connectivity
    156–157; empathy 170–173; equity
    168–170; inclusivity 151–156; management
    124; practice implications 178; summary
    173; top-down and bottom-up approach
    173–178, *174*; transparency 157–163
printing revolution 1
problem-solving 80, 155–157, 168
process review and restructure 83–84, 99
processual antecedents 94–100
Prochaska, J., *et al.* 49
Procter & Gamble 54, 135
productivity, gains/losses 19, 106–107,
    111–112, 158
Professional Services Enablement 97
profitability 32
programme management office (PMO) 164
psychological capital (PsyCap) 104
psychology 60–62, 110; antecedent conditions
    62, 90; system overload 77–79
publishing industry 52
Pugh, D. 125
PwC 30

Rafferty, A.: *et al.* 93; and Restubog, S. 92
Ramoly, R. 82–85
Randle, R., and Flamholtz, E. 52
Rayton, B., *et al.* 76
reciprocity 64–65, 96, 118, 153; mutual
    147–148; theory 140
recognition 169–170
Reed, M. 25

relatedness 61
relationships 95–99, 102, 119, 168; building 140–141, 144, 155–156; stakeholder 123–124
relativism 26
reliability 27
reputation economy 20
research and development (R&D) 18
resilience 102–104
resistance concept 171–172
resources 61, 64, 168–169; allocation 125; caravans 62; degradation 16–17; personal 102–104
responsibility 84, 90, 130
restructuring 79
Restubog, S., and Rafferty, A. 92
retaliation 156
retention 77
return on OC engagement (ROCE) 112
revolution 1; fourth industrial 11; populist 15–16; printing 1; scientific 21
rewards 169–170
rights: intellectual property (IPR) 109; voting 155
Robinson, D., et al. 64, 150
Robinson, I. 88
robotics 12, 18, 21
Rogers, J. E. 162
Rosenfeld, I. 141
Rosenthal, S., and Pittinsky, T. 125
Rosenzweig, J., and Kast, F. 26
Rothbard, N. 34
Rubin, H. 122, 146
Ruebottom, T., and Auster, E. 123

Saks, A. 34–35, 88, 94–95, 141
satisfaction 4, 29–31, 60, 65–66, 70, 111
scepticism 76, 146
Schaufeli, W.: and Bakker, A. 68, 96, 111; et al. 34–36, 39–40, 81, 93; and Hallberg, U. 34
Schneider, B., and Macey, W. 35, 38–39, 66
Schrage, M. 54
scientific revolution 21
Scroggins, W. 134
security, cyber 12–13, 17
Seidman, D. 20–21
Self Determination Theory 61
Self-Destructive Habits of Good Companies (Sheth) 2
self-development 132
self-efficacy 88, 147
self-employment 34, 63
self-expression 34
self-image 68
self-organization 27

Seligman, M. 60
Senior, B. 51
sense-making 136
Seo, M.-G., et al. 173
serendipity 28
Shamir, B. 134
Sheth, J. 2
shopping, online 52
side-bets theory 66–67
Siegrist, J., et al. 77
Siltaloppi, M., et al. 95
Singh, N. 164
Siri 12
Six Sigma 56
skills: digital 20; emotional 20
Slind, M., and Groysberg, B. 164–165
smartphone 12
Social Exchange Theory 64–65, 70, 91, 95, 169
Social Identity Theory 90, 95–96
Social Impact Theory 147
Social Information Processing Theory 92
Sonnentag, S. 169
South Africa 82, 169
Sparrow, P., and Balain, S. 33
spectre of uselessness 80
spending patterns 14
Sperry, D. 108–110
Spotify 2
stability 42, 53, 89
Stace, D., and Dunphy, D. 155
stakeholders 2–6, 29, 56, 94–100; leadership and change 130–136, 144, 148; mapping 98, 123; and OC engagement principles 150–178; power and influence 124–131, 129; relationships and management principles 123–129; theory 123
status quo bias 136
Steidlmeier, P., and Bass, B. 121
stockbroking company case study (Mauritius) 82–85
stories 161, 166–167, 170–171
Stoughton, A., and Ludema, J. 131
streaming services 2
stress 36–37, 61–62, 65–66, 79, 82, 86, 104, 110, 130, 156, 171
Sundarajan, A. 14–15
support 83, 98, 138, 140–141, 148; social 96–97
surveys 30; database 33; employee types 30–33
Sustaining Change in Organizations (Hodges and Gill) 137
Sweeney, F. 166–168
Sweetman, D., and Luthans, F. 104
symbiosis 34

systems 26–28; complex adaptive
(CAS) 27–28

Talking Walls 156
Tamkin, P., *et al.* 135
targets, performance 56
Taris, T., *et al.* 70
TaskRabbit 20
Tata Group 163–164
Taylorism, digital 19
teamwork 20
technology 10–14; advances 16–17; digital
11–14; virtual personal assistant 12;
web-based 161
Terkel, S. 62
Tesone, D., and Gibson, J. 75
Thank You For Being Late (Friedman) 2
theoretical perspectives 4–5, 42–58; complexity
46–47, 56–57; contingency 47–49;
cross-cultural 5; cyclical change 49–50;
either/or 55–56; engagement 59–71;
occurrence rate 53–58; planned change
44–46; processual 49; scale and pattern
50–51
Theory of Reasoned Action (TRA) 37
theory of self 33
Thibodeaux, M., and Kumar, K. 130
Thomson Reuters Corporation 84
Thornhill, J. 11
Tinker, T. 25
Too Much Change (Moorhouse Consulting) 78
TopCoder 20
Toyoda, A. 54–55
Toyota 54–55
trade wars 16
training programmes 13, 145, 167; provision
case study 97–100
Trans-Pacific Partnership (TPP) 15
transactional engagement 180; costs 10;
performance targets 56
transformation 2, 27, 43, 51–54, 97–100;
leadership 119–121; Task team 166–168
transparency 5, 27, 84, 98, 159, 167, 173,
180; communication 157–163; and
uncertainty 157
TRS Foods 54
Truss, K., *et al.* 80, 111
trust 83–85, 90–93, 96–99, 108, 120, 168;
building and maintenance 141, 155;
judgement dimensions 91
Tsoukas, H. 26
Tucci, J. M. 132
Twitter 27, 76

Uber 13
Ultrecht Work Engagement Scale 3

uncertainty 2, 19, 37, 42, 46–48, 79, 91, 94,
103, 136–140, 147–149, 157–160, 168–172;
and OC complexity 136
unions 97, 100, 166–167
United Kingdom (UK) 15
United Nations (UN) 15; world urbanization
prospects report 15
United States of America (USA) 11; House
Oversight Committee 54; Technology CEO
Council 11
unpredictability 43–46, 56
Upwork 20
urbanization 15
uselessness 80

Vakola, M., and Nikolaou, I. 173
validity 154
value-added services 155
values 27–28, 68, 89, 130, 182; control 27;
jam 164
Valve (software company) 106
Van de Ven, A. 49
Van den Broeck, A., *et al.* 61
velocity trends 9–23, *10*, 28, 43, 51; as crucibles 9; demand 20–21; demographic 15;
digital disruption 11–14; economic 14–15;
employment deals 21–22; environmental
16–17; impacts 17–22; labour supply 19–20;
nature of work 18–19; technology 10–14
verbal communication and stories 160–161,
164–165
vigour 35
Vince, R., and Broussine, M. 45
virtual personal assistant technology 12
vision 109–110
Vodafone 13, 23n5
voting rights 153
Vroom, V. 169
VUCA (Volatile/Uncertain/Complex/Ambig-
uous) 181
vulnerability 90–91

Wang, L., and Chen, J. 102
Ward, M. 130
web-based technology 161
Wefald, A., and Downey, R. 75
Weick, K. 46
Welch, J. 54
well-being 78, 107, 110–111
Wellbourne, T. 78
Wellins, R., *et al.* 111
Western Electric Company 60
What Happened? (Clinton) 1
Wheatley, M., and Frieze, D. 147
Whelan-Barry, K., *et al.* 158
White, K., and Jimmieson, N. 158

Whitman, M. 54
Whole Foods 29
Wi-Fi 19
Willis Towers Perrin 31, 107
Willmott, P., and Hirt, M. 10–11
Wilson, M. 104
Winslow, J., *et al.* 140
withdrawal 37, 98–99
Witzel, M. 2
Woollard, S., and Clinton, M. 77
work 17–22; demands 20–21,
    60–61; dirty 62–63; emotionally
    intelligent 18;
    employee flexibility 18–20; employment
    deals 21–22; knowledge-enabled 19,
    43; labour supply 19–20; nature
    18–19; online platforms 20; and professional

relationships 22; velocity trend impacts
    17–22, *see also* environment
Work Foundation 91
workaholism 69–70, 80
Working the Shadow Side (Egan) 130
Workplace Employment Relations study 153
World Bank Group 16
World Health Organization (WHO) 110
Worley, C., and Cummings, T. 49

Yandex Data Factory 11
Yoder, K., and Decety, J. 170
YouTube 17, 27
Yukl, G. 118

Zak, P. 140
Zanini, M., and Hamel, G. 43

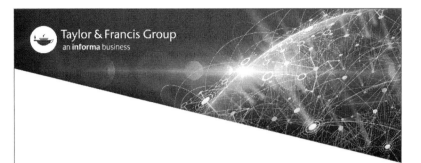